ON THE EDGE

ON THE EDGE

A
HISTORY OF
POOR BLACK CHILDREN
AND THEIR
AMERICAN DREAMS

Carl Husemoller Nightingale

BasicBooks
A Division of HarperCollins*Publishers*

Designed by Ellen Levine

Library of Congress Cataloging-in-Publication Data
Nightingale, Carl H.
     On the edge : a history of poor black children and their American dreams / Carl H. Nightingale.
          p.   cm.
     ISBN 0–465–03651–1 (cloth)
     ISBN 0–465–05219–3 (paper)
     1. Afro-American children. 2. United States—Social conditions—1980–   3. United States—Race relations. I. Title.
E185.86.N54   1993   92–56177
305.23'08996073—dc20   CIP

96 97 98 ◆/RRD 9 8 7 6 5 4

CONTENTS

DEDICATION

To My Young Friends and Neighbors in Philadelphia

This book is filled with things I have learned from you over the last
five years. I dedicate it to you, with all my deepest appreciation, and
all my best wishes for you.

At the same time, I would also like to rededicate myself to our
friendship. Learning about each other, becoming close friends, and
sharing good times and hard times and even ordinary times with you
has been a deeply treasured privilege for me. Just as our friendship
began well before I ever thought about asking you to be part of this
book, and just as the things we accomplished together have been
much wider-ranging and more important than this book, so I hope
we continue to be friends and continue to work together long after I
finish it.

When I first started working on the book, I intended it to be a
book about African-American children who lived in Philadelphia
about forty or fifty years ago. Like many books about African-
Americans in the United States, it was to be filled with statistics and
with information I learned from historical documents of the 1950s
and 1960s.

I first met you in the summer of 1987, about the time I was busy
getting the statistics out of the computer and reading the documents. Our friendships grew, later we founded the Kids' Club in
the neighborhood, and all along we got to know each other increasingly well. For me, our friendship was the most important part
of what we did together, and I did not intend it to be part of a

research effort. However, I quickly found out that I was learning much more from you about what it has been like for African-American children to grow up in Philadelphia than I was learning from the statistics and the historical documents and even from my university professors.

After a while, I began to think seriously about how I could pass on to other people some of the many things I had learned from you. I decided that this book might be a way to do it. So, I asked your parents for permission, and when they gave it, I asked you what you thought about being a part of this book. At the time, I pledged that I would not use your real names in the book, nor reveal any detailed information about where you live, so that you could continue to lead your lives in privacy even if many people read the book.

All of you gave me permission to include true stories about your lives in this book. Some of you suggested "book names" for me to use.

I trust your decision to give me permission. But at the same time, I know many of you have some mixed feelings. First, in the book I occasionally write very openly about things you sometimes feel embarrassed about, like poverty, welfare, violence, or family troubles. You have told me sometimes you think these things are "bad" or even "crazy," and you have worried that I might "write something bad" about you in the book. Also, I have gotten to know you pretty well, but I do not by any means know everything there is to know about you. And though you have told me many things about times before I met you, I was never there. Sometimes you have worried that I might not have every single thing exactly right. Most importantly, you have sometimes told me that you do not think a white man like myself can ever understand what goes on in a black neighborhood—and that "nerdy professors" like myself can never truly understand anything about what it is like to be as "cool" or "all that" as you.

All of these are important concerns to have. They are very important for me, because I have always wanted this book to strengthen our friendships, not stand in the way of them. We have talked a lot about these concerns, between ourselves, with the other adult members of the Kids' Club, and with all your families. I hope we can continue to talk about them.

As you know, I cannot claim to understand everything perfectly. I can only promise to write what I have learned from you as truthfully and as honestly as I know how. Also, I can only hope that our friendships, and the book itself, may contribute to understandings between white people and black people in this country, and between adults (even professors!) and the coolest of kids. So as I dedicate this book to you, I have dedicated myself to keeping that promise and keeping that hope.

I wish all of you the very best anyone can ever wish for the very best of friends.

Philadelphia, 1992

ACKNOWLEDGMENTS

This book owes its very creation to several quite different and extremely wonderful communities. Not only did these communities give me shelter and encouragement while I was writing, but they treated me to six years of extraordinary conversations without which the book would not have been written: cafeteria lunches and academic conferences at the departments of history at Princeton University and the University of Pennsylvania; strategy sessions in the offices of archivists, social service agency directors, and other professionals; and, most important, neighborhood get-togethers in Philadelphia: backyard barbecues, block parties, basketball games, tutoring sessions, trips to the park, picnics in the woods, and days at the beach.

Daniel T. Rodgers's contributions to the book as my doctoral adviser in the history department at Princeton, and as a teacher of the highest order, have been countless, diverse, and profound. His encouragement of the project and his energizing commentary jumpstarted the thing on numerous occasions, and he avidly supported my use of both ethnographic and social scientific techniques in a work of history. His call to historians to look at the upbringing of children for a new perspective on the American working class— along with Herbert Gutman's masterful analysis of the "Afro-American slave class," the work of Elliot Liebow, and of Lee Rainwater and his team of researchers—inspired my own analysis of the cultural and emotional dimensions of the inner-city experience, and it allowed me to make the connection between anthropological concepts like the life cycle and historical ones like class formation. The final organization of the book, which grew out of my dissertation, also owes much to several particularly brilliant pieces of Professor Rodgers's advice.

Gary Gerstle contributed immeasurably to the project as well, not only as first reader on my dissertation committee, but also as a long-time adviser with a contagious commitment to social history. In addition, he gave me a useful opportunity to rehearse some of the material in lecture form to the undergraduates in his course on twentieth-century American society. His enthusiasm for my project pulled it through many a morass.

Toni Morrison has shown more convincingly than anyone else just how factors like violence and family life fit into the complex experience of poor African-American communities. Her novels and powerful characterizations constantly provided antidotes to caricature, romanticization, and the dreary language of social science. Her commentary on the manuscript in an early form encouraged me to investigate the impact of mainstream culture on inner-city kids in broader ways, and she provided much of the inspiration for chapter 6.

Thanks as well to Michael B. Katz for keeping me up to date with the most recent social scientific literature on race and poverty, for reading and commenting on the introduction, and for offering encouragement. A number of ideas concerning conceptual language were honed in conversations with him. His editorship of a collection of essays giving historical perspective to the debate on the American urban crisis helped me form my own critique of the idea that cities somehow enjoyed a golden age before 1960. Professor George Gerbner of Penn's Annenberg School of Communications helped me to sort out many of the issues concerning mass-media violence that appear in chapter 6. Paul Carton helped me further refine some ideas on these matters, and provided me with some other invaluable pieces of information.

Evelyn Brooks Higginbotham, of the University of Pennsylvania, the outside reader on my dissertation committee, and James McPherson, the fourth reader, offered interesting perspectives on my historical argument, provided generous encouragement, and helped shape this work's final form. I also appreciate very much the enlightening advice offered by Professors Paul Jefferson and Roger Lane, both at Haverford College, by Kenneth L. Kusmer and by Professors Albert Raboteau and Nell I. Painter at Princeton

University. Steve Fraser, my editor at Basic Books, offered priceless encouragement and the best in criticism; his wise advice definitely made this a much better book.

Sessions of the Princeton Graduate History Association, and of the Work and Welfare Seminar of the University of Pennsylvania's Program to Reassess and Revitalize the Social Sciences (PARSS), also helped me better articulate my thinking on a number of subjects.

This book was born in Temple University's Urban Archives, where Fredric Miller and David Weinberg introduced me to the archives' collections of case reports concerning children who had grown up in Philadelphia immediately after World War II. Over the next four years, Theresa Davis, George Brightbill, Brenda Wright, and Cheryl Johnson all helped make the task of dissecting, copying, refiling, and storing the huge document collections possible. Their patience and professional help are very much appreciated. Thanks also to Father Avery, Father Betts, and Constance Medaugh at Episcopal Community Services, Thomas E. Weber at the Big Brother/Big Sister Association of Philadelphia, and Gerson Green at the Greater Philadelphia Federation of Settlements for their organizations' permission to review the confidential material in their collections. Their assistance made this project possible.

The quantitative data on race, poverty, marriage, and family that are so crucial in outlining the central problem of the book in part I appear only because of Doug Mills, of Princeton University's Social Science Users Service at the Center for Information Technology. His extraordinary wizardry, his boundless indulgence for my ineptitude at the computer, and his kind willingness to drop anything to listen to me whine were essential ingredients in my initiation into SPSSX and the "Public-Use Micro-Data Samples." Mills and the rest of the SSUS staff deliver what can only be called the quintessence of research assistance for students.

The quantitative information on Philadelphia homicide and suicide rates that I incorporate in chapter 1 and the appendices exists because of the record keeping of Arnold Selig, statistician at the Philadelphia Department of Public Health's Division of Health Program Analysis, who kindly made the data available to me. The staff at the reference desk at the University of Pennsylvania, especially Mark Colvson, kindly endured my constant requests for census materials; Mark also supplied me with invaluable bibliographic information on African-Americans and consumer culture. The staffs of the National Clearinghouse for the Defense of Battered Women and the Center for Effective Public Policy on occasion generously offered me the use of their office space, and in particular, I am grateful that they allowed me to print out drafts of chapters on their laser printers. Jeffrey A. Miller and his catering company kept me alive by giving me work (and leftovers!) throughout my life as a graduate student.

In Philadelphia, many volunteers and friends of the Kids' Club provided advice, wisdom, and moral guidance. My love and appreciation to Sue for her undying insistence on advocating for the children in the neighborhood. Because of her searching misgivings about the project, she was able to ask all the hard questions. Whatever level of honesty this book has attained is largely a tribute to the remarkable, if often tough, lessons I learned from her. Susan Meeker was a fantastic friend: she invited me on many sanity-restoring twilight strolls through the streets of the city, kindly shared many of her thoughts about the Kids' Club and the children themselves, and contributed encouragement and creative ideas for the book. Julie Cristol supported the Kids' Club in so many ways over the past six years. Her friendship through the toughest times, and our annual day-long cookie baking sessions (!), were great sources of sustenance for me. I also send my love, respect, and gratitude to other volunteers and neighbors of the Kids' Club: to Cheshire Agusta, Evelyn Campbell, Jackie Dale, Richard Gilbertie, Susan Jordhamo, Lynn Phillips, Brian Sherwin, Liz Sgrillo, Charles Wakefield, Sr., Charles Wakefield, Jr., Frannie Wakefield, Nancy Wakefield, Reggie Wakefield, and Emma Williams. Their support and their ideas, their depth of commitment and their energy throughout six years have taught me many invaluable and marvelously unforgettable things, and I will never be able to thank them enough for their friendship.

David Dorsey read a number of chapters in draft form and he treated me to long, fascinating conversations on the consequences of Aid to Families with Dependent Children, the ethics of ethnographic research, various general questions about poverty. Jon Liebman offered searching critiques of early drafts, and he generously listened as I free-associated endlessly about statistical variables and standard deviations. I am also very grateful for the discussion he and Anne Fine organized in their dining room one January evening that helped me so much in articulating the principal ideas for this book. T. L. Hill and John Carson generously gave me critiques of the book's conclusion, and during the hectic final months of writing, Alana Atchinson was a terrific friend in spite of my general kookiness. Many of the ideas I elaborated in the book were first tested out in chats with Joe Adler, Alisa Belzer, Ellen Berkowitz, Linda Bradley, Lynette Bradley, Dawnn Marie Bradley, Roberta Braxton, Sheila Braxton, Silvia Braxton, Georgette Brown, Geoff Clark, Bill Coleman, Mark Colvson, Ruth Cummings, Jim Goodman, Rob Gregg, Lucy Hackney, David Hahn, Kristen Herzl, Jim Hickman, Alyssa Hinton, Martha Hodes, Diane Hubbard, Jerry King, Nina Lerman, Jeffrey Miller, Diane McFarland, Gertrude McFarland, Julie Mayer, Catherine Peyroux, Douglas Porpora, Alonzo Potts, Jenny Price, Matthew Price, Marla Stone, Sara Swenson, Amy Verstappen, Edith Walker, and John Wertheimer.

During the many years it took to complete the book, my father Dale Husemoller, my mother Jeanne Nightingale, my grandparents Barbara and Philip Nightingale, my sisters Anna and Greta, my brothers Erich and Kurt, my in-laws Alison, Pato, and Peter, my nephew Adrian, and my nieces Colette, Paloma, Atena, and Annika have been sources of undying support. They tolerated my chronic absentmindedness with cheer, gave me interesting suggestions on drafts they read, and offered their impressions and advice on life in my neighborhood. Now that the project is finally finished, I can only hope to become as good a family member to all of them as they have been to me!

I have chosen to dedicate the book to the people who have taught me the most of all in recent years—the young people I met and became friends with in my Philadelphia community, their parents, and my many other wonderful neighbors. From the kids I have learned in amazement not only how hard it can be to grow up in America but also how astonishingly triumphant the youthful human spirit can be in the face of adversity. From all my neighbors who helped support the Kids' Club morally or financially, or by becoming tutors and mentors, I have also learned how great a neighborhood can be when its residents blend their energies, talents, and capacity for love. The memories of the last six years are forever indelible, and I look forward to more living and working together—and more growing up together.

ON THE EDGE

INTRODUCTION

This is a history book about some American children. But *American* is not the word most Americans commonly use to describe them. Overall, the nation's preferences run instead to phrases like "alienated youth," "ghetto kids," "them," or "you people," and in more hateful moments, "punks," "wolf packs," "welfare queens," or "niggers." Scholars and other experts on inner-city affairs have also developed a terminology filled with derogatory phrases implying that poor black kids, like the ones described in this book, exist in a realm far outside ordinary definitions of America: "Dysfunctional youth" is one of these supposedly objective concepts; "tangles of pathology" and "contagion" are others. But the favorite term nowadays is "underclass," a term one liberal scholar defined, in part, as "a vile and debased subhuman population."[1] Americans do have access to more respectful names for the kids in this book: "*African*-American" is one of them. But "*all*-American" (as in apple pie or the kid next door) is almost never a first choice.

Even the children profiled in this book tend to choose other names before they call themselves "American." "Jitterbugs" is one name they preferred in the past (it was popular in the 1940s and 1950s, when the story of this book begins). Since then other kids have tried on "cats," "hipcats," "dreamgirls," "hustlers," "gowsters," "mackmen," "flygirls," "b-boys," "round-the-way girls," and even "baaad niggers." "Underclass," not surprisingly, has little appeal.

Omar Wilkins, one of the main characters in this book, decided it meant "the place under the floor of the classroom where they put the bad kids." But despite the fact that the kids in the book all grew up in Philadelphia, Pennsylvania, a city sometimes called the "birthplace of America," I sometimes get the feeling that, for most of them, "American" might sound too "nerdy"—a little like last years' sneakers, it wouldn't quite fit.

For a number of important reasons, however, this avoidance of the name "American" is difficult to understand. As you read this book, you will discover much about its main characters that is unmistakably American (at least, in the most common usage of the term, which refers to things from the United States and ignores the rest of North America and all of Central and South America). All of the kids in the book have loved television, for example, and action-adventure movies, popcorn, basketball, boxing, and football. They have all loved to shop, especially for clothes (in recent years, they have actually tended to avoid last year's sneakers like the plague), and one of their most enthusiastic fads was a T-shirt with Mickey Mouse on the front. They also like Coca-Cola and McDonald's, sometimes with a passion, and like most other Americans, they are fond of fancy cars, especially American-made ones (at least until recently, when their inclinations, like those of many other Americans, shifted somewhat to foreign models). Although some of the kids prefer to be known as citizens of something called the "hip-hop nation," most tend to sound like so-called red-blooded, patriotic Americans when asked about various issues. For example, they tend to revere the army and the marines; during the cold war they hated Russians; and during the gulf war many of them wore a red, white, and blue T-shirt with "Support Operation Desert Storm" on it. Finally, the kids described in this book think a lot about race and racism, which have qualified handily for the title of the ultimate "American obsession."

So, why don't we proudly proclaim that inner-city black kids like the ones in this book are just as much "made in the USA" as anyone else in America?

One reason is that, despite sharing a number of predilections with most other Americans, the kids have also been severely "alienated" from the American "mainstream." For example, all have grown up poor, largely because most of the best kinds of jobs that were once close to where they live have recently left their neighborhood and relocated to places that are hard to get to, sometimes even to countries halfway around the globe. As a result, the kids' parents have not had consistent sources of good income. And though most of the kids have occasionally dreamed "American dreams," it has been rare for them to realize those dreams in any consistent way (except maybe on the occasional days when they get enough money to go shopping). Most of the time, they and their parents have had to rely heavily on welfare, thus attracting the scorn of the great majority of Americans who have always believed that anyone can make it in America with a lot of hard work and a little good luck.

Also, all of the kids I describe in this book were born with dark skin, and since the majority of Americans have a lighter shade of skin, the kids have been in the "minority" (a word, incidentally, that Omar Wilkins, one of the main characters, finds infuriating and demeaning). Racial segregation has helped dig what one recent filmmaker has called a "Grand Canyon" between inner-city kids and the suburban neighborhoods where most Americans live—even though most of the kids I have met in Philadelphia would prefer to move out beyond the city limits to "decent" houses.

Patterns of racial segregation have grown more complex, and perhaps even more alienating, in recent years. Many members of the black community have left segregated areas of the cities, usually for mostly black suburban areas. The brilliant sociologist William Julius Wilson hypothesized that this emigration has made it more difficult in recent years for poorer African-American kids in inner cities to have close contact with the black community's traditional grassroots leaders and "mainstream role models."[2] Meanwhile, schools in neighborhoods doubly segregated by race and class tend to be lousy, and though many of the kids in this book were born easily as smart as any other American, their talents have not been trained enough for them to qualify for the kinds of jobs that would allow them to realize and sustain their American dreams.

But there is another, perhaps more powerfully driving reason for the general reluctance to call the kids described in this book Americans: In recent decades, the majority of Americans have grown more prone to see poor black children as the principal components of a serious national threat.

Some of this fear is due to disturbing trends that can be measured by statistics. Since World War II, and especially since the late 1960s, families in poor urban black neighborhoods have been increasingly likely to be run by a single parent. This has been unsettling to many

Americans: our national sense of comfort often seems deeply dependent on memories of growing up in so-called nuclear households—
and the idea that the only viable families are those with two parents.

A more disturbing statistical trend, though, is the one showing
that during the late twentieth century, poor black children growing
up in the inner city have been increasingly likely to be killed by
other members of their community. Most of Philadelphia, for example, understandably shook in fear when a wave of unprecedented
gang violence overcame the city's poor African-American neighborhoods during the late 1960s and early 1970s. During the 1980s a similar outbreak of violence, which killed young people at an even
greater rate, erupted as rival drug-dealing outfits used automatic
weapons to control the streetcorner trade in crack cocaine. Many
times this violence took the lives of innocent bystanders, and some
of the violence spilled over into less poor black neighborhoods and
white neighborhoods (the number of robberies committed by black
people against white people has gone up substantially in recent
years).

Inner-city violence has taken other forms as well. In the late
1960s, black neighborhoods in many of America's cities went up in
flames as many young black people took to the streets in uncontrolled rage. Then, in April 1991, when four Los Angeles policemen
who had been videotaped ruthlessly beating a black man named
Rodney King were acquitted by a suburban jury, thousands of people, again including many young poor African-Americans, expressed
their anger by looting stores, burning buildings, and severely injur-
ing or killing innocent people.

Many Americans—whether black, white, Asian, or Latino—have
grown increasingly fearful of getting mugged, "car-jacked," looted,
or killed by poor black kids on city or suburban streets. Locksmiths
are doing increased business, as are security guard companies and
the people who put up bars on the windows of houses. Sometimes
the measures people have taken to protect themselves from danger
have in turn posed their own dangers to community life and even a
sense of American national community. City dwellers have bought
record numbers of guns in recent years, for example, and municipal
governments in Los Angeles have begun responding to pressures
from their more privileged citizens to erect walls around certain sections of the city, just like the ones already provided by increasing
numbers of private suburban developers.[3] Also, huge numbers of
well-to-do people have simply left the cities altogether, often leaving

America's centers of culture and history without a sorely needed revenue base.

While the desire for safety in today's American cities is very understandable, fear has much too easily slipped into hatred. The rise in inner-city violence, and in urban crime generally, has too often been the excuse for white Americans to revive old, awful stereotypes about the inherently violent nature of black people, especially young poor black men. Scholarly concepts like "underclass" have been heavily freighted with racist insinuations like these. And ever since the riots of the late 1960s, the same old fearsome racial images have been invoked by increasing numbers of Americans, from the ordinary to the most powerful: from the mobs of white city dwellers who have harassed and killed innocent black people; to the many police officers who utter racist insults while on patrol, harass young black men, use excessive force, and too often kill defenseless blacks in racist furor; to the politicians—school board chairpersons, big-city mayors, and U.S. presidents—who have recently employed a variety of "crypto-racist" and just plain-old racist techniques to get themselves elected.

When they are not pandering to American racism, many of these same politicians, and many scholars too, have decided that the best way to deal with inner-city violence is by hiring more vice-principals in charge of discipline, more cops, more "tough" judges, and most importantly, by building a huge number of new prisons. Into that "strengthened" criminal justice system, and into those prisons, they have packed one-fifth of all the young men, and many of the young women, of African ancestry who live in the United States—including several of the kids I introduce in this book.

Poor, on welfare, left behind by emigrating employers and community leaders, racially excluded, feared and despised by many Americans, then thrown into prisons: how could the children described in this book be more alienated from the American mainstream than that?

In fact, it was only by getting to know some poor urban African-American children much closer up that I could grasp just how thoroughly American their lives have been. At the same time, I also came to believe that we cannot understand the drastic social changes and the increases in crime and angry rioting in the inner city—nor can America begin to examine what makes it so prone to explosions of racial hatred—unless we realize just how deeply the violence of inner-city community life has been connected to some of the late-twentieth-century's most familiar American dreams.

The first group of inner-city kids I got to know well came of age during the late 1950s and early 1960s. I learned about their lives from the hundreds of case records left behind by four private Philadelphia social welfare agencies dedicated to children's needs. The caseworkers from these agencies were very diligent reporters. In their case records they wrote extensively about the daily lives of people who would otherwise have left few written traces, and the reports often include children's own words in direct or indirect speech. From the information in the reports I was able to reconstruct large segments of kids' youthful biographies. I became familiar with Johnnie "Bojack" Dungee,* the gang warlord (whose life I have come to see as something of an emblem of childrens' experiences growing up in a late-1950s inner-city); with Ida Mae King, the girl-gang member; with Darrell Smith, the enthusiastic "jitterbug"; and with a fascinating group of youngsters I call the "Settlement Boys."

While I was busy reading about children from Bojack's Philadelphia in case records, I met a second group of inner-city kids—this time in person. Our encounter began in the summer of 1987, when Omar Wilkins and several other members of his family, who lived near by my house in Philadelphia, offered to mow my lawn. When I proved to be an enthusiastic customer, they came back to visit more often. When they found out I had some tools, they brought by their BMX bikes for repairs, and their friends started coming, too. I can remember the names and faces of about sixty children whom I met over the next six months, but I became especially close friends with the kids and parents of four extended families—the Wilkinses, the Greenes, the Barkleys, and the Pattersons. At first I grew particularly close to the indomitable leader of the local crowd of youngsters, Chauntey Patterson.† Following Chauntey's suggestion, a group of neighborhood adults and I founded a loose volunteer organization (called the "Kids' Club" in this book) that was designed to find alternatives to violence and drug dealing by helping kids with homework, school attendance, recreation, and employment. Later, Chauntey went to jail, and most of the other kids moved out of his neighbor-

---

* All names of the children described in this book have been changed, in agreement with their parents in the case of kids from the neighborhood where I lived, and with the appropriate agency in the case of the kids described in the social workers' reports.

† Chauntey is pronounced "shawn-TAY."

hood. Though I have kept in touch over the years with most of the kids from my early days in Chauntey's neighborhood, I have gotten to know the Wilkinses best, since they remained, for the most part, in the immediate vicinity. They include Omar, whom I already introduced; his older brother, Fahim; his younger sisters, Theresa and Saleema; his cousin Towanda; and Towanda's older twin brothers, Georgie and Andre. Over the years all of these kids and I have built and maintained very strong and complicated friendships. Omar and Fahim lived in my house for a while when things were not working for them at home, most of the other Wilkinses visited daily (often bringing other friends and relatives with them), and I saw the Greenes, Pattersons, and to a lesser extent, the Barkleys (who moved back to their native South Carolina) periodically. Over the years we have worked hard together and played hard together. At times we have trusted each other, worked together, learned from each other; at other times we have been through major life crises with each other, gotten frustrated, furious, and burned out by each other. Through it all we have built strong friendships, and adult volunteers of the Kids' Club have also gotten to know the children's parents and other adult relatives very well. A year or so after the Kids' Club was founded, I decided to ask parents, then the kids themselves, for permission to write about our experiences. Though I occasionally asked individual children for assistance on specific matters relating to the book, our relationships never took on the strict form of an academic research project. However, our lives together as friends and co-workers have taught me most of what I know about inner-city America.

The kids growing up in the black Philadelphia of Bojack's day and the kids I met in Chauntey Patterson's neighborhood have been, in many ways, just like all other kids. They love laughing and playing, they have all sorts of wide-eyed dreams, and they are often astonishingly caring, creative, and curious. At the same time, though, it is clear that these kids' hopes and longings have been severely and increasingly circumscribed by a tragedy of historic proportions, one that has cast its pall on the life of their communities.

Part I of this book is dedicated to tracing the complexities of this historical tragedy. From about 1955 onward, key relationships within poor black families, especially between adult men and women, and between fathers and their children, have indeed experienced an unprecedented period of stress and transformation that has dwarfed the most closely analogous changes in family life among other groups of urban poor people. At almost the same time, an extraordinary surge in fatal violence began to overwhelm traditions of cooperation and collaboration in African-American neighborhoods. Between Bojack's day and more recent times, when Chauntey and his peers began to come of age, inner-city kids like them have been increasingly likely to have to endure the tribulations associated with rapidly changing families and all the dangers of inner-city violence. At the same time, they have also had to struggle with all the powerful historic forces that too often lead them to act out against their own communities and themselves.

In chapter 1, I outline the historical timing of the erosion of community life in poor African-American urban communities, and I document the exceptionality of that experience. In the same chapter I describe how so-called street-smart values espousing manipulative and aggressive behavior make up an important part of many inner-city kids' struggles to articulate their own ethical conscience. Kids' own personal tendency to act out in ways that threaten community life have also depended greatly on personal subconscious struggles as well, specifically, their struggles with often-overwhelming memories of painful emotional experiences. Finally, I argue that explanations for the drastic erosion of community life in late-twentieth-century American inner cities must include an analysis of the sources of aggressive values and the reasons for increasingly widespread memories of pain in the upbringing of young poor African-Americans.

The forces that exclude poor African-American children from meaningful participation in American economic and social life have indeed had crucial effects on the progress of inner-city desperation and community change, and on inner-city kids' moral and emotional struggles. In chapter 2, I find much evidence to agree with William Julius Wilson when he tells us that the "deindustrialization" of America's cities has contributed strongly to the drastic changes in inner-city social life. Poverty and job loss have left the kids described in this book with deeply painful feelings of frustration, disappointment, humiliation, and shame, and these emotions have in turn deeply affected their behavior toward members of their families and communities. However, the progressive alienation of poor city dwellers from the opportunities of mainstream job markets does not explain why black people's late-twentieth-century experiences of desperation and community change have been so much more drastic than those of other groups of urban poor people. And I am not convinced, for a variety of reasons also outlined in chapter 2, that other trends that have further alienated inner-city kids from the mainstream—such as increased welfare dependence, the emigration of middle-class black role models, or autonomous cultures of the poor derived from earlier urban experiences or from the rural South—help much to explain any of the specific personal characteristics of poor urban black people's recent collective experience, nor why it happened when it did, nor even why poor black people have suffered in recent years so much more greatly than other poor people.

Theories of alienation leave a lot of the story out, and in part 2, I argue that a more comprehensive explanation of the inner-city tragedy must delve into the ways that inner-city kids have actually become more American, not less, during the late twentieth century. The recent history of the ethical and emotional experience of poor African-Americans and the recent history of their communities cannot be written without understanding how some of mainstream America's most familiar and compelling institutions, ideals, and images have helped to raise inner-city children. American ideas of social control through "law and order," American racial imagery, American consumerism, and American traditions of violence have all had important (and in some cases, increasingly important) parts to play in the growing tragedy of neighborhoods like Bojack's and Chauntey's.

One crucial historical intersection between mainstream culture and the lives of poor black children has occurred in their relationships with some of the most important institutions charged with social control in the inner city. In chapter 3, I argue that the parenting philosophies of many poor African-American parents today, and the mandates of most urban police departments, juvenile court justices, and prisons, have centered around the idea that the control of aggressive or community-threatening behavior demands some form of didactic use of violence or incarceration. This idea has been derived in part from age-old American notions about the need for forceful parenting, and it has also been buttressed in recent years by mainstream America's desperate attempt to respond to urban violence through law-and-order policies. This kind of moral education has helped make cooperative values universally familiar, but hollow and uncompelling in kids' eyes. Also, because of its strictly behavioristic suppositions, such an approach has done little to help kids gain any self-awareness of the painful emotions that so often lie behind their aggressive behavior.

Chapter 4 contains a close examination of the recent historical career of American racism as experienced by inner-city children. I argue that racial exclusion must be recognized as a principal reason for the extraordinary nature of black inner-city communities' experience of desperation. Despite very real positive changes in American racial attitutdes during the years since the civil rights movement, kids still encounter expressions of racial hatred, live in racially segregated neighborhoods, and endure the suspicion widespread among many people in positions of authority. These persistent forms of racial exclusion have eroded the best efforts of educators and black political and cultural leaders to inspire racial pride among poor African-Americans, and inner-city kids have universally continued to grow up feeling the nagging feeling that blackness is something to be ashamed of. Thus, racial alienation in all these persistent forms adds to kids' emotional memories of humiliation and their widespread tendency to resent suspicion.

However, American racism has not merely affected kids as a force of exclusion: the idea that black people, and especially black men, are somehow inherently violent has been resurgent in the mainstream American mind during recent decades. Especially during the 1970s and 1980s inner-city kids, particularly boys, have taken to defiantly glorifying the caricature of the violent, oversexed black man and have transformed the so-called baaad nigger into a hero. In doing so, they not only have found a way to achieve a sense of compensatory personal adequacy in the face of racial humiliation but also have created an important basis of moral legitimacy for violence derived directly from a mainstream image.

African-American inner-city kids have also become eager practitioners of America's ethic of conspicuous consumption. In chapter 5, I trace changes in the inner-city's experience of American abundance. From the late 1960s on, mainstream marketers have targeted black inner-city youth for promotional blitzes, and, following the leadership of the sports-apparel and cheap-jewelry industries, they have strived to give specific material shape to young black people's desire for compensatory status. To counter feelings of humiliation and frustration derived from poverty and racial exclusion, kids like the ones described in this book have enthusiastically embraced the American consumer culture—hundred-dollar sneakers, sports jackets, gold, and all. At the same time, however, the self-absorption, aggression, and material expense associated with conspicuous consumption has undermined the long-term viability of these coping strategies, both for kids' own sense of well-being and for their commitment to cooperation in their families and communities. The growing number of killings associated with status symbols like sneakers and gold chains only attests to the extent to which mass consumption has, under the desperate circumstances of the inner city, turned into a passion to kill.

Young African-Americans growing up in inner cities have also come into increasing contact with newly glorified versions of the age-old values of American violence. These values have a variety of ancestries, whether they were born in slavery, the genocide of Native Americans, frontier lawlessness, racial violence, men's violence against women, state violence against working-class people, Prohibition-era gangsterism, or cold-war militarism. In the late twentieth century, the media of American mass culture have grown increasingly fond of sanitizing and celebrating each of these American traditions of violence, and they have disseminated them to ever-expanding audiences of children. My argument in chapter 6 is that, in the process of distributing these values to a mass audience, America's violent television shows and its blockbuster action-adventure and horror film images have replaced the streetcorner and African-American folkloric forms as the most important source of legitimacy for street-smart values of social manipulation and violence.

New pairs of sneakers every month, Mickey Mouse T-shirts, glorified caricatures, "racial obsessions," "patriotism" and "law-and-order" ideas, and long lines of young African-American people outside showings of *Terminator* or *Nightmare on Elm Street* are all important to the inner-city story. In the past thirty-five years, poor African-American children have increasingly and enthusiastically sought out these essentially American values, self-images, and grand delusions as principal means of expressing and compensating for the awful hurt they have felt growing up poor, jobless, and racially outcast. Thus, although economic exclusion from job markets and social exclusion need to take a central place in our explanations for changes in poor urban communities, the twentieth-century history of black inner-city culture has not been, overall, one of increasing isolation, but one that has proceeded from relative isolation to greater participation in the larger American culture. But in their embrace of the values associated with American law and order, racial caricatures, abundance, and violence, black inner-city children have also increasingly lost contact with more autonomous African-American traditions such as expressive religion or the rituals of "toasting" and "playing the dozens" that may have actually been more successful in curbing violent expressions of pain. Mainstream American values and self-images have, if anything, been much more likely to encourage imitations of violent and armed expressions of pain, and much more likely to cause confusing and painful dilemmas of identity, than the more cathartic, less violent and less heavily armed, more imagined and ritualized forms of traditional folklore.

The increasing presence of mainstream American cultural forms in inner-city life offers the best explanation for why urban African-Americans' experience of poverty, joblessness, and racial exclusion (all of which black people have, after all, lived through in earlier times, sometimes to greater degrees than they do now) has been so filled with changing families and so tragically filled with violence in the years since World War II—and why that tragedy has worsened during, of all times, the years since the civil rights movement.

It is time to find new names for the all-American kids I describe in this book and for their extraordinary experience of being both maliciously cast out of the country's mainstream and thoroughly and enthusiastically included in it. Our new vocabulary—scholarly and otherwise—does not need to add to the excoriation that America has already too willingly heaped on its poor African-American citizens. Though it needs to be candid about violence and desperation and the complex human story behind the historical tragedy of the inner city, it also needs to be subtle enough both to decry urban violence and to provide for a more direct path between fear of urban danger and the desire for understanding, not a direct route between fear and hatred. What I offer as an alternative set of words are the stories and lessons I was taught by some inner-city kids. I hope these will help—even if just a little—to give more Americans new kinds of voices in their conversations about and with the American people they have most often and most viciously ignored and despised.

PART I

THE DIMENSIONS OF A HISTORICAL TRAGEDY

1

The Explosion of
Inner-City Desperation

In the summer of 1961, sixteen-year-old Johnnie "Bojack" Dungee grew out of being just a schoolyard bully. His fists, fortified by a "certain large ring" that bore the menacing head of an elephant, had already earned him grudging admiration and fear from other kids his age. But now it was time to parlay his reputation into more serious pursuits. As his mother despaired for his future, the social workers from the local chapter of the Big Brothers Association (who had known Bojack since he started robbing parking meters at age ten) closed their case in complete frustration. Bojack had become a bona fide "jitterbug"—"the first lieutenant and known warlord of a very large gang"[1]—and the police reported that they were watching his every move.

By 1961, the mostly black Philadelphia neighborhood where Bojack lived had begun to be a very dangerous place. Five years earlier, the city's juvenile court had found it necessary to devise a new statistical category of deadly weapons charges to fit changing times. And at first count, 130 of the 151 people arrested for "possession of pistols, revolvers, and zip-guns" were young black men.[2] These racially skewed numbers may reflect the Philadelphia Police Department's notorious inclination to harass African-American kids like Bojack. But other, more sobering statistics existed as well, and these were harder for prejudiced officials to fudge: 1960 was the first year in Philadelphia history that homicide was the leading cause of death among young African-American men.[3]

A quarter century later, during the summer and fall of 1988, twelve-year-old Chauntey Patterson came of age in a way similar to Bojack's experience. Chauntey's rite of passage was also a blustery, defiant, confused, and aggressive affair. It started on the "Avenue" near his house, where he answered calls for crack deliveries that came in on the corner pay phone; it ended shortly afterward when he was sent to the juvenile court's Youth Study Center, a concrete-and-chainlink holding tank that the city of Philadelphia had built since Bojack's day to contain the growing number of kids arrested for violent crimes. The facility had already been overcrowded by the late 1960s, when African-American gangs like Bojack's suddenly began to multiply at an uncontrollable rate, which helped boost the likelihood of homicidal violence to a level never before recorded in Philadelphia. A lull in the killing then ensued, but by 1988, the year of Chauntey's first visit to juvenile jail, young African-Americans in Philadelphia were once again dying at each other's hands in unprecedented numbers.

The late twentieth century has been a period of historical tragedy for poor urban black American communities. Since about 1960 key relationships within families, especially between adult men and women, and between fathers and their children, have undergone extreme stress, highlighted by the virtual disappearance of marriage as an institution among poor black people. Also, an extraordinary surge in levels of fatal violence has threatened to overwhelm not only the traditions of cooperation rooted in African-American extended families, active neighborhood organizations, and churches, but also main-stream institutions of social control operating in inner-city communities—like schools, social welfare services, police, and the courts. These late-twentieth-century changes were both historically unprecedented and exceptional: poor, urban African-American communities felt their tragic effects much more profoundly than did any other poor urban group.

Looking back before the Second World War, family structure in urban African-American communities had changed relatively little since at least the mid-nineteenth century. As the sociologist Frank Furstenberg and his colleagues at the Philadelphia Social History Project discovered, most of Philadelphia's black families in 1850 and 1880 lived in households with two parents.[4] Thus, marriage, whether formalized or common-law, apparently remained a fairly widespread institution in the cities, despite the ravages visited upon black family life by slavery, and despite migration from the countryside to urban areas. In addition, fathers evidently tended to live with their children or with their wives' children.

African-American households as a whole were more likely to be run by a single parent than were those of white families in nineteenth-century Philadelphia. However, the family structure of poor black and poor white single-parent families differed very little; suggesting that poverty was one of the main reasons for the end of marriages or for fathers living apart from children. An even closer look at those single-parent families revealed that by far, most of the women who ran those families were widows. Thus, marriages and fathers' relations with their children seldom ended for social reasons—that is, because men deserted their family responsibilities or were asked to leave—but rather because of health-related and demographic reasons, namely, the high rates of sickness and death among poor men.[5] Also, life in immediate families—whether including one or two parents, and their children—also seems to have been interconnected in very important ways with the lives of extended relatives. Indeed, censuses from the late nineteenth and early twentieth centuries show that black extended families more often lived under the same roof than did white families, and that extended relatives in black families more often took on the responsibility for fostering relatives' children than did white families.[6]

Other bits and pieces of information from early-twentieth-century surveys, plus detailed data from the 1940 U.S. Census, suggest that little changed in urban African-American family life throughout the first half of the twentieth century. Information from the so-called long-form census questionnaires from 1940[7] reveals a portrait of urban black life that is strikingly similar to what Furstenberg and his colleagues found in Philadelphia sixty years before: most African-American households contained two parents, rates of single-parent households were similar among groups of poor people, and most single parents were widowed women.[8]

Other aspects of family life seem to have remained relatively stable even to the present day. Anthropologist Carol Stack, and other scholars who lived and worked in African-American neighborhoods during the late 1960s and 1970s, found that women in black extended families maintained strong networks of mutual responsibility into the late 1960s. In the 1990s, all of the children I met in Philadelphia lived in extended families who, despite their extreme poverty, often practiced what Stack called "the cooperative life-style of the poor," providing family members with child care, foster care, transportation, and help in managing family crises.[9]

If extended families maintained many of their traditions in post–World War II Philadelphia, however, immediate families were changing rapidly and in unprecedented fashion. First, the proportion of black households nationwide that included both parents declined suddenly and precipitously during the 1960s and even more quickly during the 1970s (see appendix A, table A.1). In the process, the historical similarity between white and black poor people's family structure disappeared. The proportion of white single-parent households among the poor population rose from 15 percent in 1959 to about 25 percent by 1985. Among blacks the portion of the poor living in families headed by a single woman skyrocketed during the same years, from 25 percent to almost 60 percent[10] (see figure 1.1).

This transformation could no longer be attributed solely to health and demographic trends among the poor. It reflected deep changes in the nature of familial relationships. The collapse of marriage was the most important immediate reason for the decrease in two-parent

FIGURE 1.1
Proportion of the Poor Population Living in
Households Run by Single Women, by Race, 1959–1983

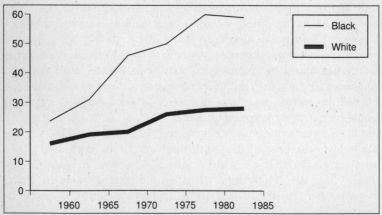

Source: Mary Jo Bane, "Household Composition and Poverty," in *Fighting Poverty: What Works and What Doesn't,* ed. Sheldon Danziger and Daniel Weinberg (Cambridge, Mass.: Harvard University Press, 1986), p. 216.

families.[11] From 1940 to 1980, poor African-American women who had married were increasingly likely to be separated or divorced, and poor African-American women in general became dramatically less likely to choose to marry at all. Indeed, separation rates among poor blacks grew so fast that they increasingly diverged from those of poor whites. Marriage rates among poor urban black women also decreased much more quickly than among poor urban white women. By 1980, only 12 percent of poor urban black women aged fourteen to forty-four were married (see appendix A, table A.2).

No longer were most women who ran single-parent households widows. By 1960, the largest group of both white and black poor women who ran households on their own were women who were separated from the men they had married. However, from 1960 to 1980, there was a growing divergence in the circumstances under which poor black and white single women formed their families. By 1980, following the rising white divorce rate, the largest group of poor white single mothers were divorced women. But because of the huge decline in marriage among poor black women during the same years, almost half of poor urban African-American single mothers formed their families by having a child and then not marrying or living with the father (see appendix A, table A.3).[12]

Indeed, another change in the poor urban African-American family was the decreasing likelihood that fathers would live with their children, and probably also a decreasing likelihood that they would offer their children economic support. The census does not record how absent fathers have behaved toward their children, but the marital status of single mothers can give us some idea of the relative risk single mothers run of not receiving paternal support. In 1985, the Census Bureau contacted a large sample of poor women who ran households on their own to determine what kind of economic support they could expect from the father of their children. In their report, they found that, of all poor single women who ran households of their own, separated women and women who had never married were by far the most likely to report that they desired child support, but had failed to get it because they were unable to locate their children's father. Reflecting differences in marriage rates, poor black women were twice as likely as their white counterparts to say they were not getting support because they could not find the father of their children.[13]

The sudden transformation of poor black families in the 1960s and 1970s coincided fairly closely with the explosion in inner-city violence. Before 1960, the year when things started to change dramatically for the worse, black communities in cities had in fact endured higher rates of violence than most other communities.[14] During the nineteenth and early twentieth centuries, the overall rate of homicide in the United States and other industrial societies had declined steadily—and would only begin to rise again in the decades after World War II in a pattern historians call the "*U* curve"[15] (see figure 1.2). The experience of African-American communities, though, had been quite different from any such general trend: murder rates among blacks actually rose fairly constantly from the mid-

FIGURE 1.2
The "U-Curve" in Western Violent Crime Rates,
Plotted against Select Homicide Rates
for Whites and Blacks in Philadelphia and New York City
1830 – 1990

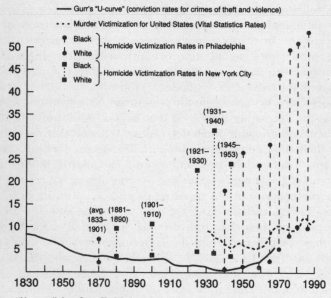

Sources: "U-curve" data from Ted Robert Gurr, "Historical Trends in Violent Crime: Europe and the United States," in *Violence in America,* ed. Ted Robert Gurr (Newbury Park, Calif.: Sage, 1989), p. 22, fig. 1.1; vital statistics data for the U.S. from Margaret Zahn, "Homicide in the Twentieth Century," in *Violence in America,* p. 219; New York rates from Gurr's calculations (based on Eric Monkkonen's research) in "Historical Trends," p. 39; Philadelphia data for 1833–1901 from Roger Lane, *Violent Death in the City: Suicide, Accident, and Murder in Nineteenth Century Philadelphia* (Cambridge, Mass.: Harvard University Press, 1979), p. 43; for other dates, data from Philadelphia Department of Health, *Annual Birth and Death Reports for Philadelphia,* volumes for 1940, 1950, 1960, 1965, 1970, 1975, 1980, 1985, 1989.

dle of the nineteenth century onward, and in Philadelphia by 1950, they stood at a level ten times as high as those of whites.[16]

However, even this long, steady climb in rates of fatal violence among African-American Philadelphians did not presage what occurred after 1960: from 1960 to 1970 the overall murder rate in black Philadelphia more than doubled. A dozen somewhat less grim years followed, but in 1988, the year of Chauntey Patterson's first arrest, murder rates once again broke city records (see figure 1.2).

Some of the sudden increase in fatal violence during the 1960s did reflect growing warfare between rival black "turf" gangs. In Bojack's day, gang wars had begun to take the lives of growing numbers of young black Philadelphia men. From 1968 to 1975, over 150 gangs, each identifying with a particular streetcorner, fought a series of vicious, deadly clashes against their rivals—and against Police Commissioner Frank Rizzo's notoriously brutal "Philly's Finest"— using knives, revolvers, and the favored zipguns (which could be made at home from pipes, nails, and rubber bands).[17] Among teenage African-American boys (aged fifteen to nineteen), homicide rates in the early 1970s were three times as high as in the late 1950s (see table 1.1).

As Philadelphia's turf gangs dispersed, died out, grew out of the habit, were broken up by police reprisals, or were brought to their senses by highly effective community organizations like the House of Umoja,[18] violence among teenagers in the city declined somewhat, helping to account for the period of relative calm in Philadelphia streets during the late 1970s and early 1980s. Meanwhile, though,

TABLE 1.1

Average Homicide Victimization Rates among Philadelphia Teenagers Aged 15–19, by Sex and Race, Selected Periods 1957–1990

	Boys		Girls	
	Nonwhite	White	Nonwhite	White
1957–60	42.6	2.6	5.4	0.9
1961–65	56.1	3.3	6.4	0.4
1966–70	105.8	6.4	9.6	2.2
1971–75	152.8	11.6	18.2	4.6
1976–80	71.5	17.3	7.9	2.4
1981–87	59.0	16.2	10.4	4.1
1988–90	153.9	33.5	20.5	7.5

Sources: Average rates of death caused by homicide in Philadelphia calculated from Philadelphia Department of Health, *Annual Birth and Death Reports for Philadelphia,* for each year from 1957 through 1990. Average rates calculated on estimates of population aged 15–19 and analogous U.S. Census figures as listed each year in the *Annual Birth and Death Reports for Philadelphia.*

the ringleaders of the trade in illegal narcotics, which had grown during the heroin craze of the late 1960s, began to revamp their marketing strategies.[19] Sales of crack cocaine, which soared in response to that drug's cheap price, its easy high, and the vast market of increasingly desperate buyers, have required well-organized and labor-intensive distribution strategies. The result for inner-city Philadelphia, which has seen a growing conflict between Jamaican dealers, a local "Junior Black Mafia," and semi-independent dealers like the revived Zulu Nation turf gang,[20] has been disastrous new increases in violent death, especially among teenage boys and men in their twenties. With the fire of semiautomatic assault rifles endemic to some neighborhoods and indiscriminate drive-by shootings more commonplace, it has become increasingly likely for bystanders, often children, to be mowed down by accident.[21] A full 80 percent of all teenagers murdered in the United States in 1990 died of gunshot wounds.

However, the rise in violence during the 1960s, 1970s, and 1980s was not at all confined to Philadelphia, nor was it solely the result of the increasing accessibility and use of firearms. Murders that did not involve guns also increased to unprecedented levels nationwide during the 1960s and early 1970s. Also, violent death became more common for people who had little or less to do with gangs or drugs: young women, middle-aged women (a population whose murder rate reflects trends in domestic violence),[22] and children under the age of four (whose violent death usually results from child abuse). In another sign of spiraling desperation and violence, the black suicide rate in Philadelphia, which has historically always been lower than the white rate, increased threefold between the late 1950s and 1990, and over fourteenfold in the same period among African-American male teenagers (see appendix A, tables A.7–A.9).[23]

Growing evidence also shows that the extraordinary levels of violence suffered by African-American communities cannot be accounted for solely by high levels of black poverty. We will probably never know for sure when murder rates among poor urban African-Americans began to exceed those among other poor communities. According to the journalist Charles Silberman, late-twentieth-century Latino communities have tended to have higher poverty rates, but considerably lower murder rates, than black communities. My own comparison of homicide rates in 1980 Philadelphia census tracts in black, white, and Latino communities with equal poverty rates revealed similar results.[24]

* * *

The realities behind these cold, hard statistics have resonated in the homes, streets, and schoolyards of African-American inner-city childhood. Poor Philadelphia black kids like Bojack and Chauntey have been increasingly likely to become tragic "statistics" themselves. Even if they have managed to escape that fate, the odds are that such children have experienced the violent death of a close relative, have suffered through their parents' acrimony, or have entertained wistful thoughts about a father who was unable or even unwilling to support them.

But the connection between childhood and the statistics is even more profound than that. For one thing, abandonment of family responsibilities and homicidal violence have made up only one part of the varied range of behavior that has threatened the social life of inner-city neighborhoods like Bojack's and Chauntey's. Communal life in those neighborhoods has also been interrupted very often by a variety of much more ordinary and less consequential noncooperative and violent acts—such as manipulation, defiance, verbal abuse, and fighting. The extent of these kinds of day-to-day interactions has been reflected in the variety of slang terms poor black children have created to describe social life in their communities. More important, though, children growing up in the world of late-twentieth-century inner cities have also inevitably faced two deeply confusing and painful personal struggles whose outcome greatly determines the extent to which they make aggressive behavior part of their own daily habits and social styles. The first of these personal struggles, occurring on a conscious level, involves the conflict between two equally familiar, but often contradictory, value systems: on the one hand, an extremely complicated set of street-smart values that decree an edgy mistrust of others and a cynical sense that manipulation and force win out, and on the other hand, ethical traditions that advocate cooperative responsibility and mutual obligation toward family members, neighbors, and peers. At the same time that kids struggle to resolve the contradictions of these value systems, they also wage a second internal struggle on a subconscious level: this one involves kids' attempts to cope with often overwhelmingly painful emotions they have collected throughout childhood in the reservoirs of their emotional memory. In order to explain why kids themselves have become all too likely to act in ways that undermine their own communities, we need to investigate the details of these personal struggles.

Since World War II, folklorists, ethnographers, and linguists have been impressed by the extent to which young black people's street slang has focused on acts of manipulation, defiance, boasting, and flight from sexual and social responsibility. Some of this language may owe its origins to the age of slavery, when black people played manipulative tricks on their white masters. But by the 1950s, when the folklorist Roger Abraham began his stay in a poor black Philadelphia neighborhood, nineteenth-century terms like "shuckin' and jivin'." applied to the deceptions and manipulations that devious black hustlers, numbers runners, pimps, "mackmen," "hipcat studs," and con artists played on other black people.[25] In the "toasts," boastful rhymed orations that were passed down from generation to generation and performed by young African-American men on streetcorners, characters like the Signifyin' Monkey, Stackolee, Honky-Tonk Bud, and the "cold-blooded mack" prostitute Duriella du Fontaine were celebrated for their abilities to lead others by indirection and force. *Signifying*, the word most commonly used for the Monkey's practices, was the stock-in-trade of all protagonists of the toasts, who celebrated their exploits at "staking my claim to a piece of the game" and at forcing women to accept lives as prize trophies in the "stables" of their sexual conquerors:

> *Where the jungle creed says the strong must feed*
> *On any prey at hand,*
> *I was branded a beast and sat at the feast*
> *Before I was a man.*
> . . . . .
>
> *In the gaudy display of the midnight ray*
> *Lit up like a Christmas toy,*
> *I made my play for female prey*
> *At the time I was just a boy.*
> . . . . .
>
> *Now it wasn't by chance that I caught her glance,*
> *'Cause I intended to steal this dame;*
> *So I smiled with glee and said, "Golly gee,*
> *It's time for the kid to game."*[26]

Another term for manipulation, "copping a plea," was derived from the legal maneuver by which accused people could diminish their sentences by pleading guilty to lesser charges. By the late sixties, according to the ethnographer Thomas Kochman, it referred to ways of "inducing pity" in an aggressor or a more powerful person to get what one wanted.[27] The linguist Edith Folb, who lived and worked during the late 1960s and most of the 1970s in South-Central, a gang-racked poor black neighborhood of Los Angeles, wrote that "fully a fourth of the vernacular expressions" she recorded "describe or characterize some form of manipulative or coercive activity." The most commonly used terms for manipulation included "gaming," "shaming," "slicking," "zooming," "blowing on" someone, "gigoloing" someone, "tripping out" someone, and "fucking with" someone's "mind."[28]

The most commonly used general term for manipulation in postwar poor African-American communities has been, of course, the "hustle." When the kids in Chauntey's neighborhood first met with interested adults in 1988 to name our newly founded community organization, the most popular suggestion was the "————Street Hustlers." Although the name was eventually rejected (mostly because of adult pressure), the kids' identification with the term persisted. "After all," then eleven-year-old Chauntey Patterson reminded everyone (to murmurs of agreement), "we all hustlers!" Language describing forms of hustling has a wide currency in Chauntey's neighborhood: "sweating," "fronting," "putting on airs," and "perpetrating the fraud" (pronounced by little kids, with even more poetic effect, "perpetrating the fog") or just "perpetrating." To "gag" people, "baste" them, "cap" them, make them "catch the vapors," or leave them "with their nose wide open" are ways of exulting in the success of a hustle—itself sometimes known as the "hype" (as in the rap group Public Enemy's hit song "Don't Believe the Hype") or a "gag." A hustler is most commonly judged on his or her ability to be "slick." Hustles that are too transparent are usually put down by words like "he think he slick," or "man, you ain't slick."

The most common use of this language occurs in boys' or young men's relationships with women. From very early on, boys and girls learn that manipulation, violence, and coercion are common—if not always widely valued—ways of maintaining control over family, marital, and other heterosexual relationships. Fourteen-year-old Fahim Wilkins, a friend of Chauntey's, once laid out his plans for wooing a girl to bed in this way: "First I'm a crack on her, then I'll g her up, then I'll fuck her." "Cracking" and "g-ing" (short for "gaming," a term derived from pimping), or "working a girl," involve different forms of manipulation (called "sweating," or "getting on her cock" [either vagina or clitoris]) and boasting ("fronting" or "putting up a front"). Sexual conquest is an extremely important part of proving a boy's masculine adequacy and his prowess as a "b-boy" (short for "bad boy"). The very terms boys use for girls carry coercive overtones. Girls almost always get called "bitches," "hos," "chumpies," "hotties," or "slimmies" in conversations between boys. Boys often gloat about the number of "seven-digits" (phone numbers) they have collected from girls, and some boys keep running records of these conquests on pads of paper they carry in their pockets.

An ethic of conquest that forbids expressions of emotional vulnerability toward girls, coupled with a thoroughgoing sense of mistrust, also dictates boys' thoughts about intimate relationships and marriage: Omar Wilkins, Fahim's younger brother, has vowed repeatedly that he would "never, never trust a slimmy, never. They always after your shit, then they dump your ass." He is fond of making fun of an older brother of his and Fahim's, a young man who has agreed to take responsibility for a child of his girlfriend's by another man. "Rent-a-pop," Omar calls him, as he dissolves into gales of laughter, "he a rent-a-pop!" From very early on in their sexual awakenings, boys subscribe wholeheartedly to the idea that relationships with women are to be kept nonbinding, primarily sexual, devoid of pledges of responsibility (except as manipulative devices), and strictly temporary. This "fuck 'em, fill 'em, leave 'em" attitude most definitely contributes heavily to the continued growth of the number of homes run by single women in the neighborhood.[29]

The aggressive side of the streetwise ethic of inner-city childhood has been as pervasively mirrored in street slang as the manipulative side, but the culture of aggression has been much more complex and multifaceted, and its values have extended across a wider spectrum, from benign verbal abuse to the openly predatory and homicidal.

Like manipulation, language for verbal abuse in black inner-city communities may have roots in the earliest history of African-American folklore, especially practices that involved blacks' relationships to whites on slave plantations: historical folklorists have collected the lyrics of countless slave songs that contain veiled denunciations of their masters. By the 1930s, in urban black neighborhoods, historian Lawrence Levine found that derision and put-down had become central to an important folkloric practice involving social encounters between blacks, namely, the ritualized insult games known as the "dozens" or "playing the dirty dozens."[30]

Other scholars have documented instances of similar games, called by a variety of names, being played in different places at different times in the post–World War II years. Roger Abrahams heard the dozens called "sounding" or "woofing" in late-1950s Philadelphia. "Sounding" was still the current term in Philadelphia and New York in the late 1960s, when William Labov began his sociolinguistic inquiries there; and ethnographer Ulf Hannerz found the term "joning" to be more common in Washington, D.C., during the same period. Linguist Edith Folb listed a huge variety of terms in her lexicon of Los Angeles slang from the 1970s, including "screaming," "vibing," "capping," "cutting," "chipping," "cracking," "shooting," and "droppin' lugs."[31]

In keeping with this tradition of linguistic invention and variety, very few of the terms referring to verbal insult that I learned in Chauntey's Philadelphia neighborhood coincided with those that folklorists had documented ten years earlier. "Bussing," the most common general term Chauntey's peers used for insult and verbal put-down, has a number of synonyms: among others, "messing with," "talking trash" (or just "talkin' about" someone), "picking," "dissing" (a common rap term derived from *disrespecting*, I have been told), "illing," and "getting in (someone's) face" are a few of these terms. Though the game is no longer played in quite the ritualistic way that Abrahams and Labov observed during the 1950s and 1960s, prowess at insulting is still highly valued. In many cases the insulters were referring to the poverty, the skin color, or the sexual availability of their victim's mother:

Your mom so fat she jumped up in the sky and got stuck.

Your dad so skinny he use a Cheerio for a Hula Hoop.

Your mom so dumb she try to put M&M's in alphabetical order.

Your freezer so empty, I looked in there and saw the roaches ice-skating

One day I came to your house to use the bathroom, and your mom told me it was the first bucket to the left.

There wasn't any toilet tissue, so she said, "That's okay—just slide down the bannister."

Your house so cold that when I came over to watch the basketball game, the Sixers were wearing mittens.

The close resonance between terms for verbal abuse and those describing fights—like "popping," "dropping," "bum rushing," "rolling on," "fucking (someone) up,"—is not merely linguistic: in Chauntey's neighborhood, the trading of insults often provided the context for outbreaks of physical violence. By contrast, during earlier years of the post–World War II era, dozens playing may have served a cathartic function that prevented actual fights (see chapter 6 for more on this change).[32]

Fighting has, nonetheless, been a ubiquitous part of inner-city black childhood throughout the late twentieth century. The values that prescribe physical violence are varied, and different groups of young people, with different age and gender compositions, subscribe to different sets of these values. The most widely acknowledged moral justifications for fighting and violence have been for self-defense, for deterrence against other aggression, and for the decrying and avenging of an individual's or a group's victimization. Kids of all ages and both genders have endorsed the view that physical and verbal retaliation is a fundamental right; in most cases, but especially for boys, it has been a moral imperative. Proper retaliation, furthermore, has often been seen to involve an escalation in hostility; for example, a dirty look or a particularly cutting insult (especially one made by someone the avenger does not know) warrants, even requires, physical violence.

"During [her] growing up years," Etta, a client of the Episcopal City Service's Sheltering Arms program during the fifties, "recalled that she was always fighting someone, partly because she was picked on for things that were not her fault."[33] The intensity with which inner-city kids have clung to this imperative to return aggression in kind or by besting it can be seen in instances when adults seeking to instill cooperative values tried to prevent acts of revenge seeking. Duane, one of Bojack's fellow clients at the Big Brothers Association in the late 1950s, "said he didn't like to fight especially but people [were] always bothering him." When the caseworker "told Duane that fighting should be resorted to as a solution only when there is no other alternative," Duane sidestepped the issue of more cooperative alternatives and claimed that the severity of his victimization justified his fighting: "Duane insisted that others molested and annoyed him to the point where he felt it was necessary to fight."[34]

In Chauntey's neighborhood fights of revenge could break out daily, among both girls and boys. My most eye-opening experience of the power of the ethic of retributive violence, however, came in an argument I had with a young cousin of Fahim and Omar Wilkins. This youngster, Rasool, had been at the local swimming pool with his two younger brothers, aged eight and six. According to his report, "forty big boys" began to "instigate" with him and his brothers, and when he started to defend himself, his six-year-old brother did not join in, but instead cowered in a corner. Recalling this, Rasool became furious at his youngest brother, calling him a "punk" and shouting at him that "blood always swings together! Forty guys were there and you should have jumped into it." Indignant, I admonished, "Rasool, you have no right to force anyone to fight. I can't believe what I'm hearing you say, especially to a six-year-old!" Rasool's response outflanked me neatly and logically: "What do you mean *force* him? I shouldn't have to force him. He should just have jumped in without being forced."

Another universally shared ethic of aggression concerned the value of violence as a form of entertainment. Philadelphia news reporters who covered gang activity in the 1950s and 1960s repeatedly noted that street wars provided a diversion from the boring streets of places like North Philly. One of Bojack's fellow "little brothers" for example, robbed a store at gunpoint in 1958 "because there was nothing else to do."[35] This same refrain was often invoked as a reason to build more recreation centers and ballparks in black neighborhoods, something that occurred with increasing frequency as black politicians began to achieve prominence in Philadelphia politics during the seventies.

In Chauntey's neighborhood, however, the most avidly anticipated forms of entertainment—outside perhaps violent adventure films, professional wrestling extravaganzas, and boxing matches—are streetfights themselves. Once when I was quietly talking with some girls on my front steps, two of their friends suddenly raced up to us, breathlessly yelling, "Quick! Them two ladies fightin'!" Our conversation ceased instantly as all of the kids tore around the corner. When I went to see what was happening, I noticed that a huge crowd of adults and kids had gathered in the street to watch the two women slugging it out and causing an uproar. Incidents like this occur about once every four or five months on my block (more frequently in the surrounding area), and for several days afterwards, everyone talks about them in much the same way as about horror flicks. Omar is perhaps the most prurient streetfight fan I know. He frequently wanders over to a local drug corner to watch gunfights from his cousin's nearby living-room window. He also finds other people's victimization absolutely hilarious, and he will often laugh out loud while he is

telling me stories about fights, or sometimes go to great lengths to
deride other kids who have gotten hurt. Once, a tutor at the Kids'
Club told Omar that she had seen a man assaulting his wife, and
asked him what he would do if he witnessed domestic violence. Omar
guffawed and said loudly, for all the other kids to hear, "I'd get some
chairs and put 'em out there. Then I'd sell tickets!"

The widely shared values of aggression for revenge and entertainment in neighborhoods like Bojack's and Chauntey's have formed
the bedrock for a set of more severe ethical codes, ones that prescribe actively offensive, predatory, and even homicidal violence.
The currency of these values has been much more bounded by gender, and maybe even age, than others: they have been almost exclusively the province of young men.

In the 1940s and 1950s, these values belonged to the kings of
street culture—or the "sporting life," as it was often still called—the
"jitterbugs" and "hipcats." Many reputed young "jitterbugs" came to
the attention of Philadelphia social service agencies: like Bojack,
they were very often (but not always) members of turf gangs. Jitterbug boys wore their hair greased and "marcelled" (straightened),
and they sometimes flaunted expensive and brightly colored suits,
shoes, and wide-brimmed hats. Some of them crafted zip guns or
carried revolvers acquired through mail order or on the street.[36]
Other highly visible older male teenagers and young men also
gained notoriety in the sporting life as numbers runners, heroin
pushers, or pimps. In all the 1940s and 1950s Philadelphia casework
reports I read, I found no references to girls as jitterbugs. However, a
half dozen or so references appeared to members of "girl gangs"
(usually affiliated with the gang boys they were involved with roman-
tically). The members, along with their boyfriends, "carried knives,"
or they fought with other girls. But girls usually got a reputation for
being "bad" through sexual activity, and especially through unmarried pregnancy, rather than through violence.[37]

Bojack had begun to enter this world as a schoolyard bully. After
he had achieved great success in the game of revenge and deterrence by using his fists and elephant ring and "everybody at school
[was] afraid of him," he could move into more predatory pursuits:
"He is able to have all the sandwiches and all the soft drinks he wants
just by asking for them," wrote his caseworker. Later, his mother
reported that "he had been involved in a fight in the neighborhood,
and . . . that the mother [of the victim] had come to her and said
that Johnnie had practically killed her son."

Since the Big Brothers caseworker who recorded Bojack's life gave up in frustration as his charge plunged into the maw of gang violence, we do not know specifically how Bojack's social consciousness developed as he passed into his late teens. However, other bits of evidence from other case reports of the fifties and sixties do demonstrate how gangs could make predatory ethics into codes of moral obligation, employ them in their own designs on other gangs' territory, and even use similar values to punish cooperative behavior:

> Harry said that the boys from A Street and B Street never got along and were always fighting against each other, and he did not join the gang and the boys in his neighborhood called him chicken. The boys in A Street attacked him because he was from B Street.[38]

> Leroy said several weeks ago a teacher asked if he knew who had caused a particular disturbance at school. . . . He gave the teacher the names of the boys who were responsible and later these boys wanted to fight him. He said they chased him, caught him and hit him a few times before he could get away again.[39]

> Only last week George's boyfriend Alvin had been hit in the head with a stick and cut at the nape of his neck to within a few inches of his jugular vein. He said this had so scared Alvin that he has not been back to school since then. On the days he goes he does not sign the daily record because the boys in the gang look at the daily record and see who is at school and in the evening these boys are singled out an beatten [sic].[40]

When Ida Mae, once a knife-carrying girl-gang member, had a baby and "determined to have nothing to do with this gang again," she and her boyfriend, Alfie, were forced to stay inside, "except for short walks during the day," because they "were both in . . . bad graces." Her boyfriend ended up in Philadelphia General Hospital when his irate former gangmates attacked him and shot him in the thigh.[41]

Open advocacy of homicide also played something of a part in gang culture at least as early as the mid-1950s. The sociologist Lew Yablonski, who worked as a social worker for a gang prevention program in New York during the 1950s, remembers one member of the "Kings" lamenting a missed chance to kill someone: "That would have given me more of a build-up. People would have respected me for what I've done and things like that. They would say, 'There goes

a cold killer.'" Later, at a highly publicized trial of black gang members accused of killing a white boy, one of the accused told police
that he "always wanted to see how it felt to stick a knife through
human bone."[42]

Ethnographers and folklorists living in Philadelphia during the
1950s extensively documented similar values in the toasts. During
the 1950s, the toasts still often paid homage to Stackolee and Shine,
the mythic black badmen who first appeared in African-American
folklore during the 1890s. Stackolee's most famous exploit was the
murder of his best friend; some versions also tell of his descent into
the underworld, where he raped the devil's wife and scared his children, then took Satan's pitchfork and "ruled hell" himself. The
toasts of the 1950s also included a variety of other heroes known for
murderous pursuits. When Badman Dan, a character from one of
the toasts, challenges Two-Gun Green over a woman ("I walk a
barbed wire, a tiger in each hand, / I'm that bad motherfucker, Badman Dan"), his adversary responds, in classic toast fashion:

> Now sit down mister, and listen to me,
> While I run down by pedigree.
>
> I'll have you know I'm Two-Gun Green
> The baddest motherfucker the world has ever seen.
>
> I was weaned of the tit of a wild boar,
> And I cut my teeth on a Colt .44.
>
> I can be mean without trying.
> I'm a bad motherfucker and I don't mind dying.
> . . . . .
>
> If I catch you fucking with my whore,
> I'll make room in my private graveyard for just one more.
>
> Dan made his pass at those last words,
> And Green's two .44s was the last sound he heard.[43]

In Chauntey's neighborhood, predatory and homicidal values are
distinctly gender-specific. Girls do not depend heavily on prowess at
fighting for a sense of feminine identity, and though many girls do
fight and value violence, their justifications rest on less gender-
specific codes that, for example, prescribe violence for retribution,
entertainment, or, as we shall see, discipline of younger children.

However, young women often take pride in their "attitude," a quality men also sometimes claim to like in a woman. In one of his most popular raps, for example, L.L. Cool J nostalgically remembered the "round-the-way girls" of his neighborhood, whom he liked for their hairstyles, "bamboo earrings," and "bad attitude." Round-the-way girls also sometimes feel obligated to fight rivals interested in the men they are involved with. As "nasty girls" or, as the graffiti on a mailbox in Chauntey's neighborhood has it, "raw girls," young women sometimes also pride themselves in sexual adventure and their ability to manipulate men.

It is among boys and young men, however, that the link between gender identity and predatory violence is most clear. A wide variety of terms has been invented to describe this aggressive code of masculinity: "hard," "fly," "cool," "with it," "all that," "down," "safe," "fresh," and most tellingly, "bad." For "bad boys" (sometimes shortened to "b-boys") boasting, defiance, verbal abuse, manipulation, and prowess at fighting are some of the most important measures of masculinity. Like the jitterbug of the 1950s, b-boys of the 1980s and 1990s also parade their "badness" by the clothes they wear—in Chauntey's neighborhood, usually expensive sneakers, gold chains, and designer sweat suits. A failure to seek violent retribution, a taste for entertainment other than the most violent kind, and sometimes even an unwillingness to use firearms can bring teen boys' masculinity and heterosexuality into question, and subject them to epithets like "nerd," "corny," "sissy," "bitch," "pussy," "faggot," or "gay." The pressure to yield to "hard" ethics can be unyielding and abusive. "Those dudes in school were callin' you brushy and bristly," Omar once yelled at his cousin, "and you ain't even said nothin'! Man, why you always actin' like a girl? Girl! Andre the girl!" ("Brushy" and "bristly" are insults sometimes directed at kids who have not been able to afford a haircut.) Omar and Fahim have an older cousin whose lessons in the hard knocks of manhood the younger boys fear and sometimes resent. He is known for surprising them from down the street with the order to "hit the deck!"—a signal that they are supposed to get down on all fours on the pavement and do thirty pushups. Once when Omar, Fahim, and their two cousins were busy with some peaceful pursuit, the older cousin ordered them to fight each other. Meanwhile, he watched, insulting them and egging them on. Later they met me and complained bitterly. I sympathized with them, but the conversation ended with them all agreeing that "he just wants to make us sure we tough. It's rough in our neighborhood, and we have to learn how to be a man." In another incident I escorted an eight-year-old boy to his home after he appeared on my porch crying because he had received a punch in the face. His uncle greeted him at the door and told him, "Come on, buddy, you gotta start learning you can't run away like that. Take off your coat and get out your fists. You gotta be responsible for yourself if you gonna take the first punch like that!"

The standard by which men and boys are judged on their ability to be aggressive also limits and stigmatizes cooperative or affectionate behavior. Boys who so much as compliment another are disgustedly said to be "sweating him" or are derided for "being on his tip" or "jocking him." Since these terms also refer to boys' flattery of girls, they may also imply that verbal expressions of friendliness between boys are strictly for homosexuals—and most kids in the neighborhood tend to view homosexuality with utter contempt. Indeed, *gay* and *faggot* rank among boys' (and girls') most potent fighting words.

In Chauntey's neighborhood, prescriptions for homicidal violence in the service of masculine hardness find their ultimate expression in the lifestyles and values of drug dealers. Chauntey himself probably taught me more than anyone else how values of manipulation and violence could help create a drug dealer. When I first met him, around Christmas of 1987, I had already heard many rumors from other kids about his Bojack-like reputation as a neighborhood bully and a sexual adventurer. He first came by my house to demand repairs on a new BMX bike he had just acquired—not from Santa Claus, but from a negligent "white boy" who had left it unlocked at a nearby mall that Chauntey often made his hunting ground. Over the next month or so he gave me a full demonstration of his merciless, charismatic wit, as well as his inexorable temper. He could boast imaginatively about his own exploits and make the superhuman seem convincing, slyly manipulate anyone else to do what he wanted, verbally abuse his peers into willful submission, and defy adults in ways that often reduced them to complete fury. When I invited Chauntey to visit my house later on, he made off with all sorts of odds and ends from my desk drawers.

At age eleven, however, Chauntey Patterson was already headed toward other, even more violent places. Indeed, he did little to conceal his ambitions: he would lean out of my pickup truck window to shout insults at drug dealers passing by in souped-up Mercedes and signal his fearlessness and availability. Other kids would grumble, half in disgust and half in admiration, how Chauntey would act "like an ol' head on the avenue" whenever he sensed opportunities from older "clockers," the name kids used for crack pushers. He grew increasingly contemptuous of the Kids' Club that he had originally suggested, and that I was then beginning to organize with other children and adults in the neighborhood. His change of mind about the club derived partly, no doubt, from its implicit challenge to his control over his once relatively subservient peers.

In August 1988, perhaps to prove his continued influence, he led an expedition of younger boys and girls through a window of my house and made off with some classic kids' loot: peanut butter, jelly, some cookies, and a couple of fistfuls of loose change. When we brought him to task for this incident, he declared that he was tired of me and of "little kids' stuff" like the Kids' Club. In response to my admonishments, he slapped on his Walkman earphones, sucked his teeth, and told me arrogantly, "No one tells me what to do. I got too much backup around here. I got a posse down the street gettin' ready to kill somebody." A few days later I looked across the street to see him wearing a trench coat and wrap-around shades, nuzzling (what I think was) a full-sized Uzi squirt gun, and staring at me menacingly. Shortly after that, he was spotted for the first time up on his favorite avenue waiting for the corner pay phone to ring with orders for cocaine deliveries. To demonstrate his solidarity with the group of older boys who had adopted him, he began wearing mismatched sneakers—one of his own and one belonging to his "boyz"—and imitated their practice of spraying red dye on a tuft of hair above their foreheads. Also during this time, Chauntey broke into my house again, this time using a crowbar, and made off with a VCR, a considerably more grown-up kind of hustle than that of a few months before.

Soon thereafter the cops came looking for Chauntey. According to wide-eyed and breathless reports from other kids, he either was caught selling drugs or he stabbed someone in the stomach, or worse. "Some crazy stuff," was what I got from Chauntey himself when I saw him a year or so later, on furlough from the Youth Study Center and reform school (he would be in and out of custody for the next five years). "I want to kill somebody," he told me on a later visit. "I need to kill somebody so people will know I'm a bad-assed motherfucker. Maybe I'll kill you." Chauntey Patterson, like all of the other children of the eighties in his neighborhood, had never even heard of the mythic Stackolee (as we shall see, TV and movies have provided them with a different cast of violent heroes). However, Chauntey could certainly sound like a modern version of the old hell-raiser: "I am," he once told me with menacing eyes, "the brother of the devil!"

As complex and varied as they are, street-smart values of manipulation and aggression do not by themselves account for the full range of values that inner-city children have learned about and incorporated into their social consciousness during the late twentieth century. All inner-city kids from the 1950s and 1960s whom I have read about, and from the 1980s and 1990s whom I have met personally—even the toughest "brothers of the devil" among them—have also felt it necessary to integrate ethics of cooperation and social collaboration into their moral world.

The contradictions between cooperative and aggressive values could lead children into serious confusion and despair.[44] Ida Mae, the girl-gang member turned teen mother, constantly waffled between the violently enforced rules of her peer group and those of her stern (and anxiously upwardly mobile) southern-born parents. When she got pregnant, her family despaired all the more for her, and her gang, as we have seen, started putting violent pressure on her to stay. In a sorrowful moment she told her caseworker that she "felt she was too mixed up."[45]

One "jitterbug" and gang recruit named Marty found the solution in a kind of moral ambivalence, as one conversation he had with his family services social worker indicates:

[Marty] liked going to church and . . . he often made little offerings. . . . He saved the 25¢ his mother gave him just to put in the offering. . . . I [his caseworker] asked him why he didn't put in the other money that he got from the other boys when he helped them rob; and he said, "Oh no, that is bad money; that is not honest money." I smiled at Marty and asked him why he thought this money was bad and not honest. He said because that was stolen money and that was not right. He said that the other money his mother had earned and worked hard for it, and he felt this was honest money and he could offer it to God. I asked him if he knew that this was true . . . and that God was watching and would know when he would offer dishonest money. He said, "Oh, we don't believe in God." I asked him who he meant by "we," and he said their [gang] leader said there was nothing like God, and Marty said that the leader said that if they do something bad and they can get away with it, then it was wrong and if God was there they would all fall dead; and he said another thing, if they take the name of God in vain by saying "honest to God" and if you still don't die then there is no God. I looked at Marty and said, "Do you believe in this?" He said that he did. [In a later session, Marty] said well there are times when he wants to do something good and he does bad, and when he wants to do bad, things seem to be doing good, so he just does not know what to do. I said I did not understand; I would be pleased if he could tell me again. He said well ma'am when you do everything right, then everything goes wrong, and when you do everything wrong, everything goes right. Oh, is that what he thought? he said yes ma'am. He said like when he did something wrong, there is something inside of him that didn't want to do it. For instance he felt like one Marty telling him not to do a thing and another Marty telling him to do a thing.[46]

In another case a Big Brother reported that he had introduced his teenage charge, who was a member of a gang, to Sunday school at a local church. Later at an interview with the head caseworker, "Jerome mentioned that he really enjoyed attending . . . because he made a lot of friends there. He said that he was apprehensive about going because he feared they might ask him where he has been and he would not want to tell them that he had been in a correctional institution." In the same interview, Jerome's caseworker "urged him to consider abandoning his 'processed' hair. Jerome said his [gang] friends would laugh at him and his girl friends would quit him if he changed his hair style." Some weeks later, "he complained of the bad character and poor influence of his [gang] friends, but still [wanted] to maintain his association with them." For the remainder of his career with Big Brothers, Jerome demonstrated in many ways that "he [seemed] to be torn between the pull of this 'good group' and the gang with which he [associated]." He committed himself alternately to graduating from high school and to dropping out, finally in desperation admitting that he had been "wasting his life," but saw no way "improve his situation."[47]

Among more self-assured teenagers in the 1950s, like Bojack himself, kids showed their familiarity with cooperative norms by explicitly modeling their streetwise ethics on the specific cooperative policies and values they wanted to defy. Boys and young men transformed insubordination at home, truancy from school, assignment to a probation officer, and lengthy arrest records from measures of deviance to gauges of "rep."[48] Gangs would relish their assignment to a city gang worker as a sign they were a "down" club.[49] Bojack showed similar familiarity with the cooperative values he was turning upside-down: he had "been asked to stop wearing a certain large ring," but he continued to wear it "in defiance of the school authorities." This was the elephant-head ring he often used as a weapon, and when the caseworker "spoke to him about such a lethal looking ring," Bojack "copped a plea," after a fashion, using his knowledge of the caseworker's values to disguise his offensive violence as self-defense and avoid a sterner reproach: "I need it for protection," he said. The caseworker saw through the ruse, though, and "asked from whom—the youngsters who [wouldn't] give him the sandwiches during recess? [Bojack] started to laugh," and said he hadn't "had to punch anybody and innocently explained that they just gave him whatever he asked them for, and he was at a lost [sic] to explain why." Bojack and the caseworker "laughed together and found this very amusing."[50]

In the months before Chauntey became a drug dealer, he and I spent a lot of time together, and I got to hear his personal ethical conversation firsthand. He often tapped his talents as a charismatic leader and applied his sense of humor to organize cooperative activities. Once when I first got to know him, and certainly before I had any claim to being a positive role model in his life, he gathered together six or seven other kids on my porch and launched into an eloquent speech about how "all I want is to be able to live in a decent neighborhood where there ain't nobody sellin' drugs and beatin' up on everybody and where blacks and whites and purple and green live together and I can have a family and nobody gonna hurt my kids." He even managed to throw in a little Martin Luther King, Jr.: "I want my kids to be known by the content of they character, not the color of they skin." Later, as I mentioned earlier, he would be the first to suggest the idea of organizing a kids' club in the neigborhood, in his words, "to help the kids with they homework."

Like Bojack, Chauntey could also use his knowledge of cooperative standards to defy and manipulate the authorities who tried to enforce those standards. His particular technique was slightly different than Bojack's: he was the ultimate practitioner of what I came to call the "reverse accusation"—responding to reprimands for his behavior by charging his accuser with violations (often fabricated) of cooperative norms. But, more often, Chauntey's familiarity with cooperative norms would come up as one side in an internal debate that seemed to be going on constantly inside his head. He used to draw and spray paint "C.A.D." on a number of prominent places in the neighborhood. In one of our more trusting and close moments, he told me that the abbreviation stood for "Chauntey against Drugs." Some weeks later the message had changed to "Chauntey and Drugs," encircled with a heart. A few weeks after his second arrest and just before his fifteenth birthday, he gave me a long, rambling speech in which he alternately announced his intention to get a job and get down to a "decent life" and mused over his prospects at selling drugs in his new neighborhood. He remembered all the "crazy" things he had done while he lived down the street from me, but I could not tell whether he thought they were wrong. In the three or four times he used the word *crazy* he would alternate between pronouncing it disparagingly and saying it with an obvious sense of self-satisfaction. Finally, he resigned himself to the observation that he wanted to be "good," but he did not know why he had done "all that crazy stuff."

Other children in Chauntey's neighborhood found other ingenious and idiosyncratic ways to resolve the contradictions of their moral worlds. Chauntey's amazing younger sister Kimberly found the double standards of female identity to be a useful vessel for a dual social conscience. On the street-smart side, Kimberly often tapped into the archetypal sexual seductress. Defiance would overcome her like an intoxicant, and she could either lash out at other much younger kids or bawdily goad boys into fights (and probably sex, though my knowledge of incidents like these are based on the hearsay of eleven-year-olds). Sometimes she would just yell nonsense at the top of her blueswoman's lungs and intersperse that with, "I'm nasty, nasty, nasty," or with snatches from songs like "for I'm a hell of a woman, and I need me a hell of a man!" On the other hand, in order for her to "act good," at least around me, she seemed to have to exaggerate another female archetype, the dutiful daughter and responsible mother. When she took on this role, she would put on huge, angelic smiles. On several occasions she took my arm in hers as we walked down the street, and she once told me, "My mom and my aunt had a meeting about it and I supposed to be nice to you, and if I ever cuss I'll give you a dollar."

If Kimberly relied on gender roles, Fahim Wilkins used racial stereotypes to "resolve" his moral conflicts. It helped that he had a white friend around the corner who was a classic square. Fahim, who was good at imitations, would take on this white kid's sincere manner and high-pitched voice as a way of disguising his own often serious expressions of cooperative values as a joke at the expense of "white nerds." Whenever he would offer to help around the house or teach some little kid how to play basketball, out would come his white-nerd imitation, which became such a habit that he could even use it comfortably in "hard" company, apparently without fearing rebuke from his peers. Of course, when he needed to be a b-boy, out would come his "tough face," and an equally overacted persona that he himself sometimes called the "bad nigger."[51]

Despite kids' intimate familiarity with cooperative values (as well as with the more manipulative and aggressive kind of culture), street-smart ethics do in fact often serve as blueprints for violent behavior. Indeed, in one form or another, similar values can no doubt be found hovering around every act that breaks social trust or threatens community life in the inner city. But the fact that kids actively try to integrate both aggressive and cooperative values into their social outlooks and personalities suggests that values, and kids' familiarity with them, may not be the only ingredient in their complex tendency to behave violently. What made Bojack act as if might made right in the schoolyard? Why did he become a gang warlord and flout the cooperative ethic that his mother and his school sought to inculcate, one he clearly understood? What underlies Kimberly's and Fahim's elaborate switching of social masks? And why did Chauntey become a drug dealer, intent on killing, when he dreamed of living in a neighborhood that would be safe for his own children?

Kids' conscious, moral energy has not been the only driving force behind their own personal tendencies to act out. Like all violence and social betrayal among humans, that among young people growing up in late-twentieth-century inner cities also reflects individuals' subconscious emotional struggles. And poor African-American children in Bojack's Philadelphia and in Chauntey's neighborhood have all lived often deeply painful lives.[52] Feelings of sheer humiliation and embarrassment, disappointment and frustration, grief and loneliness, and fear and anxiety (especially concerning suspicion, rejection, and abandonment) have filled inner-city black kids' emotional memories to extraordinary depths. Because, as we shall see, kids have persistently experienced one kind of pain or another in their relationships with virtually all of the most important people, institutions, cultural forms, and social structures that they encounter as they grow up, almost all of kids' daily interactions with others, no matter how insignificant, run the risk of reminding them of past painful experiences and of rekindling painful sensations. Chauntey was my most revealing teacher about the connections between painful emotion, aggressive values, and the grim statistics of the late-twentieth-century inner-city tragedy. Indeed, his transformation from neighborhood bully to drug dealer was not only the product of a rational choice of ethical alternatives: it also involved the overwhelming emotional crisis he endured that summer of 1988, when he was on the eve of his twelfth birthday.

The agony of that summer had long been foreshadowed. I had already gotten my first sense of Chauntey's pain on the day early in our friendship when I had caught him rifling through my desk drawers. Other kids assured me that what happened to me was not new—that I should not trust Chauntey and should never invite him again into my house. When I tried this tactic, he became furious, telling me he didn't care whether I let him in the house and he didn't need me anyway; at another time, he threatened to throw one of my heavy adjustable wrenches through the front window. I decided that it was time to bring this behavior to his mother's attention. She became furious at him, calling him a thief and threatening to "fuck him up good." I told him that I would close my house and tool shop to everyone in the neighborhood until Chauntey brought back the things he had stolen; I thought all the kids on whom his popularity depended would pressure him to relent so they could get their bikes repaired. As I walked away, Chauntey's current sidekick lobbed an iceball in my direction and threatened to "get me next time."

That night I flipped on public television to a show called "Growing Up Suspect" that described how black Ph.D.'s were indiscriminately treated like criminals by New York City store owners. The feeling of being constantly mistrusted was visibly painful to the men in the show, and I wondered if Chauntey's behavior was an expression of a similar feeling. After all, most of the people in the neighborhood, his mom, and now I myself all treated him as untrustworthy. Maybe our expectations of him brought up so much resentment that the only way he could respond to our rebukes was by behaving in ways that only reconfirmed our suspicions. I decided to see if I could become a source of trust in Chauntey's life, and if that was possible, whether that would help him begin to change his habits of stealing and maybe even his other aggressive propensities. I wrote him a note: "I *don't want* to mistrust you or *suspect* you all the time. For me, it's not the way to treat anyone. . . . I am not treating you right by mistrusting you. But you need to help. I will not be able to treat you right unless you begin to treat me right too." The next day, Chauntey apologized, saying, "I've thought a lot about it, and I've decided to play it safe." I told him I thought it would "take a lot of work for both of us," and he agreed. For the next four months, Chauntey and I did work hard together. When I could, I gave him free passage throughout my house, invited him to friends' houses and to my workplace, all places that he knew signaled my trust in him. For four months, as far as I know, nothing was ever missing in his wake.

During those months, however, I discovered that his resentment and anxiety about suspicion were not the only painful feelings he carried. He had vivid memories of frustration and disappointment, and eruptions of his violent temper often coincided with moments when, for example, I or someone else could not provide him with material things he often had to ask for, like food or kerosene or laundry money. Embarrassment and humiliation also frequently welled up in him, especially when he contemplated things like welfare, the roaches in his house, the behavior of some of his family members, or sometimes even the color of his skin. Other kinds of pain arose as well, though somewhat less often: loneliness, fear, and grief.

His frequent experiencing of these feelings was compounded by the lack of places he could depend on for understanding and acknowledgment of his pain. His mother, for one, also suffered from similar feelings, and she believed as strongly as many other parents in Chauntey's neighborhood, that misbehavior like Chauntey's should be punished with force, not met with any attempt at emotional understanding. For lack of anyone better, Chauntey increasingly sought me out to acknowledge his pain, and our friendship deepened emotionally. During the four months that he and I worked on our relationship, built on trust and a rudimentary understanding of each other's feelings, he began to show, on a number of occasions, a capacity for admitting his vulnerability and dropping his tough, protective mask. I remember him one day after school sauntering into the catering company I worked for with the defiant, sullen, "tough face" he always put on when greeting other kids. When he saw an enormous bowl of frosting waiting for him, the b-boy's tough face vanished, and he dived into the bowl like an eager eight-year-old. He would often openly admit his friendship for me, and for the first time since I had met him, even playfully show physical affection, by jumping on my back and burying his head behind my neck.

But the relative absence of sources of affection, trust, fulfillment, and pride was not the only reason that Chauntey was prohibited from coming to terms with his feelings. The very power of the pain he experienced made it correspondingly difficult to sustain any acknowledgment of his vulnerability. Furthermore, as a young man, he was discouraged by the behavioral codes of his gender role from acknowledging any pain. Chauntey's peers and family members strictly enforced these rules, which castigated crying, demonstrations of affection, and enthusiasm as signs of weakness or effeminacy. As a result, he often had little choice but to repress his hurtful emotions, hide them, disguise them, or protect himself from them— and doing so made it less likely that he would find any relief from them. For boys and men the only approved ways of managing feelings were essentially protective and repressive: concealment, boasting, lying, and of course, aggression in all its forms.

By the summer after I met Chauntey, all of the forces acting on his emotional life, helped along by codes of protective and aggressive behavior, conspired to make him seek out the values and the life of the drug corner. The first blow came from school, when Chauntey found out that he was not going to pass seventh grade. He had always been good at boasting about his schoolwork, but once when I had the chance to speak with his teacher, I found out that he was several grades behind and that he had deliberately lied to me about his age, to make me think he was at the right level. He was also flunking all of his classes and was being a holy terror in the classroom. Later, Chauntey was kicked out of summer school, because, as the principal informed me, "his teacher came to us highly recommended. We have been looking forward to having that teacher with us. But that teacher left after two days with your friend in his classroom."

If school brought Chauntey's already vulnerable sense of adequacy further into question, events in his family life redoubled his sense of embarrassment. Chauntey had once told me, in one of his more vulnerable moments, "Man, if I lost my family? If my mom died, man, I don't know what I'd do. I love my family." In that spirit, he proudly invited me to his family reunion on Memorial Day of 1988. But that very night, his mother did not come home with him from the party, in what had already become a pattern of increasing absences. Although he continued to hide his mom's crack habit, it had gotten out of control (I learned about this much later from one of Chauntey's aunts). The family began to collapse, as his mom invited his aunt and seven troubled young cousins to share the one-room apartment Chauntey, his mother, and his three siblings inhabited. Shortly after, his mom and his aunt began leaving all eleven kids alone for longer and longer spells. When they were gone, when Chauntey's older sister moved away with her new baby, and when his older brother was arrested for helping steal a car, Chauntey occasionally took charge of the household. He did not take the overflowing of twelve years' worth of disappointment, rejection, loneliness, or humiliation well at all. In the ensuing rash of violence and thievery of that summer—much of which, as I have mentioned, was directed against me—our fragile relationship based on trust and emotional understanding completely collapsed.

I saw less and less of Chauntey after the day he appeared across the street with the toy Uzi against his cheek, but my sense was that his association with older drug dealers served some very important emotional purposes in addition to signifying his break with a less hostile set of values. The group he hung with was called "The Family," and I have no doubt that, knowing Chauntey, he had much to do with the choice. He once enthusiastically told me that one of the members of the group, the guy he traded sneakers with, had a sister who was married to one of Chauntey's sister's ex-boyfriends. This made the two boys "cousins," he told me. No doubt he also could expect much from his "boyz" in the way of moral approval for his ways of repressing and protecting his deep-seated pain. Dropping out of school and spending less time with his mother also probably lessened his need to wrestle with feelings of humiliation. Income from drugs allowed him to show off newfound riches that also obviated any acknowledgement of his deep embarrassment about poverty. Indeed, by openly expressing aggressive values and aspiring to be a "bad motherfucker," he had found a value system that gave a totally different recipe for personal adequacy than the one he left behind, one that not only concealed humiliation, fear, and loneliness but also allowed for violent expressions of his overwhelming frustrations. Moreover, the new recipe for adequacy, unlike that suggested by his schoolteachers, for example, was one for which he could easily secure all the ingredients.

Feelings and values thus connected to create aggressive behavior in a number of ways. The explosive physical sensation of some kinds of hurt, such as frustration, resentment, or fear, could alone have made individuals like Chauntey more prone to aggression. But conscious ethical codes of behavior also dictated exactly how such kids could or should behaviorally express their feelings. The likelihood that Chauntey would express his painful emotions in violent ways was indeed partly restricted by a cooperative ethic in his community.

Also, values that applied specifically to him as a young man pre-
scribed that he express his frustration, disappointment, and resentment over suspicion through aggression. At the same time, to cope
with other emotions like humiliation and loneliness, he sought out a
social milieu where he could act out roles that gave him a compensatory sense of personal adequacy, in this case through boastful pos-
turing, fancy clothes, the backup of his boyz, toy Uzis, labels like
"bad motherfucker" or "baaad nigger," and homicidal threats.

Other children in Chauntey's neighborhood all began to accumu-
late painful feelings like his at early ages, and all were very familiar
with numerous ways of expressing, coping with, and compensating
for that pain. The particular ways they incorporated different techniques into their personal social styles changed as they grew up, varied considerably by gender, and no doubt reflected the extent of
their hurtful emotional memories.

Infants, toddlers, and kids under about eight or nine usually have
not yet shed universal, nonaggressive expressions of emotional vulnerability, like crying and open calls for hugs, and they still respond
to affection with the equally universal language of smiles and lit-up
faces. The signs of deep pain are already hard to miss. Whole groups
of little kids who are playing together in Chauntey's neighborhood
will drop whatever they are doing whenever an adult who has a reputation for being affectionate drives up the street, and they will race
each other to be the one to open the car door, or be the first to be
picked up or given a hug. There is nothing of the social reticence of
most of the middle-class children I know: the crowds that have
greeted me on occasion often include children I have never met.
One four-year-old boy—who seems already to have lived a particularly troubling young life, and who has already become a master of
getting into trouble and of completely steeling himself in the face of
my frequent reprimands (which he mostly simply ignores)—once
gave me an incredible send-off as I got into my truck to do a few
errands, complete with hugs, handshakes, and his insistence that he
kiss me over and over on my knees.

If boys like this eventually go on to recognize these kinds of
expressions as unsuitably effeminate, girls have the comparative psychic advantage of being somewhat less bound by tyrannical limits on
expressions of pain and on requests for affection. Fahim's fourteen-
year-old sister Theresa Wilkins gauged the strength of her friendship
with her peers by whether they kissed each other on the cheek in
greeting. Fear of abandonment is very strong for both Theresa and

her younger sister Saleema, and they often verbally express deep worries about whether their mother or their Kids' Club tutor will remember to call them or show up at appointments. "Don't leave me," is a common exhortation from both girls and boys to their peers or adult friends; a common accusation, which carries significant moral responsibility for the person accused, is "Man, I can't believe you left me." The advantage of greater avenues for psychic expression is no doubt reflected in inner-city African-American girls' much lower rates of court referral and violent crime, and also in their higher rates of high-school graduation and employment. But a slightly wider array of options to express pain does not by any means always reduce the power of girls' painful memories sufficiently to avoid inauspicious outcomes. Even then, though, aggressive behavior is not necessarily a crucial ingredient. In fact, one of the most important ways that many inner-city girls deal with pain may be one involving expressions of deep desire for affection. Three teenaged girls from the four extended families I got to know in Chauntey's neighborhood have since had children of their own. Though all of these births were due to many complicated events, sometimes outside of the girls' control, their respective decisions to go through with a birth probably derived at least in part from the affection they thought they could expect from an infant and from the aura of adulthood they hoped could come from being a mother.

Values of aggression and aggressive behavior do enter into girls' compensatory identities in the neighborhood, despite boys' and men's dominance of those forms of expression, and despite the wider array of expressive opportunities available to young women. The "attitude" of the "round-the-way girls" and the overt sexuality of the "nasty girls" both counter, in ways similar to the ethic of the "b-boys," the daily risk of dealing with resurgent memories of humiliation or other emotional vulnerabilities. Like Chauntey's and other boys' practice of aggressive ethics, attitude and a glorification of fighting skills among girls usually get perfected around the age of puberty. Some especially distressed girls, like Kimberly Patterson, make aggression a major part of their daily habits. However, by and large, girls resort to violence for a psychic rescue much less frequently than do boys.

Indeed, almost every parent in Chauntey's neighborhood whom I have spoken to about child rearing has assured me that boys are much more difficult to raise than girls. Even at age two or three, before male restrictions on emotional expression begin to constrict their behavior, boys already begin to practice many of the basic poses and rules of masculine self-expression they will later perfect in adolescence. By the fifth or sixth grade, inner-city elementary schoolteachers regularly report, the bright eyes of their boy students start to glaze over in preparation for assuming a "tough look." And at about the same age, boys in Chauntey's neighborhood start to control crying or even smiling in public, and they begin to spurn affection. Despite these trends toward repression and aggressive expression, some boys still manage to subvert the restrictions on open expressions of vulnerability well into their teens. Fahim's white boy act was one of these strategies: it disguised Fahim's own articulation of fear and his search for affection in a b-boy's trademark put-down of whites. In private, the teenaged Fahim also continued to seek affection and attention in the manner of kids much younger than he, asking one female tutor at the Kids' Club, for example, to "rub his peas" (hair) and being demonstrative even toward a few of his favorite male volunteers in the center. Omar's dogmatic adherence to b-boy repression of painful feeling made him a particularly depressed and often unfriendly teenager, though he continued well into his teens to have a soft spot that he rarely showed to anyone but his closest friends. He would occasionally, and only in deeply private moments, break out in uncontrollable torrents of embarrassed tears. These private habits may have helped both Fahim and Omar, unlike Chauntey, to resist the powerful temptations of the drug corner (their collections of painful memories also may not have been quite as extensive and severe as Chauntey's). But their relatively unaggressive expressions of emotion by no means prevented either Omar or Fahim from concurrently perfecting their own public b-boy affectations—tough faces, certain walks, lists of girls' phone numbers, boasts about sexual prowess, street-fighting skills, and blustery expressions of aggressive ethics. Like Chauntey, the Wilkins boys—including Fahim and Omar's twin cousins, Andre and Georgie—also eagerly sought a relatively stable group of "boyz" to hang out with.

Because these compensatory identities are directed so clearly at feelings associated with people's experiences of poverty and racial humiliation, many observers of similar survival strategies have hailed them as evidence that poor people clearly have not just sat idly by in the face of oppression. In the late 1960s, analysts hailed such stategies as a "creative adaptation to conditions of deprivation," and more recently some observers have characterized numerous sorts of aggressive behavior as part of an "infrapolitics" of the poor directed at "resisting" "hegemonic" forces that constrain them.[53]

My experience of life in Chauntey's neighborhood has made me cautious about applying these optimistic concepts to all of the kids' strategies for compensatory identity. I agree with both the adaptation and the resistance theorists that the strategies have been creative in ways that, especially given the circumstances, have been astonishing: the phenomenal artistry of the folklore of the urban toasts, the language of the hustler, and all of hip-hop culture have helped immeasurably to articulate inner-city young people's searches for self-worth during the post–World War II era. Also, I agree that some of the noncooperative values and behaviors among kids in Chauntey's neighborhood may very well follow directly from traditions of resistance set by the previous generations of black urban poor people, as historian Robin D. G. Kelley has described.

I have heard kids talk about shoplifting, for example, as a way of overcoming the barriers of overinflated prices. African-American kids in Philadelphia of the 1980s and 1990s may be echoing African-American's historic struggles over segregated public spaces when they take over the back of trolleys, play loud music to establish their presence in streets and parks, spray paint their graffiti signature on the walls of buildings, or hang their sneakers by the shoelaces from telephone wires. The flashy attire of today's b-boys and their implicit commentary on exclusivity and commodities keep the message of the zoot-suiter and the jitterbug alive. And kids' derogation of "white men" and, more importantly, of police officers reflects long traditions of resistance to the most visible agents of racism and social control in their neighborhoods.

Insofar as kids' compensatory identities all necessarily resist power—power wielded by those institutions that have given kids their memories of pain and denied them a sense of adequacy—then I have no problem labeling all of those strategies "political," at least in that limited sense. By other definitions of political resistance, though, some aspects of compensatory identity fit the characterization and some do not. In the occasional instances when kids incorporate values of aggressive resistance to the police and white racism into their compensatory strategies, for example, they are making appeals based on collective grievances, and they may arguably be articulating a universal condemnation of oppression. Reconquest of public space and shoplifting may share these attributes, though only if we stretch their definitions nearly beyond recognition. But violence as an expression of masculinity, conspicuous consumption, and the compensatory use of a language of racial hatred are manifestly individual acts, most often directed against or in competition with other members of the oppressed community. Through such acts individuals freely enlist, not condemn, the techniques of domination and the language of hegemonic values.

Indeed conscious political criticism only plays a minor part in informing kids' everyday attempts to "resist power," their various compensatory strategies, and their frequent moral choice to employ violence as a tactic. In all its variety, inner-city aggression much more consistently reflects a personal and subconscious struggle, one waged by individuals against the threat of complete despair.

Six years in Chauntey's neighborhood have also made me somewhat more skeptical than the ethnographers of the 1960s about the success of those strategies. I remember first thinking just how fragile Chauntey's choice of compensatory identity really was when I saw one of The Family guys angrily chasing Chauntey down the street and threatening to kill him. Life in the gang could provide fleeting moral legitimacy for the violent ways he protected and repressed his feelings, but it did nothing to reverse his lifelong experience of pain. None of the possibly comforting aspects of life as a drug dealer meant that social relationships were any easier for Chauntey. Even his increasingly ravenous attraction to women and his many opportunities for intimacy or sex only fleetingly offered the possibility for relief from hurt. Too quickly, the maintenance of intimate ties only left him open to abundant emotional risks and to demands for verbal expression of vulnerability. Faced with that threat, the ethics of sexual conquest became emotionally very compelling. Indeed, life in his family of boyz was based precisely on the assumption that intimacy was unmasculine and that trust was simply unwise. In the end, for all of its attractions, the street did little to provide a place of real understanding of the emotions that had got him there. It allowed—if not forced—Chauntey to avoid the risk of understanding his hurt and of beginning to come to terms with it less violently. It is no wonder that (as Chauntey told me a few years later) he had "no idea" why he had done "all that crazy stuff."[54]

Why Chauntey did in fact do his "crazy stuff" and why poor African-American neighborhoods have been the scene of such a devastating historical tragedy are, of course, the central questions of this book. Grim statistics and stories about children's values and feelings teach us that the explanation is extremely complex. Above all, it involves a

close look at the histories of the people, institutions, and social systems that have raised poor black inner-city children in America.
And, in the end, a satisfactory explanation for the post–World War II
tragedy of American inner cities must answer more specific questions: Why did it occur in the late twentieth century and not before?
Why did it affect poor African-Americans more than other groups of
poor people? Where have black inner-city kids learned about aggressive values—did the "street" somehow spontaneously create them, or
do they have other origins? Have these sources of ethical education
changed over time? Where have kids learned about cooperative values? Why has their education in traditions of mutual responsibility
and collaboration so often failed to direct kids' behavior? What are
the sources of pain in kids' lives, specifically, the sources of their
frustration and disappointment, humiliation and shame, and grief
and loneliness, as well as their fears concerning suspicion, abandonment, and rejection? The story of Chauntey's rite of passage from
neighborhood bully to drug dealer suggests that his painful memories were connected with many different things: his family, his peers,
other people in the neighborhood, store owners, poverty, and race.
Which of these sources of pain influences kids to the greatest
extent? Have the sources of these painful emotional memories
changed over time in ways that might make their effects increasingly
hazardous to kids' emotional well-being? Also, where have poor
African-American kids like Bojack and Chauntey learned about their
strategies for expressing hurtful emotions and for coping with and
compensating for pain? What controls whether those coping strategies actually work—for kids themselves, and for the maintenance of
their communities? Finally, what makes those compensatory strategies (like Chauntey's experience with his corner boyz) only further
undermine kids' sense of emotional self-awareness and spiral into
rejection of social responsibility and acts of violence?

Satisfactory answers to all these questions are needed for a comprehensive explanation of the historical tragedy of late-twentieth-
century inner-cities. More stories about children living in Bojack
Dungee's Philadelphia of the 1950s and 1960s, and in Chauntey Patterson's neighborhood thirty years later will begin to answer them.
But before we get to some more stories, we need to look briefly at
the progress scholars have already made in explaining the late-
twentieth-century transformation in inner-city family life and the
drastic increases in violence, and we need to determine what pieces
of the picture they have left out. Only then can we fully appreciate

the extent to which Bojack's and Chauntey's tumultuous upbring-ings—their moral consciousness, their emotional experiences, and their social habits—reflect their deep connections with a collection of mainstream America's most compelling values, images, and illu-sions.

2

The Limits of Alienation

Experts on American cities and American poverty have long argued among themselves about the reasons for drastic changes in late-twentieth-century inner-city community life. Their debate has often been passionate, because the topic requires discussion of America's most sensitive political issues. Some believe that depleted urban job markets are the primary cause of inner-city troubles; others prefer to blame racism or "self-perpetuating" subcultures of poor people or welfare and criminals' rights programs. Barely hidden behind their often-raucous conversations lie other broader and equally passionate questions: the proper role of government in society, the viability of unfettered capitalism, the usefulness of civil rights approaches to black people's progress, the moral responsibility of the poor for their lot, the importance of a unitary national culture, and the nature and future of American race relations.

However, amidst all this controversy a general consensus of sorts has arisen. Virtually all the experts, no matter their political persuasion, have agreed on one thing: violence and family change in late-twentieth-century inner cities ultimately reflect the recently growing impact of forces that alienate and exclude inner-city residents from meaningful participation in the American mainstream. Those on both the left and the right of the political spectrum have produced theories of *economic* alienation. Liberals and other left-wingers, such as the sociologist William Julius Wilson, tend to focus on the effects of poverty and joblessness, while conservatives, such as Charles Murray, prefer to dwell on what they see to be the deleterious economic incentives of the welfare system. In recent years liberals have paid

more attention to the impact of *social* alienation than have conservatives. Some have pointed to residential segregation by race as a
major cause of inner-city troubles, and Wilson has also argued that
the migration of working-and middle-class black people away from
the cities has exacerbated the effects of economic alienation on the
inner-city poor. By contrast, conservative policy analysts, such as
Glen Loury and Thomas Sowell, have preferred to characterize
inner-city troubles as deriving from *cultural* alienation—that is, from
value systems radically at odds with mainstream norms. But this idea
also has some appeal to more left-leaning experts, such as the journalist Nicholas Lemann and the historian Roger Lane, who feel,
respectively, that the inner-city values of aggression originated in the
alienating experience of the rural South and the late nineteenth-
century urban North.[1]

How well do these forces of economic, social, and cultural alienation account for all the complicated facets of Johnnie "Bojack"
Dungee's and Chauntey Patterson's young lives in their inner-city
neighborhoods? And how well does alienation explain the timing
and the exceptionality of the tragedy that unfolded during the years
between their generations' coming of age?

Clearly, much of the recent drastic change in the social life of poor
urban African-American communities has been due to fundamental
shifts in the late-twentieth-century American urban economy. Inner-
city residents have found it increasingly difficult in recent years to
achieve the American dreams of stable employment, freedom from
want, economic independence, and social mobility. Poverty, dependence on welfare, and joblessness have become increasingly common in inner-city neighborhoods and, once established, have persisted to alarming degrees. The devastation of inner-city economies
has contrasted starkly with the overall growth and unprecedented
affluence of the American economy in the post–World War II era.

Poverty itself has definitely contributed to the violence and other
signs of community erosion. Poor people are more likely than people living in material comfort to die a violent death and live in families experiencing social hardship. The case reports of the Philadelphia's Protestant Episcopal City Mission (PECM), an agency that
actively provided material relief during the early years of the
post–World War II era, documented countless cries for help from
parents and children who did not have enough to eat, who did not
have school clothes, whose utilities had been turned off, or whose

houses were overcrowded or collapsing. Babies often went without milk or food for long periods, and young mothers needed layettes, cribs, strollers, and sometimes even a house to stay in. Parents could not afford to do laundry, they often requested shoes so their children could go to school, and they or their kids often missed appointments with social workers for lack of carfare. Kids often complained about not getting presents on Christmas and their birthday, about not getting allowances, about sharing their bed with four or five of their siblings, and about being hungry so often.

In Chauntey's neighborhood I got a closer look at how kids grapple daily with poverty. The physical experience of deprivation has not changed much since the PECM case reports were written. Hunger is a daily problem for most of the kids I know in the neighborhood. They also long for things to play with, bike repairs, clothes, laundry detergent, kerosene for heat, transportation, and a warm place for hanging out or sleeping. The houses my friends live in were, and for the most part still are, in terrible shape. Most of the members of the Patterson and Barkley families lived in three of the single-room apartments in a rooming house at the corner of my street. The place had one blocked-up bathroom on each floor, was crawling with vermin, and was only intermittently heated. One of the immediate families from the Wilkins clan lived in a house the kids' grandfather had bought long ago; maintaining it had become too expensive. Over the years I have known the Wilkinses, most of the utilities in their house have been shut off, one by one, and an accidental fire left a gaping hole in the kids' room, which their father later repaired with thin pieces of wall paneling. In the winter of 1989–90, snow fell in the room one night, and stagnant water in the bathtub froze over.

Since I met them, the other Wilkinses and the Greenes have all lived in Section 8 rent-subsidized housing. Under these kinds of contracts, the Philadelphia Housing Authority guarantees about 80 percent of the rent, so long as the landlord and the tenants keep the place in good enough shape to pass a city inspection. During the late summer of 1989, the Greenes were forced to move because the landlord purposely let the house fail inspection so he could recover the property. The same thing happened to one of the Wilkins families a year later, when the landlord sent a couple of repairmen over to disconnect the pipe from the toilet to the sewer main, allowing human waste to back up into the crawlspaces between floors during the middle of August. Because the housing in my neighborhood is either unavailable, too expensive, or subject to the whims of owners, the families I know have been at great risk for experiencing periods of homelessness. Before moving to my neighborhood, the Greenes lived in the streets and in a shelter for some time, and one of the Pattersons and her children found themselves homeless for about six months after a fruitless search for housing outside the city in 1988.

In the face of their ordinary struggles to find something to eat, and in the face of other less frequent but more consequential calamities, all of the children I have met over the past five years have shown tremendous resourcefulness: they have built bikes out of abandoned parts; they have played basketball with a tennis ball and a No Parking sign as the backboard; using a piece of discarded plastic as a brush, they have created paintings with the goo left at the bottom of a half-dried can of housepaint; and they have invented games, including one played with milk-bottle caps filled with candle wax on a game-board drawn on the street with a piece of broken brick. They have collected aluminum cans to get change from recycling machines, sold things they no longer use, bagged groceries at local supermarkets, distributed advertising flyers, carried packages, mowed lawns, shoveled sidewalks, and cleaned out people's basements and alleyways for a little spending money to buy something to eat.

Kids' resourcefulness, however, has been no match for the physical toll of poverty and its constant frustrations and humiliations. A number of the children I know came into the world already victimized by prenatal undernourishment and, as a result, by premature birth or a low birthweight. Since then, inconsistent mealtimes, punctuated by feasts on hunger-numbing junk food bought with proceeds from odd jobs or the leftovers from welfare checks, have left many kids alternately drained, hyperactive, and irritable. Frustration at their parents' inability to provide and memories of those adults' defensive responses to requests for food and clothes inevitably help engender the kinds of mistrust and manipulative behavior described in chapter 1. Poverty also often engenders a deep sense of personal failure and humiliation. One entry from my neighborhood journal reads as follows:

Saleema Wilkins: Professor, are you going to write anything bad in your book?
Me: That depends. What do you mean by *bad*?
Saleema: Like about poverty.
Me: What do you mean by *poverty*?
Saleema: It's when you not living right.

In combination with frustration, the shame-laden sting of poverty pervades kids' spells of aggressive behavior. Indeed, "bussing" about other kids' mothers or houses or empty freezers—by giving the insulter a chance to dispense, rather than receive, humiliation—often makes up part of a compensatory strategy to deal with the shame of poverty. Of course, violence itself can result from all kinds of pain associated with poverty, whether the physical pangs of hunger, the sheer explosiveness of mounting frustration, or the collapse of fragile compensatory "fronts" erected to stave off humiliation.

However, poverty alone cannot explain the tragedy of late-twentieth-century inner-city community life. Overall, poverty rates have actually decreased substantially since 1959, when the government first calculated its official poverty line. The biggest years of decrease were the 1960s, when rates of black homicide exploded, and when poor African-American families began their historic transformation.[2] Also, as we know, poor black communities have shown much greater signs of erosion than other communities of American poor people.[3] Similar problems also arise with the argument that welfare programs, not poverty, explain the recent transformation of poor families because the eligibility rules for the federal government's Aid to Families with Dependent Children (AFDC) programs make it difficult for two-parent households to qualify, and hence create a disincentive for marriage. While the number of new welfare cases did increase in the late 1960s and 1970s as a result of President Lyndon Johnson's "Great Society" initiatives, and while the number of single-parent households did begin to increase at about the same time, by the mid-1970s the number of welfare cases dropped off and the pace of family transformation continued unabated.[4]

The gradual erosion of unskilled employment opportunities in industry and the growing alienation of inner-city residents from employment opportunities help much more than poverty and welfare to explain the timing of the transformation of inner-city social life. In the first third of the century, manufacturing centers like Philadelphia did offer the jobs and the income needed for large proportions of unskilled European immigrants to afford social mobility—though the opportunities were never as boundless as the mythology of the American dream made them out to be. Color bars generally kept African-Americans almost completely excluded from industrial work, especially before World War I, and relegated them to jobs in the unskilled service sector that tended to offer less social prestige and fewer possibilities for social mobility. When black people were invited to work in industry—usually to fill gaps in the work-force during strikes or periods of wartime industrial production—they faced racial hatred and violence from whites, received union memberships only very slowly, and endured manufacturers' treatment of them as a last-hired, first-fired reserve labor force.[5] These differing employment opportunities came into sharp relief during the Great Depression, when the gap between the unemployment rates of blacks and whites in Philadelphia grew from 1.6 to 1 in 1930 to 2.1 to 1 in 1940, a ratio that has persisted throughout the rest of the twentieth century.[6] The years of World War II and the decade immediately after the war did provide some glimmers of hope to urban African-Americans: during that period the federal government, under Franklin Roosevelt, made its first efforts to end the color bar in manufacturing. However, a new round of devastating economic changes lurked just around the corner. Seeking to compete more effectively worldwide, and plagued by an aging urban industrial plant, manufacturers began increasingly to look outside of American cities for their industrial sites and labor pools. Because of their unencumbered spaces and low tax rates, suburban and exurban locations became more attractive as plant sites. In other cases, the extremely low wages of developing nations induced many American employers to set up their production lines outside of the country altogether. Philadelphia lost 55,000 manufacturing jobs between 1948 and 1967, 106,000 during the next ten years, and another 67,000 between 1977 and 1987. By 1990, the city had retained less than two-thirds of the industrial jobs that it had after World War II. Although the postwar economy did create many new jobs in cities, most by far were in the service sector, which was much less well equipped to offer unskilled people any kind of social mobility. Indeed, while the number of jobs requiring some college education increased by 38 percent during the 1970s in Philadelphia, employment requiring less than a high school degree fell by 32 percent.[7]

The rise of the "postindustrial" service economy, which affected cities across the country, coincided with two other trends that made it harder for black people to find work. One was the burgeoning population of urban black communities in the wake of the so-called second great migration between 1940 and 1970, when millions of African-Americans left the farms and cities of the South for opportunities in Northern cities. The other was the simultaneous increase in the level of racial segregation and isolation of black urban communities.[8] If population growth put extra strains on the job market, the racial violence, the restrictive real-estate covenants, and the federally sanctioned racial "redlining" of credit markets that kept blacks confined into increasingly dilapidated ghettoes also prevented poor African-Americans from doing what many whites did during the 1960s, 1970s, and 1980s, namely, leave the cities to live near those jobs that had disappeared into the suburbs.[9] The landmark federal civil-rights legislation of the 1960s did help spur affirmative-action programs designed to redress the inequities of the color bar and segregation, but those programs have rarely opened doors to anyone but the more highly educated members of the African-American community.[10] Meanwhile, as sociologists Joleen Kirschenman and Kathryn Neckerman have documented, a variety of forms of racial exclusion have persisted in the hiring and promoting of less-skilled urban black people.[11]

Declines in employment among African-Americans, and especially among young people (whose share of the urban black population increased at the greatest rate of all, especially during the 1960s), were catastrophic. The black unemployment rate itself remained double that for whites throughout the post–World War II era, but at the same time, huge numbers of inner-city inhabitants began to drop out of the workforce altogether. The percentage of black people who considered themselves "outside of the labor force" more than doubled from 16 percent as the depression waned in 1940, to 33 percent on the eve of the "prosperous" 1980s.[12] Only 53 percent of all African-American men had jobs in 1983 (down from 80 percent in 1930 when the industrial color bar still reigned). Young African-American men (aged eighteen to nineteen) were slightly more likely than their white counterparts to work in 1954, when 66 percent of them found work. By 1981, that number had decreased to 34.5 percent, or about half the rate among whites.[13]

This drastic, depression-level decline in inner-city employment rates has had its clearest impact on the family life of poor urban African-American communities. William Julius Wilson and his collaborator Kathryn Neckerman have been the most eloquent advocates of the view that "the increasing rate of joblessness among black men merits serious consideration as a major underlying factor in the rise of black single mothers and female-headed households."[14] According to these researchers, as black men have become decreasingly likely to be able to count on employment during the postwar years, they have become less "marriageable" and less "in a position to support a family." High unemployment, high percentages of men out of the workforce, high incarceration rates, and high early mortality rates all have meant that, in the black community, there are relatively few men available for women in the "marriage market."[15]

The case reports of Philadelphia social service agencies from the 1950s bolster Wilson and Neckerman's claim about the importance of joblessness to family change. Most of the reports from the PECM's Family Services division concerned married couples who were having difficulties, and many of those from the PECM's Sheltering Arms program for pregnant teens chronicled the troubles girls endured while trying to convince their sexual partner to offer support or agree to marriage. Men's lack of employment was almost invariably a central issue in these difficulties, both because of the financial constraints unemployed men faced, and because of the often-aggressive eruptions of shame they felt as a result of failing to meet gender-role standards as family providers.

In response, just as Wilson and Neckerman predicted, women used employment as one of their most important gauges of men's "marriageability."[16] Girls and young women in general, as well as girls who had children by unemployed men or who were married to unemployed men, often blamed men for their failure to provide for their family. "Shiftless," "worthless," "backward," "winehead," "irresponsible," and "corner lounger" were among some of the insults they used to describe the "no-good" male partners. In their disappointment, many turned to their own extended families, to Family Services or Sheltering Arms, to the police and the courts to put pressure on men to provide.

Ironically, appeals like these to the patriarchal standards of family roles have often been seen as the principal evidence of "matriarchy" in African-American marriages, and the corresponding "castration" of black men. Indeed, women could largely count on the influence of mainstream institutions to support them in their definition of male failure and in their attempts to bring men to task for their inability or lack of desire to provide.[17] However, men in these kinds of conflicts were by no means "castrated," even if they did often exhibit clear signs of shame and humiliation. They could very easily appeal to other privileges of their gender to overcome shame and combat insults and even punishments. They could resort to a sexist vocabulary of insult to describe assertive women (complaints about "nagging" were commonly used as means to undermine women's power and incite sympathy for men), or criticize them for going on welfare or for misusing welfare money. Despite African-American women's long traditions of working out of the home, men often also turned to other patriarchal standards to criticize working spouses for neglecting the care of children.[18] Manipulative techniques also came in handy. Marckus, a young client of the Big Brothers Association (BBA) in 1962, mentioned to his caseworker having "a girl friend whom he likes very much. He said he told the girl that he is employed full time making $75 a week and she believes him. Marckus said he does not know what he will do when she discovers that he is lying."[19] In addition, men also usually had ultimate control in deciding whether or not to abandon a materially supportive relationship with wives, girlfriends, or children (few men were arrested or forced to pay support in the case reports), and their gender also gave them license to the ultimate recourse of violence.[20]

Indeed, far from submitting to "castration" by "matriarchs," men often adopted alternative "shadow values"—values that recast their standards of male adequacy from those of breadwinners to those of sexual conquerors—because of their supposed failure to provide. Ethnographer Elliot Liebow made this observation among a group of African-American men in 1960s Washington, D.C., and another ethographer, Elijah Anderson, confirmed it in his report from 1980s "Eastern City."[21] In Chauntey's neighborhood, kids aged eleven or twelve already encounter humiliating and frustrating difficulties as they search for work. Although employment vies with the ability to consume as the most important standard of economic adequacy for the teenage boys and girls in the neighborhood (see chapter 5), insults about boys' ability to hang on to a job and boys' exaggerated assurances about their financial status are significant parts of the compensatory identity, manipulation, attraction, conquest, and conflict that pervade the daily interactions between boys and girls.

Statistical data further support historical and ethnographic evidence like this. Marital breakup and delay of marriage have repeatedly been shown to correlate closely with male unemployment and absence from the workforce.[22] And the historical timing of changes in indices of joblessness closely parallel those in the degree of family change over time. Wilson and Neckerman's "male marriageable pool index," a measure of the number of employed men for every hundred women, has been declining rapidly among blacks in the postwar era, closely paralleling the decline in urban black male employment. Meanwhile, the rate of black female-headed households has risen rapidly.[23]

Despite all of this strong evidence, however, there are also impor-

TABLE 2.1

Separation and Marriage Rates among Poor Unemployed Men and Poor Men out of the Labor Force, Ages 14–44, by Race, 1940–1980

Separation (Percentages of Ever-Married Men Who Were Separated)					
	1940	1950	1960	1970	1980
Unemployed					
Black	16.2	13.5	13.1	17.9	17.7
White	6.9	7.0	6.7	5.7	4.0
Ratio bl/wh	2.3	1.9	2.0	3.1	4.4
Out of Labor Force					
Black	17.2	20.9	25.2	25.7	22.0
White	8.7	9.3	12.8	9.1	5.3
Ratio bl/wh	2.0	2.2	2.0	2.8	4.2
Marriage (Percentages of All Men Who Were Married)					
	1940	1950	1960	1970	1980
Unemployed					
Black	36.8	51.3	48.7	31.2	22.8
White	33.3	50.4	55.0	46.4	48.4
Ratio bl/wh	1.1	1.0	0.9	0.7	0.5
Out of Labor Force					
Black	21.6	15.0	8.2	7.8	11.4
White	20.1	15.7	11.7	14.9	26.0
Ratio bl/wh	1.1	1.0	0.7	0.5	0.4

Source: U.S. Bureau of the Census, "Public-Use Micro-Data Samples" (PUMS). See Appendix B for details on sampling and poverty cutoffs.

tant indications that while increasing joblessness is a crucial part of the changes in inner-city family life, it does not completely explain them. The rise in joblessness, for example, does little to explain the exceptionality of the recent history of poor black families. The census long-form questionnaires on unemployed men in urban areas suggest that being poor and unemployed or out of the workforce has very different implications for marital life among black men than does the same economic experience among white men. From 1940 to 1980, poor black jobless men, aged fourteen to forty-four, living in central cities of the Northeast and Midwest have been between one and a half and three times as likely to be separated or divorced than poor jobless white men of the same ages. Counting separation rates alone, the difference between black and white poor jobless men grew from a factor of over two in 1940 to one of over four in 1980. At the same time, the likelihood of marriage among black poor jobless men decreased from a level about equal to that of whites in 1940 and 1950 to a level less than half of that of whites in 1980[24] (see table 2.1). Neckerman and Wilson, in an article written with fellow sociologist Robert Aponte, acknowledged that "although we have evidence that male economic status is related to family structure, much more work remains to be done."[25] To rephrase these cautious remarks, joblessness remains a necessary part of our understanding of family change in poor African-American communities, but it does not suffice as a complete explanation.

The history of joblessness appears, likewise, to be an indispensable, but definitely not a comprehensive explanation for inner cities' high rates of fatal violence.[26] Measures of unemployment and joblessness, like those of poverty, have correlated only moderately with high rates of homicide. Looking at a sample of the largest American cities, sociologist Robert Sampson has concluded that joblessness only helps explain the higher rates of homicide victimization among African-Americans because employment problems are at the root of the general "social disorganization" in inner-city communities (as measured by high rates of single-parent households), which in turn breeds lots of murder. This theory does not, of course, explain why poor blacks have been more likely to live in single-parent families or "disorganized" communities than poor whites.[27]

Different researchers who have conducted chronological studies of the connection between changes in unemployment rates (as opposed to joblessness rates) and changes in murder rates have reached diverse conclusions (no doubt reflecting the varied statistical techniques and measurements now in use in the field of criminology). For example, some researchers have argued that unemployment and other economic troubles explain white homicide rates, but not black ones; that unemployment has had little effect on homicide; and that any rise in unemployment rates may, at least immediately, slow down the rate of homicide.[28] Of course, general unemployment rates do not include people who have left the workforce altogether; do not necessarily reflect the level of employment troubles faced by young males, who are most likely to be murder victims; and do not measure how long individuals have been unemployed.

Also, alienation from the job market may explain the increase in homicide better if other factors are taken into consideration. The number of young people in places like Philadelphia shot up during the 1960's, and a number of commentators have hypothesized that the larger youth population increased the number of potential relationships between young people, and thus also increased the number of those contacts that turned violent. The increased availability of guns since World War II has clearly had some impact on the level of fatal violence in the inner city, and the advent of crack-cocaine sales no doubt accounts for the timing of the most recent succession of record breaking annual homicide rates. Finally, criminologists concerned with the effects of unemployment have yet to analyze fully the impact that different economic conditions may have had on different kinds of murder, such as homicide committed during robberies, which is more premeditated and "instrumental" than is emotion-filled assault-related homicide. Different indices of the overall decrease in employment among young men, and especially African-American young men, in late-twentieth-century America may yet provide a better idea of how joblessness affects trends in fatal violence.

Other criminologists have found statistical correlations between economic alienation and violence in the inner city by measuring what they call indices of "economic inequality." Judith and Peter Blau were the first to test this approach in a 1983 study. Methodological controversies surrounding the approach arose during the 1980's, but it has recently received more consistent support in limited applications. The theory, as recently amended, is that poverty or unemployment "is not equivalent to frustration." The emotional experience of economic deprivation is equally molded by what a poor or unemployed person is led to expect in an affluent society like America: "The linkage between frustration and aggression is contingent on actor's interpretations . . . of how and why desired goals are blocked." The criminologists Jay Corzine and Lin Huff-Corzine have recently shown that measures of economic inequality between the races in American cities correlate strongly with rates of "expressive," assault-related homicide among African-Americans, reflecting their model's touted ability to predict levels of frustration and "angry aggression."[29]

Further research will be needed to see if this statistical fit also extends to change in homicide rates over time. However, if measures of economic inequality do help explain the high murder rates among African-Americans, they do so in a way that implicitly involves other, noneconomic forces. The level of perceived inequality depends not only on economic factors but also on a sense of racial grievance and on the media and the messages that expose poor people to affluence in American society. All of these things have changed substantially at the same time that the urban economy has undergone its most recent transformations.

* * *

Economic alienation alone cannot fully explain the recent erosion
of poor urban black communities. To understand why the recent
experiences of the African-American urban poor has been so much
more filled with desperation than those of other groups of poor city
dwellers, scholars, policymakers, and journalists have turned to
other theories of alienation—ones that focus less on economic
trends and more on a growing social and cultural distance between
residents of inner cities and of mainstream America.

William Julius Wilson has been the biggest proponent of the idea
that the increasing "social isolation" of poor black communities has
contributed to their recent troubles. His hypothesis arose from patterns of change he noticed in the demographic makeup of
Chicago's poor neighborhoods during the 1970s. In 1970, only one
of Chicago's so-called community areas had a poverty rate of over 40
percent, but by 1980 there were nine such areas of "extreme
poverty"—all of them neighborhoods inhabited principally by
African-Americans. What was especially interesting to Wilson about
these neighborhoods was that the increases in the poverty rate
occurred despite a relatively stable or declining number of poor
people. From this information, Wilson hypothesized that since the
civil rights movement, "working- and middle-class" black people
have been afforded new opportunities for life outside the previously
sealed racial walls of the urban African-American community.[30] As a
result, during the 1970s, the black inner city had begun to lose the
very people who once offered economic stability and moral guidance. Left behind were areas of "concentrated" or "ghetto" urban
poverty in black communities without an "important 'social buffer'
that could deflect the full impact of the kind of prolonged and
increasing joblessness that plagued inner-city neighborhoods" and
without the "mainstream role models that help keep alive the perception that education is meaningful, that steady employment is a
viable alternative to welfare, and that family stability is the norm, not
the exception." Because poor black communities experienced a
greater depletion of mainstream role models than did poor white
communities, Wilson endorsed a hypothesis proposed by the sociologist Mark Testa, namely that,

> simple comparisons between poor whites and poor blacks would be
> confounded with the fact that poor whites reside in areas which are
> ecologically and economically very different from poor blacks. Any

observed relationships involving race would reflect, to some unknown degree, the relatively superior ecological niche many poor whites occupy with respect to jobs, marriage opportunities, and exposure to conventional role models."[31]

Wilson's convictions have more recently led him to call on scholars to rally around a precise usage of the concept "underclass" (or "ghetto poor," in a more recent formulation) as denoting that group of poor people who are particularly "isolated" from contact "with the more affluent part of the black community."[32]

Wilson's idea of social isolation has been the subject of many rigorous empirical tests. The sociologists Paul Jargowski and Mary Jo Bane conducted an extensive national survey of "concentrated poverty" and found that during the 1970s there was much variation between key cities in the growth of concentrated poverty and in the proportion of poor people of different racial groups who lived in high-poverty neighborhoods. In 1980, for example, fully a third of the country's total number of poor people living in high-poverty tracts lived in just three cities—New York City, Chicago, and Philadelphia.[33] And while the proportion of poor blacks living in high-poverty areas increased dramatically in those cities—from 21.3 percent to 36.9 percent in Philadelphia, for example—increases in concentrated poverty only occurred in only about half of America's metropolitan areas, most of those in the cities of the Northeast and Midwest.[34] In cities like Los Angeles, San Diego, San Francisco, Houston, Washington, D.C., and Boston, the number of black poor people living in tracts with high poverty rates in 1980 was less than 15 percent of the total poor black population. In virtually all cities on the West Coast with over a million people, as well as many in the South, the rate actually declined from 1970 to 1980.[35]

Another important qualification that Jargowski and Bane offer in their tests of Wilson's hypothesis concerns the chronology of the process he describes, which is focused solely on the 1970s. Evidence from earlier periods suggests that the movement of nonpoor blacks away from poorer areas of the city was not new to the post–civil rights era. Looking at patterns of racial change in urban neighborhoods, including Philadelphia, during the 1940s, sociologists Karl and Alma Taeuber had found that "movement of Negroes into previously all-white areas is clearly led by high-status Negroes." The emigration of "working- and middle-class" black people away from poorer areas, in other words, did not need to wait for the civil rights movement; it had been happening within the boundaries of the cities earlier. And as sociologist Reynolds Farley suggests, "The innovation of the 1970's was not the process of selective black migration to better residential areas, but rather, blacks crossed city boundaries into the suburban ring in large numbers."[36] In addition to the flight of more prosperous African-Americans away from poorer areas, changes in the rates of poverty among urban African-Americans no doubt affected the poverty concentration in earlier decades more than they did in the 1970s. After all, the national poverty rate among blacks in 1959 (the first year the poverty line was measured) was about 55 percent, and even though that rate may have been slightly lower in urban areas, the *average* urban African-American census tract would have a much higher rate of poverty in 1960 than Wilson's "extreme" poverty areas, which were defined by poverty rates of 40 percent or more.

For the most part, the geographical and chronological variability of concentrated poverty raises doubts that growing social isolation from mainstream influences can explain unprecedented increases and exceptionally high rates of family change and homicidal violence among poor or jobless urban African-Americans today. Two of the most notorious "murder capitals" of the early eighties—Washington, D.C., and Los Angeles—were among that half of American metropolitan areas that saw a decline in the percentage of poor blacks living in high-poverty neighborhoods during the 1970s. Also, if large increases in social isolation of the poor and jobless lead to increased family change and homicide, then the percentage of single-parent households and murder rates among Latino-Americans should have been much higher than those among blacks, since a greater portion of Latinos than African-Americans lived in high-poverty districts in most cities, and the concentration of poor Latinos increased at a greater rate during the 1970s.[37] However, as we have seen, African-American single-parent rates and murder rates were substantially higher than those of Latinos in both the 1970s and 1980s. Though joblessness rates were not nearly as high in urban black America during the 1940s and 1950s as they were during the 1970s and 1980s, we do need to explain why the doubtlessly high rates, and high rates of increase, of poverty concentration in the early postwar years— brought on by increases in racial segregation, extremely high poverty rates, and the flight of nonpoor blacks from poor neighborhoods—did not lead to even slight changes in family structure and murder rates during the late 1940s or the early 1950s.

Whether or not the concentration of poverty and the resulting social isolation of poor people affect the social life of poor communities, it is becoming clearer, as social scientists continue to test Wilson's hypothesis, that poor African-Americans' disproportionate likelihood of living in neighborhoods with high poverty rates and few mainstream role models does not fully explain the uniqueness of their recent collective social experience in urban poverty. Just as African-Americans have experienced poverty and joblessness in different ways than whites and Latinos, they have also experienced concentrated poverty differently.[38]

A more important problem with the theory of social isolation is one that also plagues theories of economic alienation: none adequately addresses the precise historical heritage of values of manipulation and aggression at the heart of community-threatening behavior or inner-city kids' ways of compensating for painful feelings. The supposed social isolation of a group of people from one cultural ethos—that of the middle-class black role models—does not determine the presence, or the specific character, of another. The whole complex, varied set of street smart moral codes, such as those sanctioning aggressive behavior among Philadelphia's inner-city children, cannot have arisen spontaneously, merely because prohibitive influences did not curb them.

In the most recent arguments about American inner cities, the subject of culture has for the most part been the province of conservatives. For commentators like Glen Loury and Thomas Sowell, proclaiming the insufficiency of economic explanations for violence and family change is tantamount to proving the importance of "cultural" causes and the existence of "upside-down" values that do not depend on socioeconomic structural change for their persistence and growth. Though these so-called culture-of-poverty ideas have roots in the work of scholars of the late 1950s and early 1960s who had solid liberal credentials (the sociologist Oscar Lewis, Assistant Secretary of Labor Daniel Patrick Moynihan, and the criminologist Marvin Wolfgang, among them[39]), liberals of more recent years have tended, with some good reason, to see the cultural explanations as unfairly blaming victims of structural inequity for their own plight. Glenn Loury, among others, often wrote spitefully about "the aversion [of liberals] to holding persons responsible for those actions which precipitate their own dependency."[40] However, other problems arise with use of the culture-of-poverty concept: the principal forms of evidence most recent theorists of inner-city culture have employed to prove that a "deterioration in values" has brought about an increase in social problems are statistical counts of the very behavior that the values were meant to explain.[41] More important than the circular fallacy of the argument though, is a problem that the culture-of-poverty notion shares with Wilson's social isolation theory: it does not adequately identify what created and then transmitted the specific forms of the complicated and widely compelling ethical culture of poor African-American inner cities during the late twentieth century.

The closest culture-of-poverty theorists have come to establishing the historical source of the upside-down ideas they decry has been their effort to link them to families, and specifically to single-parent families. Daniel Patrick Moynihan was the most outspoken proponent of this theory. In his famous 1965 Labor Department "Report," he presented three premises destined to embroil his name in controversy: "At the heart of the deterioration of the fabric of Negro society is the deterioration of the Negro family"; "at the center of the tangle of pathology is the weakness of the family structure"; and, "at this point, the present tangle of pathology is capable of perpetuating itself without assistance from white world."[42] There a number of problems with Moynihan's premises, the most important of which was best documented by Wilson and Neckerman when they showed that the rate of single-parent households has indeed changed in close correlation with changes in the availability of employment. More importantly, though, Moynihan, and analysts further to the right who have since taken up his theory, have yet to document precisely what values poor African-American families actually pass on to younger generations, or how it is that the structure of single-parent families itself necessarily results in social "deterioration." Indeed, as discussed more in chapter 3, inner-city black families actually teach core values and transmit a culture that are not alienated inversions of middle-class norms, but rather represent an orthodox form of one of America's oldest traditions of child rearing and community obligation.

Nicholas Lemann and Roger Lane have recently proposed two other theories about the origins of inner-city culture, partly in response to the shortcomings of culture-of-poverty theory as a historical explanation. Lemann's argument is a revised version of an older theory that claims that the problems of urban black neighborhoods are due to the desperate conditions of a people who migrated from the rural South; Lane's focuses instead on the ways blocked opportunities and racial discrimination in late-nineteenth-century northern cities created a culture of violence that was unique to urban black communities. Both theories assume, first, that community-threatening values have been part of a cultural phenomenon that has continually regenerated itself ever since the time of its historical origin and, second, that inner-city culture has been largely independent and alienated from the influence of mainstream culture.

Lemann's idea that the exceptional experience of poor urban black communities reflects the legacy of oppression and violence of the South is not new. Southern slavery was long thought to have destroyed black families and engendered a culture of violence among both white and black southerners, and some of the classic sociological inquiries of black urban communities, like those of W. E. B. Du Bois and E. Franklin Frazier, linked urban problems to slavery.[43] These theories were dealt a major blow by social historian Herbert Gutman in the 1970s, when he unearthed much compelling evidence that black two-parent households had largely survived slavery. In reviving the idea of the southern origins of inner-city troubles, Lemann has been careful to specify that it was not slavery but the injustices associated with the late-nineteenth- and early-twentieth-century institution of sharecropping that undermined black community:

> Whatever the cause of its differentness, black sharecropper society . . . was the equivalent of big-city ghetto society today in many ways. It was the national center of illegitimate childbearing and of the female-headed family. It had the worst public education system in the country, the one whose students were most likely to leave school before finishing and most likely to be illiterate even if they did finish. It had an extremely high rate of violent crime: in 1933 the six states with the highest murder rates were in the South, and most of the murders were black-on-black. Sexually transmitted disease and substance abuse were nationally known as special problems of the black rural South; home-brew whisky was much more physically perilous than crack cocaine is today, if less addictive."[44]

An abundance of quantitative information contradicts Lemann's idea, though. Looking at family data from a variety of southern cities and small towns throughout the South in the 1880s, Herbert Gutman found that rates of single-parent households among blacks in the rural South were about the same as for whites. By comparing statistics on family life in two poor counties in rural Mississippi, the one predominantly white and the other mostly black, Gutman also suggested that little difference existed between the races in the ways poor people organized their families. If anything, poor blacks had lower rates of single-parent households than poor whites, despite a lower ratio of men to women among blacks.[45]

By 1940, measured in terms of marriage statistics, the situation had begun to change somewhat among the southern rural poor, in ways very similar to what happened in the urban North. U.S. Census long-form data on marriage and separation show that from 1940 to 1980, marriage rates among poor blacks in the rural South decreased dramatically, black never-married rates increased rapidly, and black separation rates climbed to nearly four times those of whites. Thus, the sharecropping system itself does not seem to have inevitably led to single-parent families and high rates of marital separation; in fact, the period of greatest family change among poor people in the rural South seems to have begun in earnest during the 1940s, 1950s, and 1960s, when sharecropping began to disappear—only to culminate in the 1970s and 1980s, after the institution had virtually ceased to exist.

Moreover, the tremendous changes in family life in northern black inner-city communities probably were not directly transplanted patterns that had occurred in either the rural or the urban South. African-Americans who grew up in northern cities between 1940 and 1980 experienced poverty in substantially different ways than did rural or urban southerners and even people born in the South who migrated to the North at some point. Poor northern urban black women who were born in the North were less likely in almost every census year to be married than were their rural southern counterparts, and they were much more likely to be separated.[46] If southern patterns of family life were considerably different from northern ones, the agonies of migration northward still might have helped cause the particular troubles of urban communities. Thus, the link between the South and city culture may have derived from what Frazier called the "uprooting" of a southern culture more than the culture itself. No doubt this is a very real possibility. However, during most of the years of massive migration, during World War II and during the fifteen years afterward, levels of erosion of marriage among poor southern-born migrants, though slightly higher than those in the rural and urban South, tended to be closer to southern rates than to northern urban ones. The largest wave of migration, from 1940 to 1960, thus seems to have coincided with the period of the least amount of cultural uprooting. Only in 1970 and 1980, when migration to the North virtually stopped, did indicators of the decline of marriage among southern-born residents of northern cities consistently equal or exceed those of the northern-born poor. If anything, the influx of migrants from the South brought marital disruption rates in the city down, not up.

There may be a common heritage, or common experience of some sort, at work in the parallel increases in marital disruption among African-Americans in the South and the North, but for at least the early years of the post–World War II era, something else had a particularly strong effect on social life among people who had grown up in northern cities.[47] A similar interpretation, positing both bedrock continuities and crucial changes, can be reached by looking at some of the qualitative evidence of the southern cultural legacy in the inner city. As we have seen, folklorists and linguists have made much of the survival of southern African-American folklore in the inner city and its possible implications for community life. Many characteristics of the street smart language of manipulation and aggression, and the toasts themselves, echo much older African-American oral cultural traditions, like the trickster stories and the ballads of badmen, as noted in chapter 1. Lemann has argued that black sharecroppers' attempts to "get over" on the merchant-landlord with whom they contracted may have been a model for manipulative family and community relationships.[48] Modern-day urban violence may descend even more directly from another experience common to most African-Americans: violent racial subjugation. The educator James Comer writes that slavery "was a system that promoted powerful forces for identification with the aggressor (slave master and other whites) and depreciation of and often ambivalence and antagonism toward one's self and group." Other writers have taken an opposite tack and have blamed post-Emancipation southern law enforcement for neglecting black-on-black (and white-on-black) crime and, thus, for allowing murder to become commonplace.[49]

At the same time, however, these writers and others also hold that the urban experience has substantially changed these common traditions, whether in mood, in substance, or in the ethical culture and institutions surrounding the behavior they may promote. Frazier mourned the disappearance of the "bonds of sympathy and community of interests," which he thought characterized family and community life in the South despite the frequency of marital breakup and unmarried motherhood, but which "have been unable to withstand the disintegrating forces in the city."[50] Even Lemann admitted that though the term "getting over" in its original southern usage "comes from the idea of crossing the Jordan River to the Promised Land," its "ghetto expression equivalent is not as sweet."[51] In the cities the bittersweetness and irony of the Delta and Piedmont blues, with rich evocations of male vulnerability, turned electric and harsh. People in the case reports and Chauntey's neighborhood tended to see the South as a place far away from the troubles of the city, a place to send their kids if they get into too much trouble. For one mother in the Wilkins clan, "acting southern" is a badge of respectability, a sign of cooperative values, of pride in extended family, with a tinge of religiosity thrown in. Indeed, most of the principal moral codes of aggressive behavior I found in the case reports and in my neighbor-hood—those of the turf and drug gangs, that of "cool" or "hard" masculinity—are quintessentially urban in origin and medium.

A number of scholars who have analyzed similar kinds of data over the past twenty years have concluded that something about "city life" must be included in theories of the origins of family change and val-ues of aggression in recent urban African-American communities.[52] The relatively unchanging character of southern family life during the nineteenth and early twentieth centuries, and statistics that showed that northern, urban-born children were much more likely than southern migrant youngsters to be charged with "delinquency," con-vinced Roger Lane, for example, that "the idea that criminality was imported from the South" needed to be refuted. In his opinion, late-nineteenth-century African-Americans' experiences with the struc-tures of everyday city life—including cruel economic discrimination, political frustration, and violent racial hatred—were enough to create a "criminal subculture" well before the great migration. Lane also noted that the city was the primary seedbed for the "aggressively com-petitive strain" of African-American folklore. In the cities, the old trickster tales of slavery days were replaced by the dozens and the toasts, especially those starring Stackolee. Lane even unearthed a story of one black Philadelphia man who yelled "hear my bulldog bark!" a line from a Stackolee story, as he pulled out his Colt .45 and shot his best friend.[53] Such evidence has convinced Lane that the origins of the social experience of late twentieth-century inner cities dates from before World War II, and that "current rates of criminality are rela-tively simple projections out of the past, products of a subculture long nurtured by exclusion and denial."[54] Like Lemann's "sharecropping culture," Lane's urban "criminal subculture" was defined by its essen-tial alienation and independence from the mainstream.

The life stories of children from Philadelphia in the 1950s and from Chauntey's neighborhood do provide some evidence for the validity of Lane's theory. As we learned by comparing kids from Bojack's day with Chauntey and his peers, many similarities could be found in the general characteristics of the values kids espoused. In both periods we could find codes of behavior that valued violence for retribution of wrongs and for entertainment, plus codes that sanctioned offensive acts and even homicide. However, as we also saw, specific attributes of inner-city ethical culture have changed. The disappearance of Stackolee, for example, during the same time that inner-city murder rates exploded, should give us some pause as to the explanatory power of Lane's "simple projections from the past." As we have also seen, the dozens were widely believed by folklorists of the 1930s, 1940s, and 1950s to have functioned as a nonviolent means to express feelings that otherwise might have turned into violence. In Chauntey's neighborhood, the ritualized forms and functions of the dozens have disappeared—"busses" are either remembered as old jokes, or they take the form of "fighting words" that often serve as the first step in chains of retributive violence.

General similarities in inner-city values of aggression across time do not prove that those values have always come from the same source, that individuals have always encountered those values at similar ages in their lives or in similarly compelling circumstances, or that those values have always filled the same purposes at all times for people struggling with ethical contradictions and painful emotion. Therefore, those similarities also do not prove that those values have always had the same capacity to dictate actual community-threatening behavior, and they do not precisely explain why kids have so often chosen to behave according to aggressive ethics despite their familiarity with traditions of cooperative ethics and values of mutual responsibility.

What the stories about children from Philadelphia case reports and from Chauntey's neighborhood have taught me is that the sources of both aggressive, street-smart ethics and cooperative values have changed in crucial ways since World War II. If some of the general characteristics of these kids' ethical culture does indeed hail from the urban past, and maybe even to some extent from the rural southern past, that culture has been pervasively affected by institutions, ideals, and images that have been disseminated into the inner city from outside. This is not to say that families and the cultural milieu of the urban street have not helped to pass those values on to successive generations of young people. But inner-city institutions themselves have changed over time in response to other, much more powerful institutions, ideas, and images—namely, those that have come to define the late-twentieth-century American mainstream.

By focusing on the residential propinquity of working- and middle-class blacks as the main agent of mainstream cultural transmission in poor urban communities, the social isolation theorists ignored the much more powerful influences of mainstream institutions of community control like schools, social welfare organizations, the police, and the courts—all of which have sent their bureaucratic tentacles and often forceful tactics much deeper into the lives of poor African-Americans in recent years. Inner-city children's familiarity with traditions of cooperation, and their ambivalence toward them, cannot be understood without reference to those mainstream institutions of social control and the effects those institutions and some of the traditions they represent have had on inner-city families.

The specific character of the compensatory identities that kids like Bojack and Chauntey have turned to as a way of coping with pain cannot be fully explained without examining how American racial imagery and ideas of mass consumption have intersected with inner-city cultural life. As Lane himself has argued, "The temptations of affluence" and the "impatience, especially among young people, implicit in a consumer society" may have helped cause the recent upswing in the overall *U*-curve murder rates in the Western world. The inner city has by no means been so isolated or so wrapped up in its past that it has been spared from the effects of those dramatic transformations in American culture.[55] To identify precisely what legitimized aggressive ethics themselves during a period when the traditions of African-American folklore began to disappear in inner-city neighborhoods, we need to understand how America's political leadership, American culture in general, and mainstream mass media have infused the upbringing of inner-city kids with racial caricatures and an extremely compelling set of sanitized, glorified images of violence.

Theories of alienation do in fact explain much about the tragedy of inner-city community life. The deindustrialization of American cities has crucially influenced the lives of children growing up in poor African-American neighborhoods. Also, we must consider the persistent forms of social exclusion brought on by racial hatred and racial segregation that have so affected African-Americans' experience of poverty. But these forces of economic and racial alienation explain increases in fatal violence and the erosion of community life only when viewed along with forces that have helped the inner city become more included in the mainstream. Indeed, though all American children have been exposed to this country's ideas of law and order, as well as to its racial caricatures, consumerism, and violence, poor African-American children have embraced all of these with especial enthusiasm—precisely because all of those aspects of the mainstream have provided them with especially compelling ways to express, cope with, and compensate for the exceptionally painful feelings that come from being poor in an affluent society and black in a white society. The history of mainstream cultural inclusion needs to play a central part in any comprehensive understanding of the recent tragedy of inner-city community life.

PART II

POOR BLACK CHILDREN AND AMERICA'S GRAND DELUSIONS

3

The American Traditions of Poor Black Families

To understand the sources of poor African-American children's values, feelings, and behavior, we must of course understand the nature of their family life. Like all children, kids in inner-city Philadelphia have been deeply affected by the structure of their families and their relationships with their parents. However, to appreciate fully the role families have played in late-twentieth-century inner cities, we need to keep in mind the effect of historical changes beyond families' control on the structure of households and the ways parents interact with and pass on a cultural heritage to their children. We have already seen, for example, how the transformation of urban job markets has helped change the structure of poor African-American families. The humiliations associated with enduring poverty and futile searches for employment also continue to affect parents' relationships with their children, and in the process often influence the cultural and emotional experiences families give their children.

In addition to being affected by changes in economic conditions, the structure, moral education, and emotional world of inner-city families have also reflected a number of ideals and historic traditions of the American mainstream. One of these traditions, the philosophy that the moral education and behavioral control of children requires parents to use force, has had a very specific impact on inner-city families. In turn, it has helped account for a number of the specific characteristics of the ethical culture of inner-city children, including some of their street-smart values and some of their painful emotional memories.

As the historian Philip Greven has shown, the notion that "sparing the rod spoils the child" has had deep roots in American Christian traditions.[1] The philosophy of forceful child rearing, with its premises about behavioral control, has shown gritty persistence throughout the nineteenth and twentieth centuries. Indeed, it has survived despite the birth and growth of a second mainstream idea about the moral education of children, one first put into practice by middle-class Americans during the early nineteenth century, and since given the name "progressive child rearing." This newer approach has emphasized the need for parents to identify and show sympathy for the painful emotional roots of children's misbehavior.[2] In the late twentieth century, even American families who have adopted progressive parenting practices often also practice corporal punishment of children. And America's trust in the efficacy of force and severe punishment for the maintenance of community has survived as the central mandate of many mainstream institutions of social control, most notably, the police, the criminal justice system, and the prisons. Since the late 1960s, visceral cries for law and order have increasingly become central to the country's expression of fear about social upheaval and rising rates of violent crime in cities.

Experts on inner-city family life have sometimes been tempted to understate the importance of corporal punishment in poor African-American families,[3] often for understandable reasons. Too often, evidence of beatings and child abuse in poor African-American families has been used to support theories that "bad parents" are to blame for the inner-city crisis or, worse, that some kind of racial proclivity toward violence is at work. But keeping the subject under wraps or romanticizing inner-city family life only undermines efforts to find alternative explanations and understandings of inner-city violence that help to fight insensitive or racist thinking. And among parents in inner-city families, like those described by Philadelphia caseworkers in the 1950s and 1960s and like those I got to know in Chauntey's neighborhood thirty years later, age-old American traditions of forceful child rearing have had nearly universal support. Almost without exception, parents have seen severe punishments— like prolonged isolation from friends, beatings, and other uses of force—as the best means to educate kids in values of social responsibility and respect for parents. Also, adults have widely held that the didactic use of violence is the most effective way of preserving their communities from more threatening kinds of violence, such as that perpetrated by gangs and drug dealers. The strength of parents' committment to this philosophy can also be seen in the strength of their opposition to other ideas—most importantly, those of the agents of "progressive" child rearing they have encountered in their children's schools, in social welfare agencies like the ones that assembled the case reports, and in community organizations like the Kids' Club in Chauntey's neighborhood.

The particular enthusiasm for American traditions of forceful child rearing among inner-city parents—and their rejection of "progressive" philosophies—also reflects their own experiences of indignities and powerless feelings brought on by poverty, troubles with employment, and racism. However, for both parents and children, the tradition itself, the respectability of its Christian and mainstream origins, and the official sanction it receives from the law-and-order policies of America's police, courts, and prisons all help to make the forceful child-rearing approach an important source of legitimacy for values of violence in the inner city. Also, the tradition can be used all too often to legitimate parental behavior that leaves children with hurtful and even traumatic memories. Though most inner-city families have also succeeded in providing kids with a source of pride, loyalty, and warm feelings, the practice of forceful parenting in the inner city has lain at the core of families' particular contribution to their children's ambivalence toward cooperative values, interest in aggressive values, and painful memories.

This argument, focusing on African-American families' mainstream traditions and on the importance of parents' relationships with children, implicitly criticizes another notion, one that social scientists have widely endorsed. During the past forty years researchers have almost unanimously assumed, first, that the *structure* of inner-city families—not parents' behavior and the nature of their relationships to their children—makes the most important contribution to young people's cultural and emotional life and, second, that, because inner-city families have grown increasingly likely to be run by one parent, inner-city family life and childhood has increasingly diverged from mainstream norms.

Before scholars took up the study of kids in single-parent households, urban American social service agencies, juvenile courts, and popular pundits had long frowned on "broken homes" as breeding grounds of "juvenile delinquency" and other problematic social behavior, especially among boys. Sociologists and psychologists followed with a host of quantitative studies that have documented comparatively strong statistical correlations between upbringing in single-parent households and problems at school, psychological troubles, juvenile involvement in the criminal justice system, and even murder.[4] The lessons of these statistical correlations, however, remain unclear and confusing. Since the 1950s, scholars attempting to find out just what it is about single-parent households that causes trouble for kids have come up with three different answers, each of which, successively, has dominated scholarly discussion of the problem.

For most interpreters of family structure in the 1950s and 1960s, the problem with father-absent households was inherent in their structure. Psychologists argued that such families did not offer adequate "object relations" for future "ego development and character formation," especially among boys, and that "paternal deprivation" too often resulted in "negative effect on . . . masculine development," as well as, inevitably, high rates of "delinquency."[5] (The filmmaker John Singleton has given us something of a modern visual rendition of this theory in his movie *Boyz N the Hood,* where the mother of the main character claims she cannot possibly raise a man.) Closely allied with the paternal deprivation theory in the 1950s and early 1960s was the matriarchy theory. In his original edition of *Deep Down in the Jungle. . . ,* folklorist Roger Abrahams tapped into this notion, attributing much of the "contest orientation" of the black neighborhood he studied to men's "relationship with the woman or women who raised him," which "is suffused with the problems of psychological domination and at least a latent sense of rejection stemming from his being an unreliable male." As a result, "seeking [a] heroic male environment [like gangs or the streetcorner] is in part a reaction to the emotional dominance of the mother or grandmother."[6] It was through this presumably inherent link between family structure and "personality disorders" that female-headed households became subsumed under the broader—and more insulting—titles of "disorganized," "dysfunctional," or "pathological" families. In his 1965 "Report," Assistant Secretary of Labor Daniel Patrick Moynihan regularly used the term "family disorganization" virtually as a synonym for "female-headed household."[7]

The firestorm of scholarly criticism that greeted the "Moynihan Report" resulted, among other things, in a revised, and somewhat less outwardly condemning interpretation of the statistical correlations between "father absence" and other "social problems." As the psychologist Timothy Hartnagel expressed it, "Future research must go beyond such simple categorizations as father present and father absent to an examination of those intra- and extra-familial variables which may be part of the pattern of father absence but whose effects may be masked by the father absent–father present dichotomy." In other words, the problems single-parent households face might not be inherently linked to their structure, but might result from their relatively high tendency to be poor (and hence, be more likely to change residences often); or the problems might be a consequence of kids in single-parent families being more likely to experience the death of a parent, traumatic marital disputes, or "sporadic movement of adult males into and out of the home."[8] In addition, because single mothers tend to be somewhat younger than parents in two-parent households, the behavior of children in single-parent households may reflect the relative inexperience of the mothers.[9]

Frank Furstenberg and a number of other sociologists have since produced much evidence to bolster hypotheses like Hartnagel's, and they have suggested that the statistical link between single-parent households and aggressive behavior does not uphold the theory that such families are inherently and structurally inviable child-rearing institutions. As a result, most current writers on family structure, including Moynihan, more often than not issue cautions like this: "It needs so very much to be emphasized that, as such, youths from female-headed households are not necessarily more likely to have more difficulties than other children. It seems to be more a matter of these children being more likely to find themselves in secondary situations that make for different probabilities."[10]

More recently, however, another train of thought has entered the debate on single-parent families. This new interpretation does not so much call into question the single-parent family as an institution of psychological development, but rather disputes such families' structural ability to offer children cultural guidance and control. The trouble with the single-parent household, according to one recent commentator, is that it "leaves too many children with less . . . adult supervision and instruction, less security, fewer alternatives for establishing inter generational relationships, and fewer adult role models." The sociologist Sanford Dornbusch and his colleagues have found that kids of single parents who can count on other relatives to help out with child care are less likely to act out in various ways than kids from families where the parent is truly on her or his own. This argument has recently gained endorsement from a number of prominent social scientists.[11]

The the latest theories do not fully contradict those advanced by

Hartnagel and Furstenberg, and they have not yet resulted in a full-scale return to theories of structural inviability. But syndicated columnists, members of policy think-tanks, and producers of TV documentaries have been especially prone to cite the evidence produced by social scientists over the last forty years—mixed, no doubt, with anxiety about the recent pace of family change across the industrialized world—to argue that the troubles single-parent families experience derive directly from their structure. As one such writer has concluded, "We must steel ourselves to speak the truth . . . about social norms that we know to be good for children and about the malign consequences of deviating from those norms. . . . With rare exceptions, two-parent families are good for children, one-parent families are bad."[12]

To better understand the connections between family life and the social behavior of inner-city residents, we need to know more about the kinds of relationships poor African-American parents and other adults forge with their children—whether in single-parent households or households of other forms.

The Big Brothers Association's (BBA) case reports provide one unique opportunity for exploring the link between family structure, parenting techniques, and aggressive behavior.* The agency was, after all, founded on the belief that one way of helping kids keep out of the juvenile justice system is to provide a significant male role model to boys who are showing signs of acting out and who have no father. Most of the resulting casework therefore tells the stories of kids who had gotten into trouble of various sorts, and who were predominantly from households that statistical surveys would automatically categorize as female-headed. Consequently, we get a detailed, multifaceted picture of what it was about a large and varied group of kids' lives in single-parent families that may have made these children more disposed to noncooperative or aggressive behavior.

Living with only one biological parent was, in fact, often at least part of the trouble the boys experienced in their family life. Though

---

* The Sheltering Arms caseworkers reported many similar kinds of parent-child interactions as did the Big Brothers. However, so much of what went on in the relationship in the SA reports was focused on the crises caused by the clients' pregnancies that it was difficult to ascertain in any systematic way just how much parents' interactions with their daughters actually caused any of the aggressive behavior girls were periodically involved in. Also, since the families in the SA reports were of varied structure, it was impossible to hold structure as a constant.

we cannot psychoanalyze the stories in the case reports, boys' day-dreams about lost fathers sometimes sound like the "paternally deprived" youngsters Freudian social psychologists might have pre-dicted. One widowed single mother, for example, commented to a BBA caseworker that as her son "has gotten older his feelings have changed about his father to a rather superhuman sense. Boy is still holding on to dreams about his father. He frequently shouts at her that he 'wishes his father was back.'"[13] Another boy, who had been raised for some time by his maternal grandmother and grandfather, "has not been the same since his grandfather died," according to the grandmother, who thought "this was the turning point in his life." The same boy's discipline problems at his grandmother's house seemed to evaporate when, it was reported, "his uncle has been showing more interest in him since this summer, and Douglass is pleased by this."[14] Another Big Brother assigned to a different child reported an even more dramatic behavior change in a child who had been a menace at school for most of his early years, dropped out and ran away from home for a while, was finally sent to court by his mother on incorrigibility charges, and spent several months in reformatories. Then his mother remarried ("Wilson said he is extremely pleased with his stepfather and only wishes his mother had married Mr. Daniels earlier"), and almost immediately the boy's school attendance became perfect, he passed all of his courses, and BBA decided triumphantly to close what had previ-ously been an extremely frustrating case.[15]

The case reports also include a few indications that boys' con-cerns about the formation of their masculine identities in house-holds run by women may have led to some acting out. There are a number of reports of boys' resentment of mothers' "nagging"; and, as Roger Abrahams had suggested, a few mothers accused their sons of being lazy and worthless and following the footsteps of no-good fathers.[16] One boy who showed continued defiance at home, then was kicked out of school for wearing his hair "processed" in a jitter-bug style, repeatedly spoke of his resentment of his mother's con-trol, once complaining bitterly that he always "had to do the dishes while his mother and sisters sit around."[17] Another single mother, separated from her husband for five years, said her son's defiance and belligerence could be explained by the fact that "Kenneth seems to feel that he is the man of the house and at times tries to take charge of her affairs and dominate her. She said he seems obsessed by the idea of being the oldest man in the house."[18]

And, just as theories of declining cultural control might have predicted, members of single-parent homes occasionally alluded to a diminished level of parental supervision—and sometimes, more specifically, the lack of fatherly guidance of boys. One mother wrote a plaintive letter to her caseworker explaining her son's recent troubles by pointing out that "it is very hard for a woman alone to try and rear a child, especially boy's [sic] by herself. . . . I have to be a Father and a Mother. . . . I feel as though if he had a man to talk with and discuss over his problems he would be different." A number of other single mothers, no doubt many of them influenced by the particular policies and goals of the BBA itself, issue similar appeals for a helping hand or, more specifically, a "father figure."[19]

Taken at face value, these few snippets of life in poor black Philadelphia of the 1950s suggest that structural characteristics do play some role in the child-rearing difficulties single-parent households experience. However, even in these instances, paternal deprivation, maternal control, or the lack of a second child-rearing partner do not tell the whole story of individual kids' family lives. Difficulties related to family structure itself do not come close to accounting for the diverse sources of pain and the complex cultural experiences kids encountered at home. Nor do they adequately explain why some boys from single-parent homes became consistent violent offenders while others had temporary problems at school that were quickly addressed without the assignment of a Big Brother. Also, for every boy longing for a father, there were many more kids in the case reports who obviously suffered from the presence, not the absence, of a variety of significant adult men in their lives. For all the boys who complained about "nagging" single mothers, there were also many more who either had relatively healthy relationships with adult women or had problems with mothers that were only partly due to differences in gender and to "reversed" sex roles. And, though about a quarter of all the BBA cases reports involving boys who lived in father-absent households do not mention whether the single mother managed to find other adults to help raise her children, the great majority of kids described in the reports grew up within a variety of formal or informal networks of adult relatives and friends, both male and female, who somehow contributed to their upbringing.[20]

Among the households described in the case reports, it was not just the shape of families—who was present and who was not—that created a cultural and emotional experience that made the children of those families more likely to act noncooperatively or aggressively. To the extent that families can be held responsible for their kids' behavior, the ways parents themselves acted in their marriages and relationships with other important adults and the ways they guided and supported their children, had consistent, important influences on the next generation. Though some of the problems kids encountered with their parents' behavior, particularly in parents' marital interactions, did fit into what Hartnagel called the "pattern of father absence" (that is, those problems tend for various reasons to be more likely a part of single-parent family life than they do for two-parent family life), some other crucial experiences kids lived through, as described in the case reports, could occur just as easily in families of almost any form. Indeed, when boys in single-parent households did mention problems with their family structure, they were also often taking into account the ways parents had behaved toward each other, or were assessing the character of those adults' parenting styles.

Of the 110 boys whose lives I read about in the BBA case reports from the 1950s and early 1960s, over half had lived through the separation or divorce of their parents. Another third had experienced the death of their father or mother, and several had lived through periods when their father was incarcerated or institutionalized. As Furstenberg observed in his study of adolescent mothers in 1970s Baltimore (many of whom were single parents), periods of marital upheaval or other discord in adult relationships within families very often intersected with periods in children's lives, especially adolescents' lives, when those kids acted out defiantly or aggressively.[21] Many other researchers have documented strong statistical correlations between separation, divorce, or parents' death and kids' behavior in families of a variety of backgrounds and structural characteristics.[22] Since kids in single-parent households are more likely than those who live with two parents to have experienced marital crises, the high frequency of separation and divorce may also help explain why children from single-parent households are more likely to act out aggressively than are their counterparts in nuclear families.

However, in the case reports, the ethical messages and emotional upheavals kids experienced during the collapse of their parents' relationships related to much more than the resulting shape their family assumed. These also depended strongly on the ways those various adults interacted with each other and with the children while the family lived together, during the period of domestic disruption

itself, and after resulting changes in the membership of the household. Of the boys who openly longed for absent fathers, for example, most could point to memories of paternal kindness and emotional support, were too young to remember periods of abuse at the
hands of their father, or had been separated from their father by
death and had not experienced the turmoil of marital conflict.[23]

For many other boys, adult men's flight from responsibility or violence during the drama of a relationship's breakup either validated
aggressive behavior by example or became a source of painful and
resentful feelings. In many cases, for example, boys' aggression
toward others seemed to be nurtured by men's abuse of women and
children in the family. The mother of one very troubled youngster
named Arthur described her relationship with Arthur's father, and
their later separation, as "a 'hell'" brought on by the man's physical
and sexual assaults on her and her children. Later, she complained
to the BBA caseworker about Arthur's own violent tendencies and
worried "that Arthur is following in his father's footsteps." Though
the case report does not offer any evidence to confirm his mother's
observations fully (he endured many other painful experiences in
addition to those he suffered at his father's hands), Arthur's life, as
well as that of many other boys in the case reports, might very well
have fit into intergenerational patterns of domestic violence recently
documented by sociologists and clinicians.[24]

For another group of boys in the case reports, painful emotions
arose out of the neglectful ways fathers carried out paternal responsibilities once those fathers had left the home. One youngster, for
example, whose parents had recently separated, told his caseworker
"that he rarely sees [his father], and whenever he does see him and
his mother is around, his father usually leaves. He said this makes
him very unhappy." A few months later, on "the day before Xmas
when he was shopping down town, he had run into his father and
his father gave him some money, however, as soon as he saw his
mother approaching, he took the money back and turned without
saying a word and walked away. Alexander said he was very hurt
because of this incident."[25]

The breakup of parents' relationships very often also brought
new adult men into the lives of boys, according to the case reports.
Though on a few occasions stepfathers or lovers gave boys a source
of identification and emotional satisfaction—even, as we have seen
in one case, helping one boy quickly abandon some aggressive
habits—most other boys who had stepfathers found the arrival of a

new man in the house painful. One boy, a Big Brother reported, "actually becomes physically sick over the mother's boyfriend. Recently following a visit from the boyfriend, Nathan was too sick to go to school the following day and even vomited."[26] If boys felt resentment about mothers' relationships with stepfathers or male lovers, this seemed based largely on how the adults behaved toward each other and the ways the men treated kids in the family. For one or two boys the problem was that their mothers might be perceived as being too indiscreet about sex (one boy "said [his mother] still drinks a great deal and goes around with too many different men. . . . [He] said he gets along better with his mother by staying away from her as much as possible"), and others seemed clearly jealous over the attention their mothers gave to adult male companions.[27] One boy resented his new stepfather's apparently active neglect, according to his older sister, and as a result Troy became "a mixed-up youngster" who did "many things to irritate Mr. Dunning," his stepfather. His resentful activity quickly turned aggressive, upset his household, and earned Troy membership in a neighborhood gang, and then an assignment to a probation officer. At one point, the caseworker related to the officer that Troy had visited the BBA offices to talk about his troubles and "he [Troy] insisted that if he could get that 'damned man' (Mr. Dunning) out of the house, he would be all right."[28]

If parents' relationships with other adults could cause great pain for kids and provide models of noncooperative or aggressive behavior, the most enduring effect of families on their kids' behavior came from parents' relationships with their children, often supported by child-rearing philosophies that condoned aggressive parenting behavior. And in the case reports almost all parental responses to children's misbehavior, were based on two general philosophical tendencies. The first was an avoidance of emotional explanations for kids' conduct, and a focus on moral, physical, or other inherent explanations that blamed kids themselves for the ways they acted. The other, linked to the first, was the opinion that harsh punishment, most often physical punishment, was the best way to modify behavior.

Among the parents of boys who were referred to the BBA the absence of emotional explanations for children's behavior was not, of course, universal: some, mostly parents of kids who committed minor infractions, acknowledged that a marital problem, the death of someone close, or long work hours may have upset to their child. However, most parents' explanations for their children's behavior fell along a spectrum that, on its most sympathetic end, included theories attributing aggression to bad moral influences outside the home and, on its most blameful and disparaging end, on notions of kids' inherent depravity.

The company kids kept was of constant concern to parents, according to the case reports, and parents often blamed other kids for lapses in their children's behavior. In a typical passage, one mother "complained that [her son] is easily led and influenced by other boys." In another case, a father told the BBA caseworker "that he always tried to do the right thing by Stephen and cannot understand his recent truancy and bad conduct. . . . It hurts [him] to know that other children have more influence with Stephen than he."[29] At other times parents interpreted noncooperative and aggressive acts as the result of some sort of deep-seated, possibly inbred, moral or physical defect. Some boys are said to have inherited irresponsible or violent traits from fathers they had never met; another mother "thinks [her son] lacks certain basic control"; another couple attributed their son's misbehavior to his small size. The parents of one boy being tried in juvenile court for running away from home informed the judge "that some of the boy's difficulty might be due to two blows on the head he received when he was quite young," and one particularly uncharitable mother "declared that [her son] is absolutely no good and that there is no hope for him."[30]

The parents' emphasis on moral and physical roots of misbehavior, rather than on emotional causes, appeared to be justified at least in part by a second major premise: aggressive or other severe punishments should be used with children. There were some exceptions to this rule (none of them involved children who were very serious offenders[31]), but only a few parents in the case reports ever explicitly ruled out harsh punishments like long-term confinement, insults, whippings, and beatings. If parents did voice opposition to physical punishment, they were usually blamed for their kids' misbehavior by other relatives and neighbors. In general, though, neglect of children—not violence toward them—was viewed as the principal gauge of a bad parent. And any lack of will to use forceful means of discipline could be defined as neglect. The maternal aunt of one boy complained to a BBA caseworker that her sister, the boy's mother, "is too lax with Rodney and his sister. . . . She said the mother's failure to discipline the children has resulted in their bad behavior and the father's separation. She said [their father had] separated from the family five years ago following arguments with the mother regarding discipline for the children. The mother told the father that he could not beat the children if they were bad. [The aunt] said [the father] is a good man and was a good father."[32]

Parents' insistence on using severe punishment was most clearly defended in their interactions with BBA caseworkers, who tried desperately, according to the case reports to get parents to understand kids' emotions. Some parents tried to take their BBA caseworkers' advice to "have talks" with their son or "show [him] more love," but most took this advice reluctantly or inconsistently. Few found changing the emotional character of their relationship with their kids to be effective. One boy's mother called her caseworker and "said Kevin's behavior is uncalled for. She said she cannot tolerate it. She said people think she does not love Kevin, but this is not true. She said talking to Kevin has no effect upon him. She said she did not see what good would come from having him continue to talk with me or his counselor since he continues to misbehave. She said he has been to see me several times and he has not changed his behavior."[33] Another mother told her social worker in a 1960 Family Services case that her husband had been frustrated with the process of counseling her son (his stepson) about his membership in a local gang. In response, the husband could look to the authority of another mainstream institution to justify giving up the strategy suggested by BBA staff. When this boy was arrested, the stepfather "laughed and laughed about what had happened to Isaiah and then said that jail was the best place for Isaiah—it would do him good and help him grow up." Isaiah's mother was furious with her husband for ridiculing her son. However, she clearly had similar frustrations with "talking": "She tells [Isaiah] not to do something and the next thing she knows he is doing it." Said the caseworker "I wondered if she punished him a lot and she said yes; it seemed as if she was always beating on him. I [the caseworker] said I knew it was hard to know just what to do with a child who behaved this way, but sometimes they are asking for more attention with this kind of behavior. [Isaiah's] mother could not go along with this, and said that she thought he was just plain 'ornery'."[34]

When another boy, Maurice, was caught associating with some "undesirable boys" in the neighborhood, his mother deprived him of new Easter clothes and put him "in 'jail' for the next two months," later adding physical punishments to his sentence as well. The Big Brother assigned to her son suggested that her punishments "might be too severe," and that she "should give Maurice more freedom."

She replied that "she cannot do so because he takes advantage of it. . . ." She said that [the Big Brother and the caseworker] "may not understand Maurice as well as she does because if we did we would see that she has to be very hard on him." In the case report describing Maurice's home life we also get the sense that his mother had a more general tendency to avoid demonstrations of affection and positive reinforcement in her child rearing. In a later interview with his caseworker, Maurice "said he suspects that she is satisfied with his behavior because she has not fussed with him or complained about anything recently. I [the caseworker] inquired whether she has complimented him on any improvement in his behavior. He said no." On another occasion the same caseworker "asked [Maurice] if [his mother] ever put her arms around him and demonstrated affection for him. He laughed sarcastically and said she had never done this."[35]

Maurice's mother told her caseworker that her severe "punishment will either make or break the youngster." But as many other case-report parents quickly discovered, increasingly forceful punishments of kids failed just as often as noncommittal attempts at greater emotional understanding. Such punishments were the single most important and consequential familial source of resentment for boys who would often run away from home for fear of beatings or would retaliate violently, like Maurice did when he got fed up with his mother's constant physical punishment.[36] Typically, kids' resentful, defiant, and aggressive behavior would increase in response to the increasing violence of parents' reprisals, often ending in the total collapse of their relationship. This collapse took the form of either parents' abdication of their responsibilities or a seemingly hopeless descent into verbal and physical abuse and family horror.

After one of Maurice's mother's beatings turned into a fistfight between the two when Maurice was fourteen, his mother "commented that she now realizes that she can no longer control Maurice by sheer force because he is more mature and does not respond to this sort of treatment." Shortly after, Maurice ran away from home and his mother filed "incorrigibility" charges at the juvenile court. Maurice spent the rest of his teenage years in and out of youth detention centers.[37] Many other cases ended similarly: parents felt "at wits' end," frustrated with Big Brothers' sermons on affect and the need to talk things out and with the failure of their own aggressive methods of discipline, and they concluded that their only recourse was to turn over control of their children's behavior to the police and juvenile courts.[38] Still other parents, some of whom were

less disposed to expend the energy it took to mete out constant physical punishment (as one mother put it, "there are times when she
does not feel like fighting with him and gives in just to have a little
peace"), found themselves withdrawing from the scene and sometimes ending up neglecting their children's upbringing. When
another boy's stepfather first moved in with the household, he "had
tried to enforce some rules and regulations, but the boy proved
unresponsive"; and since "Mr. G. feels that Troy is old enough to
know right from wrong," he decided that he "would not bother further." (As we saw earlier, the stepfather's ensuing neglect occasioned
much resentment from Troy.)[39] No doubt some of the kids' absent
fathers had come to similar conclusions as Troy's stepfather. In a few
cases mothers complained that their sons would run away from
home to find less strict fathers, and as we have seen, some boys felt
great hurt and resentment because of the neglectful behavior of
fathers who gave them minimal or inconsistent attention.[40]

The other path for failed attempts at behavioral control through
physical punishment was outright cruelty and sometimes descent
into unremitting family warfare. Some of this may have happened
despite the better wishes of parents, like in the case of Mrs. A., who
claimed that "she started punishing [Hollis] by taking his pleasures
away, but once he made her so angry that she picked up a coffee-
table and hit him over the head with it. Mrs. A. relates that her anger
rises easily and she realizes that in this state of mind she is likely to
pick up anything and strike Hollis. She states she is training herself
to remain calm for this reason and mete out punishments, instead of
whippings." One day when Mrs. A. heard from the school that Hollis
had been cutting classes, "she related that she hadn't gone home
because she was afraid she would kill Hollis." (None of her wishes to
avoid this eventuality ever seemed to help Hollis overcome his
resentment. After a number of depredations in the neighborhood,
he was sent to his grandparents' home somewhere else in Philadelphia, where he was eventually caught stealing an automobile and was
sent to a "reform school.")[41]

Other instances of abuse seem to result from more calculated cruelty: One mother related that her ex-husband "felt . . . in the matter
of discipline . . . [that] brutality was the way to handle children. She
said he never set a proper example for them or talked with them in a
warm understanding way. She said he inflicted severe physical punishment and other types of torture when the children displeased
him. She spoke of one instance when he locked a child in the ice

box."[42] In an intake interview in 1958, sixteen-year-old Clayborne, who had been referred to the BBA by the juvenile court after a number of arrests for violent acts, warned the caseworker "that his home life is quite distrubed [sic]. He remarked that he wished [the worker] was there sometime to see the things that go on in his family. He said if [the worker] stood outside the door it would be unlikely that [the worker] would want to come in." Over the next few years Clayborne and his caseworkers would report numerous acts of brutality he suffered at the hands of his mother, often on slight provocation. After one string of beatings, his mother "grabbed him in [sic] the collar and Clayborne said, 'I am tired of this,' and this shocked her and she took a chair and broke it over his head, and then she grabbed a broom handle and beat him severely. When the stick broke she would take the largest part and continue to beat. Finally when the stick got to [sic] short she knocked him on the bed and started to choke him. Finally in desperation to get away, Clayborne hit her in the jaw and knocked her down." At a later interview, "he voiced the opinion that if his mother continues to harass and beat him with chairs and table legs as in the past he will be unable the next time to control himself." He ran away twice and got involved in gang fights, during one of which he was stabbed in the back. When he returned home after running away the first time, his mother beat him with a chair leg, thus aggravating his stab wound. While trying to escape, he apparently pushed his mother down, an act for which she would not forgive Clayborne even after the court ordered her, against her wishes, to take the boy back home. Later she beat him again for burning some rice. (Unlike many other boys in his position, Clayborne seems to have mustered some miraculous reserves of resilience and counteracted his simmering resentments toward his family. He abandoned his gang friends and returned to school, and Clayborne's case record ended on something of an upbeat note—a rarity among the stories I read—when his Big Brother helped him pass the entrance exam into the armed forces.)[43]

Among the 110 boys whose BBA case reports I read, the thirty most troubled, most aggressive, and least responsive to the association's help were those whose parents most consistently acted on the belief that cooperative behavior needed to be taught to children by noncooperative and aggressive means, and who most consistently and cruelly practiced that philosophy. Many of the kids also experienced troubles that had to do with parents they missed or that resulted from their parents' marital troubles, but in no case did those problems fully account for either the pain and resentment or the validations of aggressive behavior that the children encountered in family life. At the same time, parents' child-rearing philosophies and practices—themselves part of a tradition that had a strong mandate in mainstream culture—were also at least partially responsible for kids' universal familiarity with cooperative norms. After all, the punishments kids suffered at parents' hands, no matter how violent and no matter how much they were principally aimed at establishing obedience to parental authority, were usually meted out at least in the name of prohibiting noncooperative or aggressive behavior. They were also couched in religious terms, as for example, the desire to avoid "spoiling" children by "sparing the rod." And finally, by equating child punishment with jails and being prepared to employ the police, parents demonstrated just how closely their philosophies resonated with those of mainstream institutions of law and order. However, as instances of family warfare described in the case reports also demonstrate, forceful parenting, especially at its most damaging, reflected not only parents' conscious moral philosophies but also their own aggressive expressions of painful emotional memories. Frustration, humiliation, and a sense of powerlessness and inadequacy are written all over parents' attempts to assert authority over their kids.

The stories of children in Chauntey's neighborhood offer some other angles on the question of the relationship between families and collective experience. Of course, the eight immediate families I have gotten to know (seven of which are run by a single mother) do not make up as wide-ranging and representative a sample of family upbringing as the families described in the 110 BBA case reports. However, I have been able to get a much more in-depth perception of individual parent-child relationships in those families through my friendships with mothers, fathers, and kids than I did by reading caseworkers' renditions. Though the kids involved make up a smaller group, they are also more diverse than the BBA group from the 1950s and 1960s, who, after all, were all teenagers referred to an organization for troubled children. What I have learned from my friends confirms that kids in single-parent households can grow up in many strikingly different ways, and that the nature of parents' behavior toward their children, both boys and girls, needs to be taken into account in any attempt to understand those differences.

As reflected in the case reports, the effect on kids of having an absent parent varied. Kids who have no memories of a father, because he disappeared or died before or soon after they were born, are the ones who tend to idealize their dad. Chauntey had all sorts of stories about his unknown father's prowess, and he once told me that his family stood to inherit a million dollars and a farm from a long-lost uncle of his sister Kimberly's. When Asmar Greene was four, he had not yet met his father. That year he and I took a walk, during which he told me at great length how strong his father and his (nonexistent) older brothers were by pointing to a house and saying they were as tall as the rafters three floors up, and that their shoes were as big as the metal garbage cans that stood out front. Indeed, his dad seemed to be a greater source of solace and strength when he was absent and unknown than when he eventually showed up some years later. When Asmar got to know his father, his adulation and pride turned to disgust and disappointment. On one visit Asmar was promised some fancy clothes and money. The goods never materialized, and according to Asmar's mother, when the father returned again after another long absence, Asmar, now seven, refused to shake his dad's hand, telling him, "I know you don't love me. You aren't like a father. My uncle and my godparents love me more than my own father. That's a shame."

Kimberly's memories of her father seem to be dominated by the nature of his death: he was shot and killed, (according to some accounts, right before her eyes), when she was very young. I never learned all of the details, but once when Kimberly and her younger cousin were trading apparently playful "busses," the subject of Kimberly's dad came up. Immediately Kimberly flew into a rage and slugged the younger girl, yelling, "Don't you ever talk about my father!" I later got an independent warning from Chauntey: "Don't ever ask her about her dad. She don't let anybody talk about her dad." He refused to give me any details. Fahim, Omar, Theresa, and Saleema Wilkins all seem to have been affected in a variety of contradictory but profound ways by their father's parenting and by the circumstances of his death. He was apparently a brilliant, creative man, who taught his kids lessons on the need to avoid drugs and stay in school that they have remembered well years after his death. But he also was a leading figure in a turf gang during the early seventies, and he reportedly killed a number of people and often badly hurt his wife. According to his kids' reports, he gave them whippings they will never forget. He was pushed to his death from a bridge into the river by an old gang acquaintance of his shortly before I got to know the Wilkinses. In death he has taken on proportions larger than life in his kids' eyes—first, as a source of pride for both his artistic abilities and his "heart" (that is, his ability to fight), as well as a source of fear and sometimes resentment; and second, as a guide for doing well in school (maybe even the source of a fear of failure in Fahim's case), as well as a model for expressions of masculinity based on domination of women, hatred of homosexuality, and violence. In addition, the kids have not fully reconciled themselves to the fact of his murder, and they often expressed the thought that he may have fallen by accident; their feelings of embarrassment and hurt, mingled with well-developed anxieties about abandonment, often surface when we drive near the bridge where he died or when we talk of his murder.

Unlike the boys described in the case reports, only a small minority of kids I got to know in Chauntey's neighborhood ever experienced the separation or divorce of their parents. Most of the immediate families were formed when children were born to single mothers who had little or no contact with their kids' fathers. However, mothers' behavior in their relationship with other adult men had an important impact on kids' emotional and cultural experience within their families. I have already mentioned the very frequent episodes of domestic violence that the Wilkinses remember from before their father's death. In the house of their cousins Georgie, Andre, and Towanda, which belonged to their grandfather and which was a frequent family gathering place for all the Wilkins children, one of their aunts would be brutally beaten by the father of her kids as regularly as each payday; an adult cousin of theirs would also frequently join the melee, as would Georgie and Andre's mother, father, and yet another uncle. These family brawls left memories of brutality and fear deeply etched in kids' memories. One relatively frequent pastime, especially for the Wilkins boys, was to sit around and recall in lurid detail what had happened during various incidents.

The effect on kids of mothers' relationships with boyfriends depended largely on the behavior of the adults concerned. Chauntey, as we have seen, was very embarrassed by his mother's spells of prostitution, which apparently took place in the same one-room apartment that also served as her kids' bedroom. However, a somewhat steady boyfriend, who occasionally lived with the family for a month or so at a time, and who once found them a more spacious place to live, offered the Patterson kids a stabilizing presence; so did a boyfriend of Chauntey's older sister, a reputed drug dealer who rode around in a customized four-wheel-drive vehicle and once or twice took the kids to amusement parks in the summer.

After Fahim and Omar's father died, their mother apparently lost a good deal of her authority over the boys by getting involved with a man they thought was beneath contempt. He was, they said, "a dirty piper [crack addict] and a trash picker" who made his living by gathering junk metal in a grocery cart and selling it to local recyclers. Over the years since his father's death, Omar has developed some powerful outrage at his mother (and women in general) that may be partly linked to this relationship. While it was going on, he began spending less time at his mother's house, preferring to spend the night with his cousins Georgie and Andre at their grandfather's place.

Just as in the case reports, memories of absent parents and the marital life of adults children live with can serve as ethical validation for aggressive behavior and the source of extraordinarily hurtful emotions that surface regularly in kids' ordinary social interactions. However, also like the experiences of boys as described in the case reports, the most lasting impact of families on children in Chauntey's neighborhood comes from their parents' child-rearing practices.

Since I got to know children—including girls, as well as boys—from a wider age group than those mentioned in the case reports, I got to know a little more about the diversity of emotional and cultural relationships that parents forged with their kids. But if there was a philosophical point of departure common to the parents' diverse interactions with their children in the neighborhood, it was very similar to that evident in the case reports: the tradition that physical punishment is essential to implementing moral education and to instill in children a deep respect for the primacy of adult will.

One mother probably best expressed the general sentiment among parents in my community when she once assured me: "I always believe you gotta love 'em, don't get me wrong. But there's some times when [she smacked her fist into the palm of her other hand] this is the only language they understand." Parents universally believed that the process of "teaching kids right from wrong" involved forceful verbal and physical treatment. Like the parents of the boys seen by the BBA, adults in Chauntey's neighborhood believe that aggressive behavior, especially defiance of adults, makes kids "bad" or "evil," and that socialization is primarily a moral issue. "You know right from wrong," goes a common admonition, "so why you acting bad?" Also, like in the case reports, "bad mothers" are seen as those who neglect their children, or make them "raise themselves in the streets" not the mothers who exercise force or use other strict punishments.

Many adults in Chauntey's community fondly remember the day when anyone in the neighborhood could be trusted to "give the business" to anyone else's child when they acted out, and some saw the Kids' Club as an opportunity to revive that vision of the neighborhood. The resulting philosophical clash between the Club's African-American, long-term resident members and the white outsiders like myself, who were raised according to the so-called progressive tenets of childhood, underlay much of the troubles the organization had in involving a broad base of neighborhood volunteers. Parents' philosophies also clashed with school regulations forbidding teachers to hit kids, a rule several parents have told me they think is the reason inner-city schools have so many troubles with behavior. Again, law-and-order sentiments, including occasional references to the police and jail, were the preferred mainstream source of parenting philosophy.

Some neighborhood residents also felt that violence contributed to neighborhood stability in the form of "fair fights." This institution seemed to be on its way out when I moved to Chauntey's neighborhood. Older members of the community remembered with some nostalgia the days before guns and drugs, when the kids used to "fight fair." The rules allowed violence to settle disputes, so long as the individuals involved were of the same age and gender, and so long as neither participant used any weapon other than his or her fists. Sometimes older men would "draw a ring on the street" in preparation for a fair fight, then "bring out the boxing gloves" so that the participants could "get out what was bothering them" and avoid the possibility of escalating or fatal encounters. If the two aggrieved parties did not match up fairly in age or sex, one of them could offer a more suitable proxy, usually a relative, to fight for his or her cause.

Despite the rarity of such fights nowadays, I did, unwittingly, witness preparations for one when Georgie Wilkins, either accidentally or purposely, spilled a can of beer in the lap of a woman who lived in the next block. The woman, known for her status consciousness and for the strictness with which she raised her children, drafted her teenaged nephew to fight my friend and serve justice for the stain on her dress. The proceedings, which took place on the sidewalk outside my house, were solemn: the offended woman first stood between the two contestants and had them raise their fists, then moved out of the way as a signal for the fight to begin. Meanwhile, somebody from Georgie's family summoned his aunt to make sure the referee did her job fairly. A substantial crowd gathered, and when I decided to stop the fight by escorting Georgie home, I earned myself several months' worth of disgusted looks from its organizer. From my perspective, this "fair fight" was based on an ethic that equated justice with prowess at violent acts. It set no criteria for what kinds of disputes demanded violent solutions. (In other, usually less well organized fair fights I have seen, the fact that aggression broke out over a dispute was seen as enough reason to assume it could not be resolved in any other way.) Fair fighting also obligated proxies to fight, often against their own will, for relatives and friends who were mismatched with their adversaries. However, from the perspective of the woman who had organized the fight and who had paid scrupulous attention to its fairness, I was disrupting a time-honored institution of justice and neighborhood stability, one that old-school inhabitants of Chauntey's neighborhood viewed as a force against what they saw as increasing unrestricted violence and moral decay in their community. In fact, I may have been seen as endorsing those threatening forces. By unthinkingly escorting my friend home (instead of proposing some alternative way of settling the dispute), I had put my reputation in the community behind a child who had not respected his elders (and who, incidentally, had done so on other occasions) and who also had a healthy reputation for fighting unfairly.

The corollary to advocacy of forceful punishment was the view that adults risked, to use the biblical language common in Chauntey's neighborhood, spoiling children through affection or prolonged emotional attention. Emotional distance was sometimes rigidly enforced. Kids were constantly reminded to address adults other than their parents by using *Mr.* or *Mrs.* and then their first name, a practice called "putting a handle on a name." Neighborhood parents involved in the Kids' Club consistently advised me to deal with children's misbehavior by forcing them to call me "Mr. Carl"—something that clashed too much with my own upbringing for me to carry out. Adults in the neighborhood, like Maurice's mother as described in the case reports, also worried a lot about their kids "getting over" or taking advantage of them, which was another reason for avoiding outward displays of affection: "You've gotta feed them with a long-handled spoon," one mother counseled me, "otherwise they'll take advantage of your kindness." Others pointed to the need for kids, especially boys, to be hardened in the face of constant threats to their safety in the neighborhood.

These general precepts allowed varied levels of severity in parenting practices. Children's age and sex influenced the degree of forceful treatment. On one end of the spectrum, for example, parents' and older kids' treatment of babies often verged on a contradiction of the rule against emotional contact: newborns were passed back and forth fondly, even overindulgently, between the cradling arms of adult relatives and siblings. Part of this may come from the nature of mothers', and particularly young mothers', decisions to have children in the first place. As many observers of inner-city life have suggested, such decisions are in part based on each girl's desire to have one person in life who is her "very own" and who, at least in prenatal fantasy, can be a source of undying emotional support and status to the mother. Though this kind of motherhood has been interpreted as a sign of "inversion" of mainstream norms in the inner city, the resulting treatment of babies in Chauntey's neighborhood is more affectionate than is the parenting with any other age group.[44]

Already in babyhood, however, and increasingly in toddler years, especially for boys, kids in Chauntey's neighborhood begin to experience other practices based more on spare-the-rod, spoil-the-child philosophies. Crying babies in the neighborhood are often told simply to "shut up" or are sometimes even slapped, and when two- and three-year-olds begin to show resentment by disobeying their parents, they get fixed with labels like "bad" or "spoiled," which in turn too often become self-fulfilling prophesies. Male parents and older boys in the family often take on the task of "toughening up" boy toddlers by engaging them in play boxing matches or admiringly saying, "That little boy, he a fighter." Meanwhile, little girls usually get more delicate treatment, and though they are also sometimes slapped or spanked, they generally have more affectionate relationships with their mothers or other adult female relatives. For Towanda, Theresa, and Saleema Wilkins, for example, close relationships with female adults were developed during the long hours it took to "do" kids' hair into elaborate coiffures, during shopping trips and never-ending waits in social service agency offices together, and eventually in the context of preparing girls for an increasing share in family responsibilities for younger children. Such contacts between parents, usually mothers, and girls were the closest families in the neighborhood ever came to engaging in daily rituals of family togetherness and mutual appreciation. Few kids in Chauntey's neighborhood, for example, whether boys or girls, ever counted on consistent family meals at dinnertime. But even in their warmest moments, parent-child relationships rarely involved a lot of affection or expressions of encouragement; there was little smiling, hugging, or enthusiastic greeting between parents and kids, even after extended absences from each other. At most, mothers would occasionally use affectionate phrases like "my baby" when referring to their teenagers, or adult men would take time out from other pursuits to offer boys a lecture on some topic or another, or more rarely, play some basketball with them. For the most part, kids in Chauntey's neighborhood did their playing, joking, and laughing with other kids their own age or younger.

Age and sex were clearly not the only determinants of differences in the regularity and severity of parents' verbal and physical punishment of children. Most of the differences between parents' styles can be attributed to their own emotional lives, the extent to which they too have experienced painful experiences, and the extent to which they have gotten into the habit of expressing those feelings violently. Like in the case reports, the level of cruelty employed by parents in the moral education of their kids was very closely related to the extent to which their kids incorporated aggressive and noncooperative behavior into their daily habits and social styles.

The range of practices of forceful parenting, even among the small group of parents I got to know in Chauntey's neighborhood, is vast. Asmar Greene's mother, for example, has raised her seven kids without more than playful threats of violence and more regular, and usually fairly tenderly delivered, admonishments like "ain't she bad?" or "you old meathead!" She never has been what anyone would call a dominating or interventionist moral presence in her kids' lives—she is much too gentle, even passive, for that. Her family should fit the social-scientific model of a household without adequate cultural education, yet thus far her kids, especially the older girls, are among the most caring, least defiant and aggressive, and most morally secure of all the children I have met in inner-city Philadelphia.

The family experiences of the Wilkins children represent a varied middle ground both in terms of the severity of their parents' discipline and the aggressiveness of the kids' social styles. Among the children in the immediate family that includes Fahim, Omar, Theresa, and Saleema, a marked contrast exists between the daily behavior of Fahim and the girls, on the one hand, and Omar, on the other. This difference may be due in part to differences in the kids' relationships with their mother and their now-deceased father. Their mother has always seemed to me to favor Fahim over Omar, and to treat Fahim more like she treats Theresa and Saleema. She once told a friend of mine that Fahim was her "angel" and Omar was the bad one. Also, her nickname for Fahim suggests that he is a good-natured kook, whereas she often calls Omar by a name that draws attention to the size of his lips. Fahim has also spent much more time with his mother in pursuits that are usually, but not exclusively, reserved for girls, like shopping and caring for younger children. And he has been more successful in cajoling money from his mom, an inequity Omar resents.

While both boys remember harsh punishment from their deceased father, Omar seems to have been especially affected by an incident when his father belted him severely for putting some pillows under his shirt and pretending he was a pregnant woman. Some of Omar's subsequent rigid adherence to codes of masculinity based on hardness, aggression, and homophobia may be the result of his father's lectures on the evils of "acting gay" that he got after his whipping, lectures he can recite well to this day, many years later. Fahim by no means repudiates any of these creeds, but he is able to interact with people in much more expressive and understanding ways; his white-boy imitations, which I mentioned in chapter 1, are only one part of his repertoire of ebullient theatrics, and he is considerably more willing to show warmth and understanding toward others, and to have others show affection toward him. Omar often calls Fahim a "bitch" or "gay" for actions like these; no doubt, some part of Omar's more caustic and unfriendly social style comes from a reaction to his older brother's geniality.

In other families, close relationships between parents and children were interrupted much more often by angry threats and harsh punishments. Threats like "I'm gonna rip your face up if you're not here when I get back," or "come here before I pop you," and, of course, "I'm gonna fuck you up," often reverberated throughout the public spaces of my street. Some kids told me stories about beatings with an "iron cord" which seemed to be the preferred technique of severe punishment in the neighborhood. A few kids I met bore unmistakable and gruesome scars from this kind of punishment.

Even the cruelest treatment of children in Chauntey's neighborhood can be traced, at least in part, to generally shared philosophies of forceful moral education. Fahim's mother—who, in contrast to her late husband, is relatively gentle with her kids—once told of an incident when a friend of hers was arrested for beating her child in an alleyway so severely that the child was hospitalized. Fahim's mom wanted to know if she thought her friend had any chance in the courts. After all, she said, that kid was "a real problem child. He stole a hundred dollars from his mom once, and he was stealing again when she beat him. She was trying to teach him right from wrong." (When I told her I did not think her friend had much chance of avoiding prosecution, she tried another defense: "Well, don't you think they should know at the court that they are really good parents trying to raise their kids right even if they sometimes are bad parents?")

However, there are other circumstances in parents' lives, besides their familiarity with biblical phrases and mainstream mandates, that help determine not only how often they resort to forceful techniques but also how severely they do so. These other circumstances, in turn, may give some hints as to why inner-city parents have so enthusiastically endorsed their use of didactic violence. One common justification for being hard on kids, especially boys, is that they need to be toughened up for the life they face on inner-city streets. Parents often see it as part of their duty to help give young guys "their first knocks." Of course, parents' own emotional states are also very important in determining the likelihood that they will treat their kids aggressively. Some of the statistical correlation between single-parent households and "antisocial" behavior may be due to the extra amount of sheer work, exhaustion, and frustration that is required of parents who raise children on their own. But it is also clear from my experience that the "respectability" associated with the biblical and mainstream roots of forceful parenting sometimes gives parents a justification for taking out their own pain on their kids. The same legitimacy also makes forceful parenting a kind of compensatory identity. In an effort to achieve a reputation as upstanding members of the community, parents I know often boast about the severity of their child rearing, and put down others who neglect their kids. One of the parents who did this most frequently, in fact, was also one of the more troubled parents I got to know. She often seemed to be saying, out of desperation, "I don't have much, but I make sure my kids don't get out of line." She also had a reputation for some of the harsher punishments in the neighborhood. A need to compensate for the humiliations of poverty may also be redoubled by feelings of shame associated with racism. The African-American sociologist Janice Hale, recalling her childhood, said, "I was given very strict guidelines for behavior on the bus or in public, because for me to be loud or boisterous would make white people feel that all Blacks were that way."[45] Though the legitimacy of American traditions of forceful parenting have helped to shape inner-city families' contributions to their kids' ethical and emotional worlds, those traditions clearly have also been bolstered by other historical forces at work in poor African-American neighborhoods.

Like all other families, the families of late-twentieth-century poor urban African-Americans have had vital and wide-ranging influence on the children they raise. However, the problems thought to be principally associated with single-parent households—lack of masculine identification, boys' troubles with mothers, and the paucity of role models and family supervisors—do not appear to be as important in the raising of children as the nature of parenting practices themselves. The structure of kids' families does not make them inherently inviable, but unfortunately, parents' behavior can and sometimes does. Though overwhelming statistical evidence does support the argument that children experience greater risks in single-parent households, there is ample reason to believe that the poverty those families experience, the poorer and more violent neighborhoods they tend to live in, and their greater likelihood of household unrest can explain these correlations more than any inherent characteristic of the single-parent family structure itself. Any of these other associated variables—again, probably more so than one-parent structure itself—may in turn also make parents in those families more likely to employ violence as a child-rearing technique.

The virtually universal insistence on traditions of forceful parenting in the inner city, the varying levels of actual aggression in parent-child relationships, and the varying likelihood of aggressive practices being punctuated with periods of neglect had clear and important consequences for kids' cultural ideals and emotional memories. Philosophies of forceful parenting, and the practices based on them, have served as kids' first lesson in aggressive behavior that sanctions violence for didactic purposes. Those families who have used forceful punishments extensively also have reinforced the notion that might makes right, and they have no doubt communicated a tolerance for violence, even if their punishments were designed to discourage children's aggressive acts. In addition, a very fine line exists between ethics that value violence for didactic purposes and those that value violence for retribution and vindictive personal justice. Parents who rely on force and neglect in disciplining their children have also undoubtedly contributed in large measures to kids' feelings of humiliation, loneliness, frustration, resentment, and fear. The avoidance of affective parenting practices has certainly not helped kids confront and discuss the hurtful feelings they have experienced in their struggles with poverty, racism, and their families themselves, and families often have modeled few nonviolent means for expressing troubled feelings. Finally, some kids' interactions with especially abusive parents may have even more dire consequences for their behavior. As a growing number of criminologists, sociologists, and clinicians have shown, while victims of childhood maltreatment or sexual abuse do not necessarily end up with particularly violent habits in later life, such abuse often was suffered by court-referred children, men who batter or rape women, and adolescents who kill their parents or others.[46]

None of this evidence, however, supports the notion that either single-parent household structure or parenting practices even comes close to substituting for a complete historical explanation for the recent changes in inner-city social life or the complex cultural and emotional experience that surrounds those changes. Though romanticizing inner-city parent-child relationships will simply not do, there is no excuse for either the insulting, misogynistic theories that blame "bad mothers" for the inner-city tragedy or for the racism that often underlies those theories. What has gone on in inner-city homes between parents and children is due largely to historical factors that have origins beyond the limits of inner-city neighborhoods. Though traditions of forceful parenting need to be part of any historical explanation for families' contribution to the social fabric of the post–World War II inner city, those traditions need to be understood in terms of their own historical ancestry and persistent mainstream legitimacy. The history of traditional American philosophies of child rearing and their modern-day institutional mandate—as evident in the practices of many middle-class families, the preachings of many churches, and the law-and-order rhetoric of law enforcement and criminal justice personnel—are crucial to this historical analysis.

But historically persistent ethical traditions do not fully explain the shape of inner-city parenting styles. Indeed, as well as being immersed in mainstream ideas, forceful child-rearing, like other forms of inner-city aggression, also reflects a desperation whose roots stretch beyond the confines of families and the inner city itself. In addition to the stinging alienation of poverty and racism, other sets of mainstream values and images affect kids' and parents' cultural and emotional upbringings. And in the case of American racism, American consumerism, and American mass-media violence, the mainstream impact on poor black kids' moral education and emotional memory is not limited solely to their home lives. Other powerful child-rearing institutions—ones that have commanded ever wider audiences among all American kids in the late twentieth century—have also been at work.

4

Poor Black Children and American Racism

The importance of racism to life in poor urban African-American communities has been a subject of great popular and scholarly interest. For fifty years anthropologists, psychologists, and social scientists have offered a variety of opinions on the matter. Despite some occasionally passionate moments, however, their debate has not produced nearly as much rigorous empirical work as the debate on black families, for instance. The debate also has not offered any comprehensive answer to a set of key interconnected questions: How and where in their lives have residents of inner-city neighborhoods encountered racism? What forms has it taken? Which forms have been linked to aspects of the cultural and emotional experience that have underlain violence and family change in those neighborhoods? What is the recent history of those particular kinds of racism? Does that history help shed light on the chronology, or the exceptionality of the poor black inner-city social experience over the past fifty years?

The most thorough attention to these questions as a connected whole came from the psychologist Kenneth Clark in the 1940s and 1950s. In 1940 and 1941, Clark and his wife, Mamie, conducted their famous "doll studies." They found that starting at age three, and certainly by four, black children from both a southern community and a northern urban community had received and internalized enough information on America's perverse notions of racial inferiority to choose overwhelmingly a white doll over a black one as the doll they would most like to play with, as the one that looked like a "nice doll," and as the one with a "nice color." In a couple of cases, the Clarks noted, "children ran out of the testing room, inconsolable, convulsed in tears," when, after showing preference for the white doll, they were asked which of the two most "looks like you."[1]

Where precisely did kids get information like this? When Clark was called as an expert witness for the National Association for the Advancement of Colored People's (NAACP) successful arguments in the Supreme Court's 1954 *Brown v. Board of Education* decision, the answer was clear. Racial segregation "itself means inequality" Clark argued, and inherently teaches a message of inferiority and humiliation.[2] Furthermore, as Clark argued later in the decade, racial humiliation aggravated kids' noncooperative behavior:

> On the one hand, like all human beings, [black children] require a sense of personal dignity; on the other hand, the institutionalized forms of racist rejection deny them this human dignity. This basic conflict about the worth of self must be resolved or dealt with by these children with some type of defense. . . . Some children, usually of the lower socio-economic classes, may react . . . by adopting overt, aggressive, hostile, and antisocial patterns of responses. These destructive patterns may either be directed toward their own group or toward members of the dominant group."[3]

Later, in *Dark Ghetto* (1965), Clark summed up his view of the connection between racism and the extraordinary rates of violence in poor urban black communities: "the symptoms of lower-class society afflict the dark ghettos of America— . . . family instability, . . . unemployment, crime, . . . But because Negroes begin with the primary affliction of inferior racial status, the burdens of despair and hatred are more pervasive."[4]

Since *Dark Ghetto,* the question of how racism affects poor African-Americans has sparked much controversy and emotion, but it has engendered nothing as systematic as Clark's arguments taken as a whole. Also, the very definition of racism has changed erratically as the debate has progressed.

Daniel Patrick Moynihan's Labor Department "Report" on black families sparked the fiercest episode in the debate on racism. His famous claim, on the eve of the 1965 Watts riot, that blacks' inner-city problems were capable of "perpetuating themselves without assistance from the white world" (see chapter 2) not only insulted many people but also seemed absurd. Scholars who led the assault on Moynihan's "Report" unanimously reinstated racism as the number-one reason for various social phenomena of inner-city life. They also widened their conception of racism beyond the effects of segregation. Discussing the urban riots of the 1960s, for example, the sociologist Robert Staples thought the kind of racism that had the biggest effect on inner-city social life was police brutality, the violence that the white American "colonial" regime used to maintain its power. (He also hinted at another point, though—that the police's complete disinterest in law enforcement for the black community led to social problems.)[5] At other times, Staples and, even more eloquently, the cultural critic Michelle Wallace also pointed to the impact of racial stereotypes—most importantly, that of the oversexed and violent black male—on individuals' behavior.[6]

Some revisionist scholars, such as the psychologist Alvin Poussaint, also invoked "self-hatred" brought on by racism to explain violence within the black community: "Our conceptualization of black as evil and sinful comes to the surface. By attacking a fellow black, we may feel that we are committing a manly act, the destruction of sin itself."[7] The psychiatrist and social anthropologist Robert Coles, in his encounters with black children and their parents that would be recounted in his epic five-volume *Children of Crisis,* found that when young black kids drew pictures of themselves, they often distorted their facial features or made them indistinguishable. More often than not, they would draw themselves in the corner or down the hill from a white child; would use bright, cheerful colors to draw white kids and their neighborhoods; and would choose somber, muted tones for themselves and their own houses. Though Coles would conclude that black children who helped desegregate schools in the South demonstrated tremendous resilience in an environment of racial hatred, he could also not escape the conclusion that "the words 'Negro' and 'white' help distinguish the dreams and fantasies of children. . . . At two and three [they have] very different ideas of who they are based on a budding sense of racial identity."[8]

Sentiments like these seemed to have rubbed most revisionists' cultural nationalism the wrong way, however; in general, such researchers, including Poussaint, remained wary of notions like self-hatred. As a result, in their most detailed empirical studies of racial identity among poor blacks, like the ethnographer Joyce Ladner's depiction in *Tomorrow's Tomorrow,* these scholars emphasized inner-city children's resilience in reacting to experiences of racial denigration. They also emphasized the extent to which "black-is-beautiful" campaigns had managed to penetrate even the most despairing of housing projects.[9]

What was missing most from the revisionists' work was a sense of history: in their portrayals of inner-city life, racism seemed unchanging and absolute. To the sociologist William Julius Wilson, who issued the next important salvo in the debate, this weakness was crucial. After all, racist institutions like Jim Crow had been virtually obliterated by the early 1970s, northern housing markets appeared to be opening up for blacks outside city limits, and job discrimination, according to Wilson's elaborate statistical analyses, was on the wane. Furthermore, whites' racial attitudes (or at least what they were telling opinion survey researchers) were improving dramatically; and the mass media were allowing a much greater diversity of African-American images to grace TV and movie screens. During this era of progress, life in the inner city was getting much worse. Wilson took this as unmistakable evidence of the "declining significance of race," not only in the perpetuation of poverty but also in the increasing troubles of poor African-American communities: "Even if racism continues to be a factor in the social and economic progress of some blacks, can it be used to explain the sharp increase in inner-city social dislocations since 1970? Unfortunately, no one who supports the contemporary racism thesis has provided adequate or convincing answers to this question."[10]

Since Wilson issued this challenge there has been much excellent work on racism, racial attitudes and stereotypes, discrimination, racial identity, and the recent history of race relations, a good deal of which contradicts Wilson's suppositions. The ethnographer Jonathan Rieder and the journalist Anthony Lukas have written powerful accounts of racist attitudes in white working-class communities that not only persisted after the civil rights movement but were strengthened in response to it.[11] The sociologists Joleen Kirschenman and Kathryn Neckerman have written a fascinating account of the racial images that direct inner-city business managers' hiring practices, and they have done much to question Wilson's "declining significance" argument as far as racial discrimination in hiring is concerned.[12] The ethnographer Elijah Anderson and other more recent authors have documented a growing tendency among a much broader group of whites to connect their fear of urban crime with a resurgent racism.[13] Little has been written on the effects of these forms of racism on the inner city itself, but psychologists like William Cross have expanded understandings of racial identity beyond

Clark's notions of self-hatred and accounted for a variety of other different ways of responding to racism.[14] Despite the quality of this work, the study of the effects of racism on inner-city social life remains splintered, not only between different definitions of racism itself but between scholars of different disciplines and interests.

What would a comprehensive historical analysis of the relationship between racism, racial identity, and the cultural and emotional and behavioral world of the inner city look like? My offering here is but an initial foray, one that attempts to link up the most convincing work in a variety of fields on racism and racial identity with the experiences of children, with a particular focus on boys, who have grown up in post–World War II Philadelphia. My premise is that racism has had a number of different histories in the inner city during the last fifty years, and that these reflect changes in a variety of social groups, institutions, and cultural and social structures which have communicated information about race and racial identity to poor urban African-American children.

Kids in Chauntey's neighborhood in the late 1980s and the 1990s face many of the same forms of racial exclusion that boys described in the Big Brothers Association (BBA) case reports lived through in the 1950s. While encounters with white racial hatred have probably become less common, those encounters have certainly not disappeared, nor have they become any less hurtful. Meanwhile, the racial segregation of schools and neighborhoods continues to teach kids other humiliating lessons. Also, kids, especially boys, in Chauntey's neighborhood face America's growing tendency to associate urban danger with race—probably to a degree not experienced by their counterparts in the 1950s. In addition, both boys and girls have been affected by these negative trends as played out in mass culture, a subject I discuss more in the next two chapters.

Though kids in Chauntey's neighborhood are indeed familiar with many of the improvements in racial images that have occurred since the 1950s, the forces of racial exclusion and the perpetuation of stereotypes in the American mainstream—strengthened by the embarrassment and frustration kids experience in connection with economic exclusion—have continued to thwart their youthful efforts to construct a satisfying sense of racial identity. The humiliation that so dominates inner-city kids' emotional memories is largely the result of encounters with all forms of persistent racial exclusion, and their powerful feelings of resentment over suspicion derive directly from Americans' growing tendency to equate race with criminality. At the same time that American racism continues to contribute to the painful parts of all kids lives, some of its forms have also helped shape their attempts to construct a compensatory identity, particularly among teenage boys.

The recent history of poor urban black children's encounter with white racial hatred is difficult to document, and we have to rely on diverse scraps of evidence. In his ethnographic study of black teenagers in Louisville, Kentucky, and Washington, D.C., in the late 1930s, the sociologist E. Franklin Frazier describes boys who nearly daily encountered epithets like "nigger," "darky," and "monkey" from whites, and who were often forced to dance or fight at all-white stag parties, in addition to suffering all the legal restrictions of border-state Jim Crow.[15] Caseworkers for Big Brothers and Family Services from the 1950s were primarily interested in the ways family dynamics affected the children they worked with. As a result, they said little in their reports about the frequency with which children encountered white hatred in increasingly segregated urban neighborhoods of northern cities like 1950s Philadelphia. If the historian Arnold Hirsch's depiction of life in Chicago is any indication, though, "hidden violence," perpetrated by whites against blacks seeking housing outside the confines of segregated neighborhoods, persisted throughout the years between the race riots of the 1940s and those of the 1960s and 1970s.[16]

In the few instances where case reports mention racial issues, it is clear that encounters with racial hatred, like those experienced by the children Frazier interviewed in the 1930s, were deeply felt and humiliating experiences.[17] When Gregory, who had given the staff of the BBA's integrated summer camp no end of trouble, was taken aside after fighting a white boy, he remarked "that he doesn't care for white people because before he came to camp a gang of white boys fought a gang of colored boys and threw one of the colored boys in the river." Apparently, the counselors' attempts to help Gregory come to terms with racial issues ("we tried to make him understand that there were good and bad of all people") did not keep him from heaping racial hatred onto his black friends. A later entry reads: [Gregory was] involved in a fight with [a black] boy named Howard and he started shouting to this boy 'your black mother can have you'" and "within two hours, he was involved in a fight with Tommy Findley. . . . When I told them to stop fighting, Tommy stopped right away but Gregory threatened to get a bat and hit him and was calling Tommy obscene names. Tommy claims [Gregory] had called him a 'black spook' and 'black nigger.'. . . [Later, in the office] Gregory said "I see that big black spook out there and I'm not afraid of him."[18] In another incident at camp, another boy "was involved in a fight with a smaller [black] boy. Fight started when Daniel pushed himself ahead of the other boy in line. When [the counselor] stopped the fight and told Daniel the other boy was too small for him, he started to cry and said the other boy had called him 'black.'"[19]

The caseworkers also occasionally documented strong feelings about black physical characteristics, feelings that may in part also reflect the kinds of "color struck" distinctions in skin color that Frazier described in his study of class relationships among the black middle class during the 1950s.[20] For example, one boy described in the BBA reports developed overwhelming insecurities about his "flat nose," and the mother of another boy described at great length how her family persecuted her, then sent her out of the home because her skin was darker than her siblings.'[21]

Since Frazier's interviews and Clark's experiments, and since the period of the case reports, black leaders of many political ideologies have worked actively to counteract racial humiliation among young African-Americans. During her years studying St. Louis's Pruitt-Igoe housing project in the late 1960s, Ladner noticed that poor kids had already been able to internalize some of the spirit of these efforts to raise racial consciousness: most of the girls she spoke with were certainly able to say they were proud to be black, and some even adopted some of the language of black power. At the same time, Ladner was well aware that "there is always the possibility that much of what was expressed in positive terms about one's identity by a few of them was 'reaction formation' and that consciously they liked themselves, but unconsciously they did experience self-rejection." One girl betrayed this kind of struggle graphically: "I feel very proud of it," she told Ladner, "nothing can be done about it so I have to feel proud of it myself. . . . I wouldn't change it if I could."[22]

Kids growing up in the late 1980s and early 1990s in Chauntey's neighborhood often express themselves in a similarly ambivalent language of conscious racial pride. When asked directly if they are proud to be black, kids usually say yes, and they do not always need prompting. The movement to improve racial identity continues to affect daily life in Chauntey's neighborhood in many ways: social studies curricula in the schools serving the neighborhood, and most

other schools in the city, now set aside the month of February for
the study of African-American history; and though some of the fer-
vor of the black-is-beautiful movement has died down, the kids I
know have access to a variety of festivals and holidays that celebrate
black culture and the African-American heritage. Many kids are also
familiar with the teachings of Afrocentric thinkers, whether through
reading or through the music of rap stars like Sister Souljah, Public
Enemy, and other proponents of the so-called hip-hop nation, or in
the speeches of political leaders like Louis Farrakhan. Kids love
going to "Odunde," Philadelphia's African-American New Year festi-
val, modeled on an old Yoruba rite and held every June. There they
can buy "Black by Popular Demand" sweatshirts (which people actually end up wearing pretty rarely in my neighborhood); red, green,
and black bead necklaces; Nefertiti earrings; and leather medallions
with the shape of Africa sewn into them—all of which are popular
among local kids (and some rap stars).

At the same time though, the signs of subconscious—and not-so-
subconscious—racial humiliation are abundant. Many neighborhood residents, and especially teenage boys, see all the back-to-
Africa stuff as too "corny," and most are reluctant to immerse
themselves completely in such paraphernalia (the notable exception
being the very popular "X" hat that filmmaker Spike Lee has used as
a mass-marketing strategy for his movie *Malcolm X*). When kids
express disgust at their skin color or with their hair, Kids' Club volunteers often attempt to lift their spirits with a rousing "but black is
beautiful!" A typical response is a mopey, "Yeah, yeah, yeah, we've
heard that before."

Indeed, those campaigning to free inner-city black children of
racial stigmas and self-denigration have had to fight an uphill battle
against kids' persistent experience of white hatred. Coles, Lukas,
and Rieder have all reported that the civil rights movement, the
efforts to desegregate northern urban school districts, and the social
programs to help the black poor in the 1960s and 1970s sparked
concerted movements of hatred against blacks, especially among
working-class whites who often targeted young people for debilitat-
ing harassment and violence. Though most recent opinion surveys
have shown that whites at least claim that they see less problem in
sending their children to schools also attended by black children,
and they mind much less having black people as neighbors than in
the 1960s,[23] we know well from incidents like those that have
occurred recently in Howard Beach and Bensonhurst, that orga-

nized demonstrations of racial hatred and violence have by no means disappeared. In Philadelphia in 1985, for another example, the mayor found it necessary to impose a curfew on a white neighborhood in which a mob of four hundred people had taken to the streets to protest a black-race couple's move to a previously all-white street.[24]

In Chauntey's neighborhood, none of the kids I know has yet faced the level of violence suffered by victims of racist mobs, and none of them encounter the language of racial hatred as frequently as did the kids Frazier or Lukas described. However, almost everyone I know in the neighborhood over the age of ten, boy or girl, can name at least one time in which a white person called him or her a "nigger" out of hate. Though they hear the word much more often from black people (who, as we shall see, use it in many different ways), they readily recognize the especially spiteful use of "nigger" as white in origin and practice. And even if kids initially respond to my question, "Has a white person ever called you a 'nigger'?" by joking that "Lots of black people have," they remember those few incidents when they were riding bikes and some "white girls and boys called out, 'Hey, niggers'" or when they were "chased by some white boys— they was saying, 'Niggers go home.'" Memories of such events evoke a particularly deep sense of humiliation, pain, and sometimes anger. I have heard about a dozen stories like this from the seven Wilkins children I know well. Nine-year-old Saleema just nodded her head yes with a taut, embarrassed smile when I asked about her encounters with white hatred. Chauntey told me that white kids in his relatively recently desegregated school would occasionally schedule "nigger days" when black kids were open targets of harassment and violence—a practice that may have been passed down from more open conflicts that erupted in the 1970s when his school began enrolling its first black students.

In addition to their own personal encounters, all the kids I know are at least vaguely aware of the history of white racial violence and the very real threat it continues to pose to their safety. The tangible and sensible discomfort with which nine- and ten-year-old Omar and Fahim initially greeted my invitations to visit my house turned out later to be based on their suspicions that I and my housemates might be linked to the Ku Klux Klan. Most kids I know are familiar with the basic facts about segregation and racial hatred in the South, and some also can talk about instances of racial violence like those suffered by Michael Griffith and Yusuf Hawkins in New York City as well as others that have occurred in Philadelphia but have gotten less national publicity. Films like Spike Lee's *Do the Right Thing* and rap songs that call attention to white oppression have also helped bring home knowledge of the threat of racial mob violence to those who have not experienced it directly.

Indeed, like the children Clark interviewed and like the kids in the case reports, children growing up in Chauntey's neighborhood continue to feel tremendous humiliation concerning their race. Kids' verbal and emotional abuse is packed with racial pejoratives. Derogatory references to skin color, lip size, and hair texture often came up in "buss" contests (*peas* refers to irregular tufts of hair that would sprout up if kids did not comb regularly):

> You so black they marked you absent in night school.

> You head so peasy you gonna put Del Monte outta business.

> You so black that your momma feed you buttermilk so you won't pee ink.

> You so black you look like a piece of burnt cake.

> Your mom bottom lip so low, that every time she walks she trips over it.

> You so black you sweat tar.

Among peers, "burnt," "brushy," "monkey," "grizzly," "fat lips," and of course, "nigger" were insults that sometimes carried enough weight to start fights, much in the same ways as described in the BBA case reports. The most common race-based pejorative, however, and the one that seemed to be packed with most spite, was "black" itself. To make sure their meaning was clear, kids often combined "black" with other put-downs, like "dirty black," "ugly black," "black-assed," "black as shit," or, as in one of Chauntey's favorite taunts, "hey kid, you got a black problem?"

Girls and boys would frequently express their embarrassment over their "nappy" hair (called "nigger's knots" by some), and girls especially expressed a near-universal wish for what they called the "nice," white alternative. (Whenever girls drew themselves or their mothers, their portraits would have long, straight hair, usually curled up at the end, and kids would find any excuse to play with the long hair of some of the Kids' Club's white female tutors. See chapter 5 for more on hair and hairstyles.)[25] During the first couple of years of my friendship with Georgie and Andre, they (as well as some of the other kids, less frequently) would hoist their jackets up to cover their heads and faces whenever they met a white person for the first time.

Shades of skin color were an issue of intense, if often repressed, emotional concern for everyone I met. Among the kids I met, who were all poor, the distinction between light and dark skin seemed less one of class difference, in the way Frazier described, and more one of basic physical attractiveness. One teenage girl told me that "all light-skinned boys are decent and all black boys are ugly." As a result, she thought, "light-skinned boys always got an attitude like they all that, and they don't treat you right. But black boys treat you nicer."

Attitudes about skin color form early in life. Four-year-old Asmar Greene, whose skin is a rich, dark brown, once gave me a long, rambling speech that ended with his conclusion that "we not black people, we light-skinned. I got light skin." When I asked about his mother and then his older sister (both of whom have even darker skin than Asmar), he told me both times that "she light-skinned." Then he went on to conclude, "I don't like black people. Black people evil." Older kids made special efforts to stay out of the sun if they could, to avoid darkening their skin: one teenager told me: "Y'all won't be seeing any of me outside during the day this summer. I'm going to stay in the house all day while that sun's out. I don't need to get any darker than I already am." Indeed, as kids grew into their teenage years, they became increasingly wary of the Kid's Club's traditional summer outings to the beach, for fear of the consequences.

Emotionally scarring, if somewhat less regular, encounters with verbal expressions of white hatred are not the only ways that racism has continued to deliver humiliating messages into poor urban African-American neighborhoods. Just as the Clarks (and other psychologists and social scientists of the 1950s and 1960s) would have suspected, kids' lives and racial identities are also deeply informed by the realities of continuing urban residential and educational segregation by race. And even if white hatred did diminish any during the 1970s and 1980s, residential areas of most large American cities have remained very much divided along racial lines. Philadelphia's "index of residential segregation" actually inched up every census date after 1960, continuing to increase even during the 1980s, a decade during which most other major cities became marginally less segregated.[26] Despite limited progress in the integration of some specially targeted schools, many neighborhood elementary and middle schools, plus comprehensive high schools—those that most poor black kids attend—have remained very segregated. Though Chauntey's neighborhood is racially diverse, all the African-American children who live there attended nearly all nonwhite schools (one has a substantial population of Southeast Asian immigrants), and all have since moved to virtually all-black neighborhoods.

Clearly, racial segregation intrinsically reinforces fundamental notions of racial *difference* in kids' worldviews. Whether or not, as Clark argued in connection with *Brown v. Board* in 1954, segregation inherently teaches a message of racial *inferiority* in the minds and souls of kids I have no clear way of knowing from their stories;[27] what I can tell is that the *inequalities* kids perceive between separate black and white neighborhoods and schools do form a fundamental part of their negative assessment of their own racial identity.

Kids universally perceive their neighborhoods and schools to be "trashy," "beat-up," and "dirty"; by contrast, those of whites are emphatically "decent." This stark difference is probably the most important evidence they have to bolster a general belief that, as one of the Barkley girls put it, "all black people poor and all white people got money." In the midst of a discussion on race with Fahim and the other boys one time, I asked them, "Do you ever think you're not as good as white kids?" All said no right away, but after a moment's reflection, Fahim responded, "Yeah, sometimes. Like that white kid who lives on —— Street. He's got everything—Nintendo, a decent bike, nice clothes. . . " "Yeah," the other guys chimed in. On another occasion, I got complete disbelief from Fahim and another friend of his when I told them that there are more white poor people than black poor people in the United States, and that there are more white people on welfare than black people.

It has also been clear to me from talking to kids over the years that they have no other way of explaining the differences they see between white and black schools and sections of the city other than to hold black people as a group responsible. Fahim's mother, who spent her teenage years living on my block, once told me that the neighborhood I live in used to be "real nice. But as soon as black people move on a block, they mess it up." Omar was particularly conscious of differences in the physical shape of black and white neighborhoods: he would make mental tallies of the number of abandoned houses on blocks as we drove through them, predicting whether or not we were in a white or black neighborhood on that basis. "You can tell," he would assure me, whenever his calculations proved correct.

Fahim's lack of knowledge about white poor people did not come from lack of contact. The Wilkins family live four blocks from one of the poorest white areas in town, and all of the kids have passed through the neighborhood many times. Fahim's friend (and Chauntey) went to school there. Omar once counted how few abandoned houses there were in that same neighborhood. As Wilson predicted, children do perceive a difference between a poor neighborhood of "concentrated" poverty, like those the kids I know live in, and a poor neighborhood, like the nearby white one, that is not as "concentrated." However, those perceptions may not be determined so much by relative numbers of mainstream role models as by kids' conclusion that separate and unequal worlds validate notions of racial inferiority. And though such lessons may have slightly heightened the likelihood that kids would behave aggressively, they did so not by directly shaping a moral code of behavior but by adding yet another painful indication of immutable personal inadequacy. Also, feelings about segregated and unequal neighborhoods illustrate just how humiliation concerning poverty may help undermine efforts to alleviate the impact of racial stigmas and help increase the persuasiveness of such stigmas in the eyes of inner-city youngsters.

Given the choice, none of the kids I know would want to live in their neighborhoods for life. All have expressed dreams of eventually leaving (Theresa Wilkins once told me that "When I grow up I want to live in the suburbs") or of living in Chauntey's ideal neighborhood where people of all colors live together without violence. Their attitudes closely mirror those of the group of African-Americans polled in 1987 by the *New York Times*, 86 percent of whom responded they "would like an equal mixture of black and white neighbors."[28] Kids' wishes, however, run up against another inequality that has continued to be an essential part of racially segregated America: blacks, especially poor blacks, have less choice about where they live than do whites. The sociologists Reynolds Farley and Walter R. Allen have found that the inequality of choice not only affects poor African-American city dwellers but also constrains the options of more affluent blacks who have moved to the suburbs. In a survey conducted in Chicago in 1983, 86 percent of all black respondents agreed with the statement that "there are many areas where people try to keep blacks out" (and 94 percent of all black respondents with an annual income over forty thousand dollars agreed that "the housing market was not completely opened to blacks.")[29]

Though kids in Chauntey's neighborhood have yet to go house shopping in white neighborhoods, they have already encountered the territorial kinds of race relations that exist within America's urban sociopolitical realm. Kids experience most of their encounters with white racial hatred in connection with the unwritten racial boundaries of segregated neighborhoods. Omar and Fahim were once chased out of the white neighborhood next to theirs by a gang of kids shouting racial epithets, and once when Omar accompanied me to a shopping center in the middle of the same neighborhood, a young boy asked him, "What are you doing here, nigger?" right in front of my startled eyes.

Racial hatred, invidious distinctions concerning skin color, and separation and inequality have not been the only forms of racism and its historical legacies that today's inner-city kids have encountered. The insinuation that violence is an inherent trait of black people, especially black men, has been the one kind of racism that has grown appreciably in recent years. It has also obviously had increasing consequences for inner-city community life and for the ways poor African-American children, and particularly boys, form their sense of self.

The image of the black man as a marauding brute has a long history in the United States. Often, this stereotype has been overshadowed in the white imagination by other racial images: caricatures of slaves as docile children, minstrel show portrayals of blacks as buffoons, and in recent years social scientists' characterizations of the "castrated," or powerless, black man. However, outbreaks of virulent "negrophobia" have erupted on at least two prolonged occasions before our current episode, both during periods when politicians found that inciting fear of black men was particularly useful as a means to shore up support among white voters and to counter efforts at political reform. As the historian George Frederickson has shown, many antebellum southern apologists for slavery held that the institution was necessary to keep slaves' allegedly ruthless nature in check.[30] As the abolitionist assault gained ground during the second third of the nineteenth century and then when the antislavery Republican party gained strength in the 1850s, opposing politicians regularly appealed to voters by citing the specter of slave uprisings (most notably, the fresh memories of Nat Turner's rebellion), intimations of racial "miscegenation," and prophesies of civilization's imminent collapse. In so doing, they helped make the image of the armed black slave man—who was free to seek retributions for the abuse of black women by white slaveholding men—a nightmare for many in both the South and the North. In Indiana during the late

1850s, Democrats organized campaign rallies that featured young women carrying banners that read "Fathers, save us from nigger husbands."[31]

Then, beginning during Reconstruction and more shrilly from the late 1880s until the 1920s, virulent race-baiters created another image of "black peril" by fusing antebellum images with prevailing Darwinian ideas about "racial degeneracy," harrowing false portraits of black soldiers and of "Negro rule" under Reconstruction, and evangelical anxieties about sexuality. Eminent southern doctors reasoned that "the African's birthright" consisted of "sexual madness and excess" due to the excessively "large size of the negro's penis." Politicians like "Pitchfork" Ben Tillman, one of South Carolina's senators in the late 1800s, took up this "knowledge" to whip up fear of the black man as "a fiend, a wild beast," intent on raping the flower of white womanhood. Tillman and others led a cynical campaign to undermine the solidarity of the biracial Populist movement, to sanction widespread lynchings, to institute laws that disfranchised blacks, to seek support for Jim Crow segregation—and, no doubt, to assuage racists' guilt for white mobs' terrorizing of innocent black people.[32]

Some of these stereotypes reappeared in northern cities in the early 1900s as African-Americans began traveling north in large numbers, and as whites put up resistance to what they called the black "invasion" of their neighborhoods and public facilities. On the eve of the massive race riot in East St. Louis in 1917, the historian Elliott Rudwick noted that local newspapers inflated white fears about immigrating blacks by creating a stereotype in which "'gun-toting' was a peculiarly Negro trait." In the days preceding the Detroit race riot of 1943, Mayor Edward Jeffries received letters from white residents containing demands like "please don't force us to live among these savages" and "give us white girls a break." The historian Bruce Tyler noted that white fears' and resentments about zoot-suited black men who showed an interest in white women were whipped into a frenzy by wartime New Yorkers. According to Arnold Hirsch, during the early 1950s the University of Chicago used "near panic" about rising crime rates to justify taking a prominent role in controlling black immigration into its surrounding Hyde Park neighborhood. However, excepting possibly middle-class Hyde Park residents for whom Hirsch thinks crime was "a most emotional and sensitive issue . . . during racial succession," the link between blacks and violence seemed to take a back seat, during the early and middle part of the twentieth century, to other concerns like perceived threats to jobs, housing values, and the integrity of working-class communities' ethnic homogeneity.[33]

By contrast, during the late 1960s and early 1970s, issues of crime and violence as related to race began to grow in importance. The most recent bout of national negrophobia reflects at least in part the rising statistical probabilities of black crime such as those described in chapter 1. Though only 6 percent of all murders and 9 percent of rapes in 1990 were committed by black assailants against white victims, it has become thoroughly understandable to fear random violence from any quarter in American cities nowadays—especially given that there are few precautions one can take to avoid it—and women have every reason in the world to fear sexual assault or rape from any man, black or white. Furthermore, in 1990, over a third of robberies, many involving street muggings, were committed by black male assailants against white victims.[34] No matter what the racial probabilities are, however, they cannot be taken as evidence that black people deserve the recent upsurge in racist attitudes about urban crime. Whites, after all, have shaped the racist interpretation of those statistics. First, whites have assessed the actions of a minority of blacks and concluded that violence is an inherent racial characteristic. Second, whites have denied black people's actions the complex social, political, economic, and cultural understanding that they would naturally accord to white-on-white violence. Also, it is predominantly white people who have endowed the resulting racist insinuations with a false legitimacy by disseminating them through their language of racial hatred, the mass media, law enforcement agencies, and the most powerful institutions of national leadership.

During the late 1960s the demagogic use of stereotypes about violent black males, mixed with "crypto-racist" talk of welfare, entered into the political culture in a sustained way that had not been seen since the heyday of the Jim Crow South. This time, the language drifted up from the demagoguery of local radical racist politicians to become once again a playing card in presidential politics. Our current round of race baiting and negrophobia stems from the social upheaval of the late 1960s, particularly the urban riots, and conservative politicians' desire to capture popular resentment against radical social protest and the reforms of the Great Society. In 1968 in his law-and-order campaign, Richard Nixon initiated the use of thinly veiled racial code words that hinted at violence. Ronald Reagan imitated the practice in 1980, and George Bush took it to an especially cynical level in 1988 with his Willie Horton advertisements. Since then, words like *underclass* have been successfully integrated into other even more obviously race-baiting campaigns like those of North Carolina's Senator Jesse Helms and Louisiana's politician and former Ku Klux Klan leader David Duke.[35]

Meanwhile, the equation of black men and urban crime has become an ever more important fixture in the daily workings of American race relations. In Jonathan Rieder's ethnographic study of ethnic working-class racial attitudes, fear of crime not only pervaded white Brooklynites' defense of their neighborhood boundaries against black residents but also informed their political outlook on issues such as civil rights, welfare, and affirmative action.[36] Issues of race and danger saturate Studs Terkel's recent collection of oral histories called *Race: How Blacks and Whites Think and Feel about the American Obsession*—starting with the opening paragraph, which describes a white middle-class woman who misinterprets some helpful gesturing by a group of black men as a mortal threat.[37] In 1989, Bostonians found that they were only too ready to swallow the cynical attempt by Charles Stuart, a privileged white man who murdered his wife, to foist the responsibility for his crime onto a black man.[38] The National Opinion Research Center released a survey on "Ethnic Images" in 1990, which revealed that over 56 percent of whites thought blacks to be "violence-prone."[39]

Such attitudes undoubtedly have reinforced long-standing racism among urban police officers, which historians have documented as far back as the early years of the urban police force in the nineteenth century.[40] In recent years, studies have confirmed white police officers' widespread use of racist language while riding in patrol cars and making arrests, plus their greater likelihood of using fatal force in their interactions with blacks.[41] As the political scientist Andrew Hacker has pointed out, the long litany of names of black people erroneously killed by police, like New Yorkers Eleanor Bumpurs, Yvonne Smallwood, and Philip Panell, stands as a memorial of "victims of official white force."[42] The 1990 videotape of the beating of Rodney King in Los Angeles serves as another important reminder of the connection between racism and state repression in America.

Whether incidents like these have grown more likely today is difficult to document. In the late 1960s, urban rioting and racially coded law-and-order sentiments did cause a massive growth in big-city police expenditures, the size of which, the sociologist Pamela Irving Jackson has shown, was directly related to the proportion of a city's population who were black and Hispanic.[43] In Philadelphia, this buildup was supervised by Frank Rizzo. As a police captain, Rizzo had argued for the use of live ammunition in suppressing the 1964 riot in north Philadelphia, and as the police commissioner in the late 1960s, he had conducted armed raids of the headquarters of black militants and massive, indiscriminate sweeps of black men in connection with gang violence. Finally, as mayor, Rizzo reacted defiantly when the police department he had built faced a federal police brutality suit in 1979.[44] With his open bigotry, his refusal to discipline officers who made fatal "mistakes" in the line of duty, and his condoning of the harassment and violent treatment of many black people by the Philadelphia Police Department, Rizzo did as much as any other police chief or local politician in the country to promote white America's connection between fear of crime and racial hatred.

As they grow up, kids in Chauntey's neighborhood inherit the historical legacy of America's racialization of violence. Most older children I have spoken with know full well what George Bush was doing during the 1988 presidential campaign with the ads about Willie Horton, and they know that fear of violence underlies the hatred they encounter from whites. Interactions with the police are very important socializing experiences. All the teenage boys I know have been harassed at one time or another by police officers. Just after he turned fifteen, Omar was arrested for the first time because of "mistaken identification," as have been several of his friends. Since then he has been picked up several more times on suspicion and usually quickly released. Long before their own personal experience, though, both boys and girls have learned of many other stories of "police hassling the niggers for nothing," and they have heard of police officers using racist language. Kids also know quite well what the Rodney King beating was all about. As a result, suspicions about the intentions of police abound, and the casual passing of a police car very frequently elicits either disparaging or anxious remarks from young observers.[45]

Kids' most common experiences with connections between race and violence, however, occur in more mundane experiences. At an early age kids become very aware of the roving and suspicious glances of corner shopkeepers, and they have encountered a hundred times the gruff attitudes of security guards at supermarkets and downtown clothing stores. On dozens of occasions when I took children shopping, these guards, whether white or black, would bar kids from the entrance until I offered assurances that they were with me.

On one occasion a Kid's Club volunteer finally had to confront two white store managers who had kept their suspicious glances fastened on the two kids she was with, up and down the aisles, for the entire time they shopped.

Suspicion and surveillance of this sort are not limited to stores. Elijah Anderson has best described what he called the "street etiquette" that governed casual, especially nighttime, social encounters between middle-class whites and black men in an "Eastern City" neighborhood where the two groups lived in close proximity. In this code of interaction all young black males were viewed as potential sources of danger, though among more streetwise people the tips also included clothing and other subtler behavioral or class-related cues as well as race, gender, and age. This race-based suspicion was not usually articulated by a language of overt racial hatred: "kids" was a typical way for middle-class white and black people to talk about crime suspects, whom they all assumed were black and male. In fact, words were not usually needed at all, since in sidewalk encounters with these "kids," "eyework," pedestrian "passing behavior," and the ways people controlled their dogs all communicated their distrust clearly enough.[46]

The recent movie *Juice* parodied this race-laden behavioral protocol in a scene where a white man is shown making a nervous and exaggerated detour around a group of black men who are walking on the same sidewalk. Needless to say, the predominantly youthful black audience I was with when I watched the movie did not need any explanation for the joke! Similar incidents occur all the time in the nighttime streets of Chauntey's neighborhood. No doubt many of them reflect a calculation that includes race as an important part. Certainly, the kids I know often suspect as much, and their annoyance is understandable. Indeed, in some ways the insidiousness of American racism cannot be better understood than in connection with such common social encounters. The history of the instinctive racialization of violence, and its current mass dissemination, have loaded a racist message onto any white city dweller's efforts to take even the most sensible and mundane precautions against urban danger. Even in the absence of any conscious prejudicial suppositions (and this is itself difficult to imagine), white people who take any personal precautions in encounters with a black person cannot avoid the risk of retransmitting and even relegitimating mainstream racial stereotypes.

Racist theories of violence similarly affect other confusing experiences in poor black children's lives. Just like the rest of Americans, children in Chauntey's neighborhood have all watched the six o'clock news countless times and have engraved into their consciousness the media's icon of anonymous black men spread-eagled against a wall under guard of police officers. In fact, this image is particularly real for them, because they see incidents like this in daily life all the time, often involving people they know from their neighborhoods. Other kids, like Omar, who are interested in numbers and in counting things can find plenty in the way of information on the disproportionate levels of black crime from newspapers (or from friends of theirs whose job involves tabulating murder rates by race!). In so doing, they may also encounter the historic freight of terms like *underclass*. In the absence of any opposing interpretation of any of this "evidence," the weight of historical and current caricatures puts tremendous pressures on kids to make the same conclusions that most white people in this country have made about race and violence. But this interpretation has even deeper and more personal resonances as well: in addition to other signs of violence in the black community kids also know their own capacity for aggression, and they struggle daily to understand it. Though this capacity stems from all their accumulated feelings of pain and a complicated set of other reasons, the prevailing wisdom—coupled with humiliation about poverty and race in other contexts—makes blaming race and self all the more simple and persuasive as an explanation.

Americans' propensity for linking race and violence has directly contributed a further dose of racial humiliation to inner-city kids' emotional memories. The legal theorist Patricia Williams, discussing her own encounter with a racist store owner, called it a form of "spirit murder."[47] Indeed, of all the attributes kids linked to their racial selves, they talked most often about violence, aggression, or criminality. "It seems that black people are more violent than whites," Fahim explained to me one time after a long, frank, and (I had hoped) productive discussion of his feelings after having started a fight with someone at school. Sitting out on my front porch on another occasion, Omar noticed an unknown black man leaning against a car belonging to a white neighbor we all knew. "Shit, I know what [the white neighbor] gonna do. He'll be like, 'Excuse me, could you get off the car. I need to go shopping.' If it was a black person's car, he'd be like, 'Yo, motherfucker, get your dirty ass off my car before I shoot your ass.'" In the words of kids in the neighborhood, black people are often called "crazy," "fucked up," or "evil." On various other occasions they have told me that black people beat their kids more than white people do, that they steal all the time, and that they make meaner schoolteachers. Once when it was long past time to go, and I could not find any other way of ushering an obstinate ten-year-old Kimberly out of my house, I had to lift her bodily out of an armchair and out onto the porch. She launched into one of her inimitable nonsense-noise shrieks, which finally took verbal form outside with her repeating, "Nasty, nasty black kid, nasty, nasty black kid!"

All of the children I know are very familiar with whites' suspicion and fear toward blacks. On one occasion Georgie and I drove out to the suburbs to do a quick errand. When we had parked and gotten out, I locked the door behind me. Georgie got upset and implored, "No, man, no! Don't lock the doors! You don't need to lock the doors!" When I asked him why not, he told me, "This a *white* neighborhood." On another occasion in the suburbs, he and his twin brother had marveled at the fact that the supermarket we were visiting allowed you to take the carts out to the car. "Man, somebody going to steal they shopping carts," Georgie warned. "No they won't, dummy," responded Andre, "this a white neighborhood." "This white man was driving a white Continental up at ——— Street," Omar reported to me on yet another occasion. "Some black dude rear-ended him with a beat-up Dodge Colt. I bet that white dude was scared to be in that neighborhood [because] all he can see around there is blacks." On rarer occasions, recognition of white suspicions and fear was articulated in a language that seemed to mock African-American middle-class people's fears about being associated with poorer blacks (which Anderson discusses perceptively in *Streetwise*).[48] Chauntey seemed to have a storehouse of insights like these, no doubt culled from many adverse encounters with race-conscious block captains. One time, as we were leaving an outing to a farm some fifty miles out of the city, I finished laying down some basic ground rules for the trip, and as if he were translating what I had just said, he announced in his playful, domineering way to all assembled, and to general laughter, "Where we going is all white people. So y'all gonna have to stop acting like a bunch of black ghetto Negroes, y'all hear?" Along similar lines, Omar once told me that his English teacher, who is an African-American, had given them a talk about fighting in school: "What you all don't know," the teacher had reportedly said, "is when y'all be fighting in the hallways, the white teachers in the lounge are saying, 'Unh-huh, yep, what'd I tell you? They all like animals.'"

Though the stereotype of black violence is principally focused on black men and boys, girls and a number of the mothers I knew were also deeply affected by the suspicion they encountered. Some girls took this as a reason to focus extraordinary amounts of attention on the behavior of others, especially people younger than themselves. The first time the Barkley girls visited my house, at the invitation of some of their peers from the Greene family, the Greene girls seemed very anxious about what I would think of their friends, and they followed the Barkleys' every move. Though I did not think my newest acquaintances were crossing any borders when Rasheeda Barkley sat down at my desk and took a pencil from the top drawer to begin drawing, Keisha Greene blurted out, "Rasheeda, why you gotta act like a shoplifter?" As I have mentioned, often when parents appear to want to impress me they talk about how well they have punished their kids, or how they have set new house rules to prevent their kids from associating with bad kids. I often wonder how much of a racial subtext is involved. Among peers, the model of social interaction proffered by official suspicion gives added credence to the need for protective "tough faces," to an added concern for the way people look at you, and to an added mandate to accept the view that "you can't trust nobody." For one good friend of Fahim and Omar's, who has been very active in the Kids' Club as a peer role model, the problem of suspicion is one to be dealt with internally. Once when Omar expressed his reluctance to go on a downtown shopping spree because of storekeepers who "always be looking at you like you stole something," this friend delivered one of his most personally felt lectures: "That's cause you go in there with a guilty conscience. When you black, you gotta go in there like I do—like you ain't got a guilty conscience—and they won't even mess with you."

At the same time, boys and girls also store up plenty of indignation and resentment over the suspicion they so regularly encounter. For most kids this feeling manifests itself in explosions of anger whenever they are confronted with wrongdoing. Otherwise very kind and mild-mannered Theresa is capable of sudden and startling fits of temper that are often related to occasions when her younger sister blames her for even the slightest offense. Basketball games routinely collapse into shouting matches when particularly sensitive players are accused of cheating. Chauntey's knack for returning blame onto anyone who dares accuse him no doubt also reflects his boundless memories of resentment over suspicion. Often, when police cars drive through the street, they elicit kids' expressions of fear, or a sucking of the teeth, or a comment like, "Man, they think they all that. They don't scare me."

And, of course, kids nurture no extra love for whites or Asian-

Americans, who suspiciously watch the kids in stores and on the nighttime streets. Omar has all sorts of ideas about nasty things he wants to do to security guards, like "tearing them apart" or setting fire to their stores (he suggested this idea two years before the riots in South Central Los Angeles). Indeed, the "frustration" that was widely blamed for the flaming of South Central in 1992 was definitely not the only emotion at work: resentment over suspicion and "fuck the police" attitudes, like those expressed by such rap groups as NWA (Niggers with Attitudes) and Ice Cube, thrive enough in neighborhoods like Chauntey's to produce similar occurrences in Philadelphia at any time. (Little-known riots over police treatment of black people occurred in Philadelphia in 1980, where violence stretched over three days but did little property damage,[49] and in an old neighborhood of Chauntey's in 1985).

The unequal burden of proof that African-American kids have to shoulder in their dealings with the white world is both a source of humiliation and a direct cause of their deep resentment. But there is another way that kids, and particularly teenage boys, react to the linking of race with violence—or what the rap group Public Enemy has called whites' "fear of a black planet." This is teenage inner-city boys' practice of mixing ridicule of white fear with a glorification of the stereotype of the violent black male to create a self-image that actually helps young black men, to compensate for experiences of economic failure and racial insult.

This practice has roots that are at least a century old, dating to the appearance of Stackolee stories in black folklore during the late nineteenth century, possibly in response to America's most vicious nationwide bout of negrophobia. In the past forty years, as fear of black men has again begun to run rampant, identification with the image of the "bad nigger" (as Stackolee was often called in the early twentieth century) has taken on new forms. In his study of St. Louis' Pruitt-Igoe housing project during the late 1960s, the sociologist Lee Rainwater noted that in addition to internalizing "negative" racial identities, men often used some of the language of racial hatred in ways that lauded their supposed sexual and aggressive prowess. The psychologist Erik Erikson also alluded to what he called black men's "defiant glorification of their own caricature" in a 1968 "Memorandum on Negro Identity." Cultural critics noticed similar tendencies in the so-called blaxploitation movies of the early 1970s, and in 1977, Michelle Wallace criticized the black power movement for attempting to transform the violence and sexual conquest of a white stereotype into a source of defiant racial self-affirmation, if not a masculin-ist vision of black liberation.[50]

In Chauntey's neighborhood, some girls and young women occa-sionally connect their racial identity to a self-justifying glorification of aggression: they often link their "bad attitude" or "nasty girl" iden-tity to being black, and some wear defiant "Black with Attitude" or "It's a Black Thing, You Wouldn't Understand" sweatshirts. The edu-cational ethnographers Signithia Fordham and John Ogbu have shown how some inner-city black students, both girls and boys, have used the compensatory equation of blackness and defiance to put down peers who follow rules and who do well in school by character-izing them as "acting white." Indeed, the degree to which kids have made defiance, aggression, and pride in underachieving a stamp of racial authenticity is demonstrated by the tendency of those who succeed academically to take on what Fordham calls "raceless" iden-tities in self-protection.[51]

It is in the world of teenage boys, however, on the basketball courts and in males-only banter on streetcorners that satisfaction with blackness is most completely predicated on a glorification of caricature. One of the most important pieces of boys' cool b-boy ethic (one, incidentally, that was particularly confounding to the Kids' Club's initial attempts to ban racial slurs) was their practice of inverting the meaning of the insult that white people in the neigh-borhood perceived to be the most viciously racist of all: the word *nig-ger*—or as Fahim instructed me, "nigga, N-I-G-G-A, not 'niggUHR' like y'all white nerds call it"—could, by mixing violent racial carica-tures with an alchemical formula primarily reserved to boys among their peers, be transformed into a term of heroism. The link between the "nigga" hero's aggressiveness and racial caricature was explicit in boys' minds: all the boys I know well have bragged openly about how black men make better lovers, have bigger penises, and fight better than white men—and though they are often joking about these matters, they also take great pride in the attributes they are claiming for themselves. "Nigga" often substitutes for other ethi-cally inverted terms like "motherfucker," "pimp," or "b-boy" as a label for someone who lives up to high standards of male aggressive-ness, who does not let himself get emotionally attached to women, who thinks of civility as "licking butt," and who conceals all of his pain or only expresses it violently. At the same time, identifying with the "nigga" as hero allows kids to throw shopkeepers', security guards', and police officers' racial suspicions back "in their face."

The identity also gives kids an ethical mandate to joke about, separate themselves from, defy, or most importantly, return the force of racial stigma onto white men—who, in the "nigga's" eyes, are the ultimate "nerds," combining asexuality (or effeminacy or homosexuality), bad dressing, and fear of fighting and who, as in the title of a recent popular film about basketball, "can't jump."[52] Unlike Coles' experience with black children who drew themselves into the back corners of their pictures, most of the self-portraits boys have drawn for me show the artists in the middle of the paper with black features and a flat-top cut, in defiant drug-dealer poses, sometimes grabbing their crotch, with wrap-around shades, often outsized sneakers, a fat gold chain around their neck—and often with a gun in hand.

The importance of the connection between inverted racial stigma and the ethic of b-boy cool to inner-city children nationwide can also be measured by the subject's treatment in rap. Since first appearing in its current form in the late 1970s, rap has often strived to offer its youthful audiences images of racial pride and a critique of racism. The militantly nationalistic group Public Enemy was the first to make this message sell to a wide audience (which, incidentally, also included vast numbers of white youth). Since 1987, when millions of fans bought Public Enemy's first album, a new generation of "gangsta" rappers, the most important of whom come from Los Angeles, has also achieved stardom. As the historian Robin D. G. Kelly has pointed out, groups like NWA and artists like Ice Cube and Ice-T have continued to decry racism, in the tradition of Public Enemy and artists of the hip-hop nation in general[53]—but they sometimes even more passionately also turned the language of racial hatred on its head, transforming the label "nigga" and the violence and sexual conquest of their songs into a badge of authentic blackness. The "Real Niggaz" NWA portrays in the opening lines of their album *Efil4Zaggin* (read backwards to crack the code) are "ruthless motherfucking gangsters" who extol homicidal defiance of authority, especially the police, and violent sexual conquest (one song is called "Findum, Fuckum and Flee," and another "To Kill a Hooker—One Less Bitch"). *Efil4Zaggin* was the best-selling rap album in the spring and early summer of 1991. Like Public Enemy's recordings, it was well received by white young people, prompting some critics to proclaim that rap had lost authenticity by pandering to the violent racial caricature that mainstream America was looking for. There may be some truth in this assessment of white kids' tastes, but the charge of inauthenticity is surely wrong. In Chauntey's neighborhood, NWA's rise to cult status, followed quickly by that of other "cop-killing" Los Angeles rappers, only reflects some of the most common realities of emotional hurt and psychic survival: in the face of powerful resentment of suspicion, kids doggedly search for a salvageable racial identity by transforming stereotypes.[54]

The career of the "nigga" hero suggests just how complicated an impact American racism has had on inner-city children. On the one hand, racism has operated as a force of exclusion and alienation—through white hatred, segregation, discrimination, and rampant suspicion—and has helped to fill kids' emotional memories with humiliation and resentment. On the other hand, in a perverse way, the history of the effects of American racism on inner-city kids has also been one of inclusion—resulting, ironically, in a fragile form of personal satisfaction. Racial caricatures, after all, have been a central part of American national culture, and the identities that kids, especially boys, forge for themselves using those caricatures reflects their immersion in the mainstream as much as their exclusion from it.

However, if boys' inversion of the language of white racial hatred represents a creative way of resisting the forces of painful emotion in their lives and gives them some sense of emotional equilibrium, it also reflects the extent to which racism has tragically limited their lives. Moreover, it illustrates just how high a price kids can pay for a compensatory identity based on American mainstream images. By choosing to use the word *nigga*—with its deliberately unshed and definitive evocation of racial exclusion and stereotype—in a wry and ironic attempt to save face, kids end up accepting the word's evocation of self-contempt. The identity also helps impose a rigid uniformity on the ideal image of black masculinity, which enforces inner-city boys' all-too-prevalent tendency to repress or aggressively express their overwhelming memories of pain. Nor, unfortunately, does it do much to allay suspicious white Americans' proclivities toward linking race and violence. Indeed, if the history of inner-city social life is partly based on some sort of "cyclical" dynamic, the most important one is not a "self-perpetuating" cycle of poverty passed from generation to generation. Instead, the crucial dynamic involves white racism feeding off the self-portraits of those young black men it has trapped in the seduction of its caricatures.

Poor urban African-American kids' changing experience with racism needs to be included in our understandings of the emotional and ethical world that has surrounded occurrences of violence and family change in post–World War II urban African-American communities. Racism, in all of its many forms, has also set the historical and current experiences of poor urban blacks dramatically apart from those of poor white city dwellers. Indeed, the historical career of racism must be included as a principal reason for the *difference* between the recent social historical experiences of poor white and poor black communities. In chapter 5 I consider how, in connection with other historical events and in other historical manifestations, racism may also have contributed to the recent *increase* in family change and community violence in the late-twentieth-century inner city. Indeed racial caricature is not the only means by which the American mainstream has contributed to the legitimacy of aggressive values. The nigga hero and his close cousin, the b-boy, does not owe his complex character solely to a celebrated stereotype; he has also appropriated mainstream values of conspicuous consumption to fortify his claim on compensation for both economic and racial humiliation. Also, in concert with images from American mass-media entertainment, he has become more heavily armed and more willing to find pride in homicide.

5

Poor Black Children and American Abundance

One of the extraordinary historical characteristics of urban African-Americans' collective experience of poverty and racism in the middle and late twentieth century has been its coincidence with an age of unprecedented material abundance in America. The country's mass-communicated culture of material consumption began flowing into the lives of poor urban families during the early years of this century and then thoroughly inundated American inner cities by the 1960s and 1970s. In the process, the values of conspicuous consumption, as well as the material trappings of those values, became a growing part of poor African-American children's upbringing in inner-city neighborhoods.

Inner-city kids' *inclusion* in mainstream America's mass market has been important in determining those kids' responses to the economic and racial *exclusion* they face in other parts of their lives. And, indeed, kids' experience of exclusion and of the associated painful memories has made their participation in mass culture particularly urgent and enthusiastic, for the culture of consumption has given them a seductive means to compensate for their feelings of failure. A complete explanation of the emotional, cultural, and behavioral world of post–World War II poor urban black communities needs to examine the ways America's mass culture has shaped kids' changing economic, racial, and gender identities. This part of America's upbringing of inner-city kids may also help explain some of the historical changes in family structure and community life that have occurred in the past half century.

* * *

The inclusion of inner-city youth culture in the orbit of American materialism and consumption occurred as the result of a series of successive historical changes that began in the early twentieth century and that have overlapped since then. These changes involved the nature of poor children's economic relationship to the adults in their families, the social scope of discretionary income, the technologies of mass communication, and the degree to which the messages of the mass media were tailored to the particular needs of poor urban African-American children.

In the nineteenth and early twentieth centuries, working-class families in the urban United States often depended on the wages of their children to keep everyone fed, clothed, and sheltered. Kids often started working outside the home when they were as young as nine and ten. Throughout the first four decades of the twentieth century, however, children faced increasing pressures to abandon the workplace. During the 1910s and 1920s campaigns against the cruelty of child labor reached their peak, and new waves of immigrants from southern and eastern Europe began replacing children in industrial jobs. At the same time, industry became increasingly automated, and many child workers were replaced with machines. More years of schooling were required for success in the job market, and politicians began to pass compulsory education laws that transformed high schools from bastions of the privileged few to institutions of mass education. The scarcity of jobs brought on by the Great Depression virtually ended child-labor practices in industry. By the late 1940s and 1950s, the period described by the case reports of the Big Brothers Association (BBA) of Philadelphia and the Protestant Episcopal City Mission's Family Services division, poor African-American children faced much greater economic and cultural pressures than had their parents and grandparents to remain dependent on the resources of adults in their families until relatively late in their teen years. School administrators and truancy officers—backed up by the police, welfare departments, municipal justice systems, and later, corporate-sponsored inner-city billboards (like Nike's "Don't Be Stoopid, Stay in School") that sprouted up as industry grew more worried about the attrition of skilled laborers—enforced the notion that for poor as well as rich, childhood is mainly a preparatory time for future independent and productive roles, a time to depend on parents and consume, not produce, family income.[1]

As the institutions of child rearing and the ideologies of childhood changed, the families of the industrial working class, like those in the middle class a century earlier, became increasingly able to afford the economic costs of children's dependence on adults in the household. In the nineteenth and early twentieth centuries, working-class families barely earned enough with both parents and older children working to afford the most rudimentary of leisure pursuits.[2] With the rapid rise in incomes that accompanied World War II and the postwar boom, however, the capacity for discretionary spending spread considerably among large segments of America's population of industrial, service, and government workers. Rising incomes also triggered a massive expansion of available installment credit, which had first been marketed on a wide scale during the 1920s to make automobiles available to people of modest means, but which had expanded since, making other expensive durable goods more affordable.[3]

As the social impact of growing discretionary income and the emphasis on dependent childhood increased dramatically during the middle third of the century, so did mass marketers' ability to mold the desires of the growing crop of consumers. Though advertisers and marketers had managed earlier to get wide audiences for images and messages that glorified acquisitiveness, the mass dissemination of an ethic of conspicuous consumption in the United States really dates from the 1920s. It was then, as historians such as Stewart and Elizabeth Ewen have shown, that the star system in the movies was born, that radio first came into wide use, and that fashion advertisers captured the well-to-do white youth market with sophisticated new advertising techniques.[4] However, according to the historian Lizabeth Cohen, this growing mass-communication system did not completely consolidate mainstream marketers' control over the nature of consumer values among audiences outside the middle-class for more than a decade. Ethnic radio stations and neighborhood stores still held some sway over the consumer habits of working-class people until the 1930s and 1940s.[5]

The process was completed in the late 1940s and early 1950s, when mass marketers discovered their most powerful, most centralized, and potentially most homogenizing oracle—the television. By 1960, only twelve years after televisions were first released in affordable form, 88 percent of American homes had one, and by 1970, 95 percent. Television's capacity to reach into the privacy of all households, regardless of class and race boundaries, and the medium's consolidation of image, sound, movement, and color have firmly and inalterably established an intimate familiarity with mass-market America among the poor. Indeed, it appears that poor households and poor teenagers have been significantly more attached to TV than have more affluent kids.[6] If anything, the medium's influence increased during the 1980s, when color TVs became as widespread as black-and-white ones had been in 1970, when urban cable-television networks expanded, and when videocassette recorders proliferated.

Changes in the nature of childhood, the economic well-being of American families, and the technology of mass communication helped increase the inclusion of inner-city residents in a culture of abundance and consumption in the early post–World War II era— just as the urban industrial job market was about to begin its historic disappearing act. If a barrier remained that at all slowed mass culture's conquest of inner-city kids' desires and consumer aspirations, it was the content of the media messages, which remained almost exclusively geared to specific interests of affluent whites. However, even as the economic structure of inner-cities began to worsen, marketers began to learn much more about poor black consumers and the need for compensatory identity. Indeed, marketing strategists' attitudes toward African-American consumers changed dramatically in the late 1960s and even more so in the 1970s and 1980s.

During the early twentieth century, advertisers generally perceived African-American consumers as either too poor or too indiscriminate to be worth any special marketing attention. Newspaper owners and, later, proprietors of radio stations in African-American communities, who stood to gain much by local or national marketing campaigns aimed at their readership and audiences, could count on only a slim array of sponsors, most of whom pushed products like skin whiteners, hair straighteners, and "lip shapers" designed to mold African-Americans into the dominant—namely, Caucasian— standards of appearance and beauty.[7]

In 1931 the National Negro Business League (NNBL), representing African-American press members and merchants, and hoping to convince more advertisers to patronize their papers and radio stations, conducted the first published national survey of black consumer preferences.[8] The conclusions the NNBL reached, which have been upheld over and again in subsequent marketing reports and scholarly surveys, disproved some of the principal tenets of marketers' attitudes toward African-Americans. There was indeed a distinct "Negro market," the 1931 report concluded, but it was neither poor nor undiscriminating. Not only did blacks control over a billion and a half dollars of spending money, but their buying behavior demonstrated more interest in name brands, prestige items, and fashion consciousness than did that of whites. The report counseled that, with a few advertisements using black models and greater use of media controlled by African-Americans, mainstream advertisers could readily capture the sensibilities of blacks.[9]

The NNBL's survey was the first of many similar reports that would be published, initially under the auspices of the black press—most notably, by the Johnson Publishing Company, the creators of *Ebony* (beginning in 1945), *Jet* (1951), and the black women's magazine *Tan* (1950)—and then in the late 1950s by nationally respected scholars of consumer behavior. Some new findings from these reports were that blacks, contrary to stereotype, actually saved more money than did whites (a conclusion since disputed), and that in the African-American community, "quality is always put ahead of price since the Negro is determined to enjoy the symbols of status whenever he can, whatever the price." In addition to the race-specific strategies advocated by the NNBL, marketers were cautioned to avoid "stereotypes such as minstrels, the name George, incorrect grammar, dialect, Aunt Jemima–type Negroes, watermelon, chicken, crap-shooting, pork chops, gin, pickaninny, and Negroes as servants."[10]

Mass marketers themselves were somewhat slow to take up the challenge posed by black media owners and scholars of consumer behavior. The pioneers were marketers of prestige products who placed more and more advertisements in *Ebony* during the early 1960s. By the late 1960s marketers included a growing number of African-American models and actors in advertisements with a broad national television or magazine audience, and networks employed more blacks in the casts of movies and television serials. By the early and mid-1980's television commercials very commonly included integrated casts, African-American models were called on to portray ordinary Americans as well as consumers of prestige products in magazine ads, and blacks regularly took on starring roles in Hollywood movies and television series.[11]

Full-scale attempts by mass marketers to articulate specific material definitions of young poor black people's tastes and sensibilities began some forty years later than their first highly successful forays into the white middle-class youth market in the 1920s. Again, African-American entrepreneurs took the lead. In the late 1950s, after television forced radio into more specialized programming, radio shows and then whole radio stations oriented to black music began to appear, giving a wider audience to the products of small, financially strapped black "race record" studios that had existed since the 1920s.[12] In 1957 the entrepreneur Berry Gordy, Jr., established his Motown record company and began distributing performances by black rhythm-and-blues singers. Gordy and black radio professionals helped create the first full-fledged star-promotion system in the black musical world by the mid-1960s, some fifteen years after mainstream white recording companies had begun promoting rock and roll in a similar fashion.[13] Teen-oriented magazines, devoted to music and acting stars—which had appeared overnight during the 1950s and added an all-important visual medium to inform young, white, predominantly female fans about the exploits of such celebrities as Jimmy Darren, Elvis Presley, and later, the Beatles[14]—were not available for young black audiences until 1971, when *Right On!* was first published. Its first issues were devoted exclusively to promoting the Jackson Five, but later in the 1970s it chronicled Motown and soul in general. According to its editors, it had few, if any, competitors until the late 1970s when *Soul Team,* later called *Blackbeat,* began publication. In 1986 *Word Up!* became the first magazine to devote coverage to rap, followed later by *Rap Masters* and *The Source.*

Television coverage of black youth culture and movies devoted to black teenagers also began significantly later than the same media's attention to white young people's interests. Middle-aged people in my neighborhood remember learning the most about Motown musicians like Smokey Robinson and Gladys Knight from those stars' occasional appearances on the "Ed Sullivan Show" in the mid-1960s, and it was not until the mid-1970s that shows like "Soul Train" made their syndicated debut on local UHF stations—to further consolidate the star system in black popular music. With the invention of videocassettes, and with record companies' growing love affair with the production of musical videos, both rhythm and blues and rap found another visual medium. Since videos also made good TV, young inner-city musical artists also began making increased appearances during the 1980s on cable stations like Black Entertainment Television ("Rap City"), UHF (in Philadelphia, "Crush Raps" and "Beats and Rhymes"), and finally MTV ("Yo! MTV Raps"). In the meantime, *Sweet Sweetback's Baadasss Song, Shaft,* and *Super Fly* had led off in the early 1970s as the first successful adventure movies with black principal actors. They were followed by hundreds of imitations in the 1970s, and by the 1980s musical feature films starring rap groups like Run DMC and the Fat Boys (*Krushgroove, The Disorderlies,* and *Tougher than Leather*) were added to the canon of youth-oriented, violent adventure films best represented by *New Jack City.*

Finally, during the late 1960s, the 1970s, and the 1980s—a half century after fashion advertisers had begun to seek out the white youth market actively—mainstream apparel marketers began to address and exploit inner-city kids' need for compensatory status symbols. Their approach, using media that exclusively or principally communicate to poor urban neighborhoods, is best known by the recent controversial efforts of tobacco and alcohol companies to sell their misery-numbing products by monopolizing inner-city billboard space. A similar tack, using other media (though not always with any nobler intentions) has been employed in the dissemination of clothes and standards of African-American fashion.

Manufacturers of gold jewelry, for example, have found a powerful institution of consumer socialization in the inner-city's small streetcorner vendors and pawnshops in fading urban commercial zones. In Chauntey's neighborhood today there are a number of stores like this, most owned by Korean merchants. When paying for purchases, customers cannot miss the hundreds of huge, low-carat gold "bamboo" earrings, "fat rope" or "herringbone" gold chains with gold BMW and Mercedes logos or gold guns hanging from them, thick gold bracelets, and "four-finger" gold rings—all in plain view behind a few inches of bullet-proof glass. Indeed, walls of imitation luxury—often cast in symbols of status, excess, manhood, and violence cover the horizon every time one of my young friends goes to buy a candy bar.

Perhaps an even more successful marketing venture was launched in the late 1960s by sportswear manufacturers. Converse set the pace, then Nike and Reebok perfected the approach. Their strategy was to target the inner-city male youth market by invading the college basketball recruitment process, which has served as the primary route for playground players to become national stars. Sneaker companies had long targeted youthful basketball hopefuls (Converse's Chuck Taylor, one of the most avid salesmen, was at work already during the 1920s), but in the late 1960s Converse started the practice of wooing college basketball coaches with dinners and other favors to ensure that popular teams would showcase the right shoes when they played on national television. By the 1980s, according to an exposé by the journalists Alexander Wolff and Armen Keteyan, Nike's Sales promoter Sonny Vaccaro perfected these techniques to launch a marketing onslaught very consciously directed at inner-city youth. Vaccaro not only took college coaches out to dinner, he put them on the Nike payroll and provided them with enough complementary sportswear to woo potential players from inner-city high schools. To further ensure loyalty to his product, he had Nike sponsor high school teams and summer leagues in the inner city, with all uniform costs paid, and fought—again, with the currency of warm-up jackets, sweatpants, and Air Jordans athletic shoes—to prevent rival leagues, such as those set up by Reebok, from getting the best players.[15] As with the case of marketers of gold chains, sneaker pushers well understood inner-city kids' specific needs for compensatory status symbols and their relation to symbols of masculinity and violence. Indeed, "in their own way," wrote one recent observer, "the sneaker companies are more closely connected with young black males than any other of this society's institutions."[16]

The growing sophistication of marketing campaigns and the increasing audience themselves did not create a strong interest in material symbols of prestige among poor African-Americans. Those symbols had held special importance for black people well before the advent of mass communication. In the aftermath of Emancipation, for example, ex-slaves were often reported to have bought stylish clothes as a way of celebrating newfound freedom. According to the historian Robin D. G. Kelly, for southern black sharecroppers, coal miners, and domestic and tobacco workers "'dressing up' was a way of shedding the degradation of work and collapsing status distinctions between them and their oppressors."[17] During World War II in cities across the country, young black men, as well as Mexican-Americans and other groups, were swept up in a nationwide craze for zoot suits. According to the historian Bruce Tyler, this trend flourished despite a powerful marketing campaign launched by the War Department that forbade the manufacture and sale of the suits, which used extravagant amounts of material, in the interest of wartime austerity. Partly responding to this ban, soldiers on furlough in Los Angeles in June 1943 vented their anger on Mexican-American zoot-suiters during ten days of riots. The government's efforts may have been offset by independently produced movies like *Stormy Weather* (1943), which celebrated the black "sporting life," and by Frank Sinatra and Danny Kaye, who were said to have modeled zoot suits in some of their public appearances.[18]

For the African-American children described in the Philadelphia case reports of the 1950s and 1960s, and those living in Chauntey's neighborhood thirty years later, material values and things, particularly clothes, have also been the stuff of intense emotional importance. At the same time, there are signs of change—some more evident than others in my research—in kids' identification with commodities. First, kids have modelled their changing material tastes closely on the marketing messages that mass-merchandisers, have consciously created to meet inner-city needs for compensatory status. Second—and this is less easy to prove definitively—the importance of materialistic values to inner-city youth seems to have increased steadily throughout the late twentieth century. This increase may reflect advertisers' growing ability to target the specific needs of poor black people and, perhaps, maybe also their ability to sell the seductions of status-redeeming products to children at ever-younger ages. However, if inner-city kids have been more eager to rely on consumer items as a primary means of compensating for economic, racial, and sexual humiliation, they have also had to pay dearly for that reliance, in both economic and psychological terms. Because of the steep expenses involved in acquiring those symbols, kids have faced the risk of redoubling memories of frustration and humiliation associated with poverty and race. Furthermore, if materialist mainstream America has held out a sense of belonging to excluded and alienated kids in the inner city, other parts of that same mainstream have delivered a powerful contradictory message that has disparaged poor kids with expensive tastes. Thus, if commodity worship has become an increasingly widespread faith, it may have also become increasingly exasperating—at the same time that bleaker economic prospects and persistent racial exclusion have made it all the more emotionally compelling. In turn, American abundance has assumed an undeniable place in the history of poor urban African-American kids' social interactions with others, most importantly, with their parents, with their peers, and across gender lines.

During the war years and into the period covered by the case reports, urban African-Americans' tastes in prestige consumer goods, like those of other groups in the United States, largely followed the lead of the most successful national marketing strategies of the day. In clothes this meant fancy suits; in cars, Cadillacs; and in hairdressing, imitations of the straightened standard of Caucasian America. At the same time, the search for compensatory personal images which for many poor black Americans was intensified by humiliations suffered on account of both poverty and race, endowed inner-city consumption patterns with extra emotional and creative energy and meaning.

The market analysts who pioneered the study of black consumers during the 1950s and 1960s quickly discovered evidence that the twin burdens of racial humiliation and the agony of poverty in an affluent age influenced young black people's interest in commodities. Because of advertisers' need for data on consumer income, they have, fortuitously for our purposes, assembled otherwise-elusive data that compares poor whites with poor blacks. In 1949 and in various surveys in the late 1960s, advertisers discovered that poor black men were much more likely than poor white men to buy Cadillacs, Lincolns, and high-priced Buicks (though all poor men usually bought their cars used.)[19] In a 1962 survey advertisers found that in the "less than $3,000" income group, black women were half again as likely as white women in this group to be "fashion conscious."[20] Poor black men were found to be more likely to buy prestige goods like Scotch whiskey in 1965,[21] and in another study in 1971 poor black women were found to be substantially more likely to buy name-brand foods at the supermarket.[22]

Though some of the brand-name and luxury consciousness may have been due to traditions of wariness toward small-time white merchants,[23] other, more personally felt wounds of racism may also have been at work. During the late 1930s and 1940s, southern demagogues like Mississippi Senator Theodore Babbitt were complaining about the "uppitiness" and sexual proclivities of Harlem's well-dressed or zoot-suited African-Americans. In his autobiography, Malcolm X tells a story dating from this time concerning a black shoeshine man who won the lottery and bought a Cadillac: "'Burns them white cats up when you get something,'" Malcolm's friend told him. "'Yeah, I told them I was going to get me one—just to bug them.'"[24] The author of an article called "Why Negroes Buy Cadillacs," which appeared in a 1949 edition of *Ebony*, confirmed that "basically, a Cadillac is an instrument of aggression, a solid and substantial symbol for many a Negro that he is as good as any white man."[25]

As well as buying more prestige goods than other groups of poor people, poor urban African-American men in the 1950s—especially those who led the "sporting life"—the hustlers, pimps, hipsters, and hipcat studs (see chapter 1)—put extra energy into making their appearance noticeable. The toasts of the 1950s documented this enthusiasm for commodities thoroughly. Even the Signifyin' Monkey got fancy threads:

Up jumped the monkey from the coconut grove
You could tell he was a pimp from the cut of his clothes.

He wore a herringbone jacket with Hollywood slacks
And a raglan benny with slits in the back

A Elgin ticker with a solid gold band
And a egg-sized diamond flashed on his hand

A pocket full of money and a head full of herb
A Cadillac coupe parked at the curb.[26]

Hipsters' zoot suits had wider, sharper collars than normal suits. The pants widened at the knee and tapered into tight, pegged hems. The whole costume was topped off with a wide-brimmed hat. When zoot suits went out of fashion after World War II, somewhat more conventional suits, sometimes called "vines," became popular, with bright colors preferred.[27] Even more energy was invested in hair: Malcolm X has provided a terrifying description of the hair-straightening process, called a "conk" in his day, which involved a stinging hair lather made "of Red Devil lye, two eggs, and two medium-sized white potatoes," and later, some fancy razor work. The result was "hair as straight as any white man's" that was so striking, Malcolm tells us, that it distracted some passing drivers into having a "minor car accident."[28]

The boys growing up in Philadelphia during the 1950s whose lives were described by BBA caseworkers, encountered this same world of conspicuous consumption and also had their tastes molded by white-dominated mass advertising. The case reports, however, offer a glimpse at a different side to this history of commodity-based identity. As well as promising status redemption and a muting or hiding of poverty- and race-based humiliation, conspicuous consumption also exacted a stiff psychic and material price.

Nowhere was this more true than on the streetcorner and in the lives of teenage jitterbugs (see chapter 1). Like the hustler's world of Malcolm X's day, much of 1950s jitterbug culture was based on an initiation rite that involved growing one's hair long so it could be marcelled or processed, to imitate Caucasian hair.[29] The following passage, from the case files of the Greater Philadelphia Federation of Settlements (GPFS), which worked with groups of boys who were exhibiting early signs of gang behavior, reconfirms the impact of racial stigmas upon the desire for compensatory status symbols:

Three boys had not removed their hats. . . . Before I could get them to take them off, [the director of the GPFS], who was just arriving, asked me to tell the boys to remove them. . . . This was the first thing I took up with them. . . . I . . . discussed the wearing of hats in any public places wherever they are. Then a question by me brought out a revelation and discussion on their part that had deep significence [sic]. The question: "Regardless of how much we talk about hats, some of you will continue to keep them on. Will you tell me why?" Howard said, "I tell you Mr. Jones, I don't want people to see my head." I noticed his hair had been combed and was looking fairly neat. This made me wonder what bothered him about his hair. So I commented: "Your hair seems combed and neat. What's the trouble?" There were several chuckles, and they seemed to support him, and at the same time tell me "you ought to understand." Anyway Howard began to clear the puzzle for me. He said; "Mr. Jones, who wants to go around showing stuff like this I got? (meaning hair)." Kenneth followed with a statement that not only got the endorsement from others, but aroused my suspicion that these boys were ashamed of their hair. He seemed to also say, "you ought to realize that Mr. Jones." His statement was: "When I get all dressed up, smelling sweet, shoes shined and looking nice, I feel bad when I look in the mirror and see my nappy hair." I said to them ". . . It seems that you two are not alone. How many other boys are also having the same kind of problem?" Six or seven signified by raising their hands. Not only did they raise their hands, they made several indirect comments to one another. I suggested that it might prove helpful if we started from the beginning and discussed this thing right on through.

They heartily agreed to do so. . . . I began by saying, "guess it's kinda dissapointing [sic] to get all dressed up and looking nice, and then you look up at your hair and see it's not as straight as you wish it. I wonder if there is a solution?" Cat, who has recently gotten his hair processed said; "I got my process because all my friends had one. One thing though, they cost so much money. Then some of the teachers call you a jitter bug." "Now you really seem to have a problem Cat. You had your hair done to look nice. Now you find it's very costly and also people comment about you. What have you decided to do about it?" "One sure thing, I'm not going to get it done again." . . . "From what I can see, a process doesn't give you the real kind of hair you want, does it?" The answers were; "not quite," "A little too slick and greasy," "people talk about you" . . . "they think you are just like all the other jitter bugs." "Suppose I ask the question this way. Why do you really get a process?" "People look at you hard when you take off your hat. You don't get any place. Girls like good hair fellas better. Nobody likes nappy hair." Further discussion revealed that they had feelings about color (dark) as well as hair.[30]

Boys faced not only the seductions of status conferred by hair straightening but also frustrations about the high cost of the process. Even when a boy could afford it, the resulting imitation of the mass-communicated image was disappointing at best—only reconfirming, as Malcolm X put it, that straightened hair was "an emblem of his shame that he was black."[31] And in the long term, the process only guaranteed humiliating suspicion from America's enforcers of communal and cooperative values.

Conflicting emotions like these, surrounding other aspects of kids' consumer identities, seemed to have worn down the civility of many different social relationships in these boys' lives. Parent-child relationships became particularly vulnerable to conflicts arising from kids' material tastes, especially since the growing practice of raising children as dependent consumers had begun to put severe pressures on poor urban families. Parents' inability to satisfy their children's cravings called into question their abilities as family providers, caused kids to worry about how much their parents really loved them, and made parents the targets of kids' frustration and humiliation:

[Thomas' mother] said she feels that basically he is a nice boy but is a little spoiled. She said he is very demanding. She said he fails to understand why she might not be able to give him all of the things that he might like. . . . [She] resents Thomas' constant demand for spending money and complained that Thomas shows little regard for the fact that she is presently unemployed.

The mother seems to feel that one of Harris' biggest problems is his embarrassment over the family's low economic situation. She said Harris likes to dress well and feels terrible when he thinks he does not look presentable. . . . I [the caseworker] commented on George's recent arrest for stealing.

The BB [Big Brother] and Walter attended a Phillics Giant [sic] baseball game last night and the boy thoroughly enjoyed the experience because it was his first big league ball game. The BB commented that Walter seems to . . . be ashamed of his family. The BB mentioned that on two occasions Walter has tried to avoid having him meet his mother. I told the BB that I too noted, in a previous interview, that Walter seemed to have some embarrassment regarding his background.

* * *

DeForest said his father very seldom talks with him and never takes him anywhere. He said the father does not buy him many clothes and never gives him any spending money. The youngster indicates that a very poor relationship exists between him and his father. . . . [Later, in the same report] DeForest paid me an unexpected visit today. He was dressed neatly, but always his clothes show signs of wear. . . . He said he stopped in to wish me a Merry Christmas. He said his Christmas would be bleak. He said his family does not exchange gifts. He said there would be no emphasis placed on Christmas dinner, indicating that it would be an ordinary meal. He expected to receive no gifts.

[Howard's] aunt said that Tommy and the other children are very jealous over the fact that [the BB] treats Howard so well and buys him nice things. The children are constantly teasing Howard for having a BB, and try to drive a wedge between him and the BB.

[Robert] said, pointing to his clothes, that she [his mother] wouldn't buy him anything; and whenever he asked for something, she said that his sister needs something more than he does.[32]

One particularly trusting and expressive mother told the case-worker that "she does feel bad over the fact that she is not able to give as many things as a boy his age should have because of her limited income. The mother said she receives $50.00 every two weeks from DPA [Department of Public Assistance] and this is hardly enough to exist on. Her rent is $39.00 a month and her food cost about $35.00 a month. This leaves her with about $25.00 for clothing and utilities." Her son, Stefan, she reported, was able to get a job of his own with a "vegetable huckster." This allowed him to "purchase a new shirt and sneakers from money he earned" and to go on a shopping trip that "he enjoyed . . . very much." The job, soon fell through, however, and economic woes eventually led Stefan to steal from neighbors and apparently fueled the frustration that led him eventually to try to burn his house down.[33]

Boys' desires to consume conspicuously and their judgments, based on mainstream standards, about their parents' abilities as providers led to doubts about the legitimacy of the parents' control. This seemed true in families of any structure, whether headed by a man or a woman. In single-parent families, questions of consumption and provision (in addition to parental behavior) often underlay a boy's ostensibly gender-based dismissal of his single mother's authority or his longing for a lost father. The story of the youngster I described in chapter 3, for example, who thought of his father in "a rather superhuman sense" has a revealing subtext: "At present [his mother] receives a DPA grant and when the money runs low and the morals of the family has [*sic*] ebbed and she hears Harold say, 'If my daddy were here we would have plenty' she gets quite upset and has really flown off the handle several times."[34]

Indeed, as well as offering a new explanation for some of the problems of child rearing that have been too quickly attributed to family structure, the case reports also document a close connection between kids' mainstream expectations, parents' economic frustrations, and the persistence of forceful parenting behavior. At another interview, the caseworker reported, one mother "reiterated her dissatisfaction with Tyrone's constant demand for spending money. She said she gives him over $2.00 each week, but he spends it recklessly and comes back for more." When Tyrone's mother went to his job "in an effort to get the employer to pay her some of the money which she loaned Tyrone for lunch and carfare," the two had a "serious argument." Later Tyrone told the caseworker he felt "that he should not contribute money each week to his mother because she receives $45.00 each month from SSA [Social Security] for his care. He said he never sees any of the money. . . . At the present time he eats most of his meals away from home and [is] buying some clothes for himself. He feel [*sic*] that the $45.00 check should be sufficient for his mother." Tyrone and his mother's dispute over parents' proper role as providers and children's acceptable expectations about discretionary income eventually destroyed their relationship. Some months later Tyrone's Big Brother reported an "argument over 18¢ of Tyrone's." His mother admitted to having taken four cents, but Tyrone got so angry he turned off the house current. His mother called the police, who took Tyrone to the Youth Study Center on an incorrigibility charge.[35]

In conflicts like that between Tyrone and his mother we get a more overt glimpse of the underlying dynamics that may have helped sustain inner-city parents' forceful assertions of authority. Faced with kids' demands for material goods and spending power— demands heightened in emotional intensity by kids' powerful formative memories of disappointment[36] and, more importantly, legitimized by mainstream tenets—parents have often looked to older mainstream notions of unquestioned parental authority and forceful punishment. By doing so, they have also compensated for their perceived dwindling adequacy in a society where the economic identities of children have been transformed. Middle- and late-twentieth-century poor parents' and kids' ways of adopting mainstream ideals and, as a result, their ways of perceiving and experiencing poverty have meant that the transition to dependent and nonproductive childhood has not been accompanied by the growth of affective child rearing that characterized otherwise similar changes in middle-class childhood during the nineteenth century.[37] Poor parents, have known just how fragile the economic, mainstream moral basis of their authority really was. Thus it also makes considerable sense that poor parents espousing a culture that prized the establishment of absolute adult authority over children could sometimes, in desperation, be just as quick to abandon responsibility for their children's welfare.

Though only limited case-report documentation exists regarding the role that kids' post–World War II consumer values and their search for compensatory status symbols played in their relationships with peers, some hints of the basic patterns do surface:

[Caseworker, in conversation with BB's wife:] [Melvin] is still looking for another job as he is finding an increasing need for money. She said that he is becoming very clothes-conscious and feels that the other youngsters are snickering at his poor appearance.

[Thomas' mother said his] daughter, Marilyn, who had attended the ———— Junior High School has been transferred because she did not like it there. The real reason involved was the fact that Marilyn had inadequate clothing and felt out of place with the children who wore finer clothing.

[A Big Brother's reflection, later in the same report:] He [the client] seems to have a tendency toward being the bully. He expresses discomfort over his inadequate clothing. CW [Caseworker] related that to the BB that he had seen some of this on one occasion during the summer when the youngster had attended the club in his sister's sandals because he had no other shoes to wear.

[Caseworker's reflections:] It is a known fact that clothes are a big problem in this youngster's life and that much of his show-offness has to do with achieving some kind of equalizing status. He has been known to fight after being teased about some article of clothing he has on, and many of the reports of mischief have been centered around these factors. The BB was instrumental in that he got another outfit for him on Christmas, and it is hopeful that . . . getting him a few things will help alleviate some of the clothing problems and provide him with a greater sense of security.

I urged [William] to consider abandoning his "processed" hair. Charles said his boy friends and his girl friends would quit him if he changed his hair style.[38]

Peer pressure among black boys living in inner-city Philadelphia during the 1950s clearly entailed an ethical mandate shaped by the broader American culture of mass consumption. Indeed, the mainstream dictated that boys' search for compensatory identity through symbols of economic and racial status was not only possible but obligatory. However, as hinted in the story of the Settlement boys' discussion about their hairstyles, peer society's reliance on compensatory identities based upon consumer values came at the severe price of suspicion and ostracism from parents and the adult representatives of mainstream society.

The case report of one boy best illustrates how the combination of frustration, humiliation, parent-child conflict, desire for compensatory status through commodities, and the threat of ostracism helped create a streetcorner jitterbug—and then undermined him. Frustrated by his mother's inability to buy him what he wanted, Darrel "had been involved with another youngster in a holdup of a shoe store in an attempt to get money for clothes." After a stint in a reform school, he emerged again as a menace on the streetcorner, dressed "as a jitterbug," and emulated other jitterbugs "in words and deeds." When Darrel did not respond to the caseworkers' standard response to such situations, a speech on how Darrel should understand that these are hard times for his mother and he should cooperate with her, the desperate caseworker asked the Big Brother "to impress upon [Darrel's mother] the imperativeness of getting Darrel those things that will make him feel that he belongs, in that he tends to rebel and be negative about a great many things." In her meeting with the Big Brother, Darrel's mother, "was very earnest and sincere in her desire to provide him with things, but her financial situation hardly covers rent and food." Meanwhile, reported the caseworker, Darrel "is still very much the jitterbug and wants to wear his hair in a process (marcelled). His mother has repeatedly asked him to get his hair cut, but he relates that he is growing his hair long so the process can take. . . . [The Big Brother] feels that the boy's [sic] he is hanging out with keep their hair in this manner and he looks odd if he doesn't." Darrel's search for personal adequacy based on a perhaps overenthusiastic pursuit of mainstream, white consumption standards, and on his defiance in the face of his mother's financial limitations, eventually left him wide open to mainstream censure and disparagement. "He was spotlighted as one of the youngsters that nobody else in the class should be like," wrote the caseworker in one of the later entries of Darrel's report. "[The caseworker] has encouraged the BB to resist these efforts [to grow his hair] . . . in view of the fact it only serves to stigmatize the youngster and single him out for easy identification in a group of individuals most undesirable in our society." Shortly afterward, Darrel's Big Brother gave up his assignment in frustration. The final entry notes that some months later, seventeen-year-old Darrel was arrested and sent to the state prison at Camp Hill.[39]

Twenty-five years after Darrel's struggle to articulate an identity in the midst of Philadelphia's growing culture of mass consumption, kids in Chauntey's neighborhood face more pervasive images of abundance, and a moral culture all the more insistent on equating conspicuous consumption, personal identity, and status. The newest generations of inner-city teenagers and young adults were born after the revolution in marketing philosophies concerning the inner city, and as they have grown up, they have attracted much more scrutiny as a market niche than did the jitterbugs. Following the enticements of such merchants as jewelry manufacturers, sneaker companies, and professional sports teams, inner-city boys and girls have created a new standard of prestige suited to both teenagers and younger children. The new look, based above all on warm-up suits, sneakers, and gold, has not supplanted hustlers' and jitterbugs' fascination with prestige automobiles, fancy suits, and expensive haircuts. Instead, it has added yet another very enticing lure—"consumer socialization," the marketers call it—into the supposed glamor of compensatory commodity worship.

The jitterbug look, oriented more toward older teenagers, had relied principally on the streetcorner and a few poorly distributed "sporting-life" films for its dissemination. In contrast, the youth-oriented sneakers-sweats-and-gold look of the 1980s and 1990s, as well as the more established adult code of luxury spread through a whole variety of inescapable media. Larger-than-life sneakers adorn billboards, magazine advertisements, and television screens. Mercedes with gold five-point mag hubcaps, gold license-plate holders, a swoosh of gold paint above the rear fender, and gold monograms on the passenger door not only cruise neighborhood streets, but also appear in movies, videos, TV shows, and teen-magazine photos of rap stars dressed in designer sweat suits, Gucci sneakers, and gold jewelry.[40] The ubiquitous rap tapes that kids amplify through giant speakers lodged in their open car trunks, dance to at curbside boombox get-togethers, or fall asleep to on their living-room couch show a preoccupation with consumption and acquisition that never characterized the old soul and R&B hits or even the toasts. Singers like Cash Money, Too $hort, and EPMD (Eric and Parrish Make Dollars), and their nine- and ten-year-old fans, can be heard any time of the day rapping out lyrics, many of which sound like this example from Dr. Jeckyll and Mr. Hyde's "Gettin' Money":

> *Hey, girl, I'm Dr. Jeckyll*
> *I don't have a care*
> *I'm spendin' money like a millionaire, huh!*
> *I own a mansion and even a yacht*
> *That's right, there ain't a thing that I ain't got*
> *I drive a cherry red Mercedes Benz*
> *I got a bank that has no end*
> *I got a Lear Jet at Kennedy*
> *And it's chillin' on the runway layin' for me . . .*
>
> *Gettin' money, so much money, girl*
> *Everything is funny when you're gettin' money*
> *One Million*
> *Two Million*
> *Three Million*
> *Four! . . .* [and so on, up to *"Seven Billion / More!"*][41]

According to the memories of adults on Chauntey's block who grew up in the same neighborhood in the late 1950s and early 1960s, kids' craving for things has gotten more persistent, and demands for now outrageously expensive symbols of belonging and prestige have begun earlier in life. A couple of parents have told me, for example, that their son learned to say "Michael Jordan" before "mommy." As soon as they are able, kids begin to demand the basic building blocks of the b-boy outfit. Already at five and six, many kids in the neighborhood can recite the whole canon of adult luxury—from Gucci, Evan Piccone, and Pierre Cardin, to Mercedes and BMW (some people say these have replaced Cadillacs as "*B*lack *M*an's *W*heels"), to Eddie Murphy's mansion with two pools, to Donald Trump's massive casino, to the amount of money Bill Cosby made last year. From the age of ten, kids become thoroughly engrossed in Nike's and Reebok's cult of the sneaker: they constantly check the bewildering monthly changes in style that sneaker companies offer their inner-city customers, and they always have an eye on the feet of drug dealers for any capricious switch back to models previously deemed "played out" or for models that may have mysteriously appeared on the corner to announce new lineups. Fahim slips pieces of cardboard between the toe end of his Nikes and his feet so that the front "doesn't flat out"; other kids who accidentally step on his feet are lucky if they get away without a serious browbeating or a fight. A thread slightly out of place or a slight discoloration is enough to pronounce a sneaker "dogged" and unserviceable. Fahim and Omar, now that they have a little spending cash from the car-wash, buy a new pair at least once a month, sometimes every fifteen days. Any and all windfall spending money, goes to clothes, with sneakers invariably on the top of the shopping list.[42]

If boys invest most of their commodity worship on sneakers, many girls emphasize the gold jewelry that dangles in front of the counters of corner stores and check-cashing outlets throughout inner-city shopping districts. To help celebrate Towanda Wilkins's thirteenth birthday, one of the tutors affiliated with the Kids' Club gave Towanda her first pair of one-and-a-half-inch, heart-shaped gold ear-rings. "Now I am finally a girl," Towanda declared, trying them on in the mirror. Young women in Chauntey's neighborhood have found ways to adorn virtually every visible feature of their bodies with gold: from rings covering all ten fingers, to dozens of chains and wrist ban-gles worn at the same time, to nose rings, tooth caps, ankle bracelets, and gold beads woven into a hairdo that spell out the wearer's name. Earrings are probably the most important symbol: girls prize the largest possible models, hoops and "bamboos," sometimes inscribed with their names in elaborate gold filigree, that can be worn three or more pairs at a time and can reach to shoulder length.[43] Earrings and rings are sometimes traded as signs of intimate friendship between girls, and girls sometimes ask boyfriends to buy them expensive jewelry of some kind as a way of cementing an exclusive relationship. In turn, boys often see the amount of jewelry a girl wears as an important sign of how "decent" she is.

Clothes and other conspicuous commodities not only offer protection from poverty-based humiliation but also help kids overcome race-based feelings of inadequacy. For boys, expensive dressing is an essential to their cult of the b-boy or bad-nigga image, because it supplements his ability to compensate for humiliation due to racism with necessary protection against embarrassments that derive from poverty. Indeed, the idolatry accorded to drug dealers arises from their ability to combine the glorification of blackness—by linking race to prowess in matters defiant, sexual, and violent—with virtuoso performances of conspicuous consumption.

In their quest for the bad-nigga/drug-dealer image, boys today still face some of the problems that the settlement boys encountered in the 1950s concerning black physical features. As mentioned before, boys with dark skin and kinky hair still struggle with their self-image, despite their joking self-deprecation or embrace of caricature. The intense attention boys give to avoiding too much sun and, especially, to getting particular haircuts no doubt reflects the legacy of advertising and other media that have, overall, remained dominated by Caucasian forms. Fahim Wilkins will not go to school or be seen in public if his "hairline" along the top of his forehead is not perfectly straight, or if the "fade" on the side is showing signs of growing out. Boys and girls seem to need a "fresh cut" every week and a half or so, and have a large and specific slang vocabulary describing hair problems which sometimes merges with a derogatory language about blackness: "peas," or worse, "dreadlocks"; to be "woofin," "nappy," "bald-headed," or to have "nigger's knots."

Despite the continued dominance of Caucasian images in the mass media, however, recent mass marketers have been much more willing than in the 1950s to incorporate the likenesses of African-American sports stars and rappers into the advertising and show-business worlds. As a result, black male hairstyles that do not depend on hair straightening have gained considerable prestige. (Michael Jackson's racial nebulousness is an important exception here, but it helps prove the rule: boys I know despise his attempts at "trying to be white, and also deride him as a "faggot"—even if they still agree that "he *can* dance, though.") At least for boys in Chauntey's neighborhood, the straightened white standard and all the "greasy" troubles one needs to go through to achieve it are not nearly as important as they seemed to have been for jitterbugs in the 1950s.[44] Even if the exuberant expression of racial pride symbolized by the natural, or Afro, haircut of the late 1960s and early 1970s has more recently been universally scorned ("You're mom Afro so big, when she sits in the car it look like she has tinted windows," goes one buss), there is something in the unstraightened, close-cropped "parts," "gumby-cuts," "boxes," and "fades" of rap and movie stars that articulates some level of racial pride, or at least racial autonomy. Indeed, if anything, teenage white males have lately done more imitating of black hairstyles than the other way around.

For girls, by contrast, "kinky" hair continues to be a far more complex issue. Because hair care for black women has been a much more elaborate and diverse process, involving a much more extensive line of products and hence greater financial stakes, straightened hair, unlike processes and marcels designed for men, has retained its dominant place in the post–World War II advertising imagery of black women. If anything, it received even more media coverage when mass marketers began to pay more attention to African-Americans' specific concerns. Most very young girls in Chauntey's neighborhood wear their hair in traditional braided patterns that their mothers or other relatives create for them, and a few see it as a sign of racial pride to wear cornrowed and beaded styles ("naturals" are derided by girls too, and virtually nonexistent). However, most girls prefer one kind of straightened "do" over other options, and they see their first hair straightening, which usually occurs around age seven or eight, as a rite of passage. This preference is consistent with the self-portraits girls have drawn for me over the years, which all show the artists with hair that drops straight down the sides of their faces and curls up and around at about shoulder height.

Girls who have passed this rite of passage have two main options: either they can straighten their hair using a hot comb almost every day (especially in the summer, when their hairstyles have a greater tendency to "sweat out"), or they can go to the hair parlor to get something more permanent. There, various chemical-rinse, oil, and temperature treatments that hold for a month or so are available. In turn, these "perms" can be fashioned into such styles as "waves," "Shirley Temples," and "french rolls." Even more expensive are "weave-ins," which involve implantation of straight hair into the base of natural follicles. Hair dying, in blond or other colors, also became increasingly popular in the 1980s. Indeed, the great bulk of the two billion dollars reaped every year by licensed black hair salons and through sales of hair products comes from women's hair straightening; and blacks, who constitute about 12 percent of the U.S. population account for 36 percent of all purchasers of hair-care products.[45] Whole magazines, like *Black Hair* and *Blac-Tress* ("Starring Today's

Black Woman"), have been issued to inform black women about the latest hairstyles, and much of the coverage focuses on forms of straightening. Though some of the beauticians interviewed express hints of regret that "natural styles" are not sought out more often, the very names of the magazines and of some of the straightened cuts (one favorite style, for example, is called a "Cleopatra") suggest a different attitude that coexists alongside apology: that blacks' straightened hair—which after all is still different from white hair, and can be styled in ways white hair cannot—has become as authentically African-American and as thoroughly feminine as the spiritual bonding between daughters and mothers who braid hair in traditional fashion.[46]

No matter what racial code is assigned to hair straightening, however, its prestige offers only a very risky way for people to cope with humiliation due to poverty or racism. First, the process can be expensive. To avoid some of that burden, children often visit unlicensed beauty parlors, where lack of the right equipment puts them at risk of severe and unsightly hair damage from overexposure to chemicals or heat. Chemical perms can be very risky: though they offer straight hair that lasts a month or so, they need to be redone at least that often to avoid hair breakage. When Theresa and Saleema Wilkins's father was alive, he forbade his daughters to have perms because he feared they would lose their waist-length braids. A number of girls in the neighborhood experienced distress when their hair "came out bad" because for example, they could not afford to renew their perm, or someone at the parlor made a mistake. Kimberley Patterson's slow-growing hair certainly did nothing to lessen the anguish she lived with: her siblings and peers routinely called her "bald head" and "scrubby." Aisha Greene encountered the same problem at age seven: "Aisha is upset 'cause her hair turned out bad," her mother explained to me once when I found Aisha moping at the kitchen table. "It's all short and it falls out when she be lying on it in the bed." The only affordable (that is, no more than thirty dollars) choice for Aisha was to get "extensions" (artificial hair in the shape of cornrows that are braided into a girl's natural hair). This style was clearly a distant second-best, I discovered on a return visit to the Greene's house, when I found Aisha disgustedly tearing the fake braids out of her hair.

The emotional power of clothes, jewelry, and hair for kids in Chauntey's neighborhood—along with other consumer items that symbolize prestige among children, like BMX bikes and Nintendo video games—goes beyond their promise to conceal poverty and blackness and to tame deep-rooted humiliation. If identities based on American consumerism have gotten more emotionally compelling since the days of the case reports in the 1950s, they have also become all the more unaffordable. Though kids in Chauntey's neighborhood can often achieve moments of glamour and pride through consumption, much bigger parts of their day-to-day existence are preoccupied with dreaming about those moments, desperately trying to find ways to get enough money for the things they want, feeling frustrated with parents who cannot regularly afford food and rent, let alone discretionary items like hundred-dollar sneakers, and feeling jealous of others who have found some way to dress "fly" for their own fleeting moment.

It is difficult to exaggerate the intensity of feeling that can arise from this mixture of a seductive sense of hope and expectation (so rare in the neighborhood as it is) and reconfirmed humiliation, frustration, and envy. Once, while he was visiting my house shortly after I first met him, eleven-year-old Georgie disappeared, and only after a ten-minute search was I able to find him, hiding deep inside the hall closet of my house with old coats pulled over his face. We had been fixing up his and his brother's homemade skateboards (scrap plywood and sawed-apart roller-skate wheels), and another kid had just ridden by on a hundred-dollar Hot Rod Wheeler. Georgie, as far as I know, had not learned to write at the time, but somehow he produced me a note in red crayon that said, "I a bich cause they state bod better." The Kids' Club's early efforts in getting Fahim and Omar to start attending school sputtered badly, and for the longest time none of us could figure out why, given all sorts of incentives, lectures, rewards, and so on. The two would repeatedly lie about their attendance and end up on the absentee roles. Finally, after yet another difficult meeting, Fahim broke down in tears and told us he and Omar did not have the right clothes, which was the same reason all of his older brothers had dropped out—they could not be seen in their "bummy old rags." For two years afterward their tutors and I were repeatedly reminded not to tell anyone about what had happened that night at the meeting. Concealment, of course, did little to lessen the power of those contradictory feelings. Several years later, when Omar had perfected his ability to repress emotion in public and had developed his particularly unfriendly teenage macho "cool pose," I found him awash in tears in my kitchen. After spending close to a full year in school and doing extremely well for a while, he became unable to keep up with what he defined as minimum standards of consumption. Fahim had already given up on school in part for the same reason, and it was not long after that Omar followed suit.

Like all of the other pain that kids in Chauntey's neighborhood feel, the explosive emotions surrounding poverty and prestige commodities have perhaps their deepest consequences when they surface in interactions with others. Family relationships are particularly vulnerable. Parents relatively less susceptible to the authority of mass culture often admonish their kids for extravagant requests by reminding them that they (the parents) grew up on "dollar-ninety-nine sneaks" and "came out alright." Others, especially young parents, who are more anxious about what others will say, get together on the street to show off the latest expensive baby clothes and strollers they have bought their kid and coo at miniature Bo Jackson sneakers or infants wearing tiny gold earrings.[47] As they soon learn, however, spending at the level required to maintain a family full of b-boys and "flygirls" cannot be sustained and some parents act out their resulting feelings of shame through harsh treatment of their kids.

For their part, children are very likely to develop an ardent sense of disappointment in their parents very early in their lives that can regularly surface in relationships with others. Andre and Georgie's parents would occasionally succumb to a temptation that is surely hard for inner-city parents to resist—promising their kids a new Nintendo or some sneakers when the "income tax" (refund) comes. The news would immediately earn Mr. and Ms. Wilkins the undying affection of their kids and a sense of family solidarity that would be written all over their faces, only to disappear when the appointed day arrived and there was no new Nintendo. Georgie bears a set of jagged scars on his forearm from the time shortly after one episode like this, when he took a broken bottle by the neck and ground the sharp end into the top of his wrist. All the kids whose families I knew well lived through similar incidents: yelling matches between Fahim and his mother on how she spent her welfare check, Theresa's disgust when she found out she was not going to get a dress because her mom's boyfriend had demanded some of the family's monthly money for crack, and Omar's decision to leave his mother's house altogether because "I hate her. She always be asking y'all [the Kids' Club] for money. That's going to get around, and people'll be talking." Also, he felt that she never had enough for his school clothes.

For kids, the experience of living in a poor family amid a mass culture of abundance quickly sours their attitudes toward cooperation and implicitly provides models for verbal abuse. Parents' inability to provide the basic amenities of childhood "as seen on TV," their occasional wishful, desperate promises to the contrary, and their kids' memories of disappointment help forge a set of cynical assumptions about other people's motives in general, a first step toward the sense that one must manipulate and hustle in order to get what one desires. Kids also quickly grasp the insult implied in the advertisement of status symbols: that those who cannot afford prestigious commodities are inferior. Given the prominence of consumer-oriented media in their upbringing, it is no wonder that kids often seek to imitate that example of insult in relationships with others.

Nowhere is this last aspect of inner-city children's consumer education more evident than in their relationships with peers. If children can, in the privacy of their homes, blame their parents for many of the difficulties associated with acquiring desired material items, they have much less to fall back on when in school and on the streetcorner. The jokes and busses about economic status that fly from child to child mercilessly treat signs of poverty (the most important being the state of one's clothes) as indications of innate individual failure. "Bum," "ugly," "dirty," "dusty," and "leaking" are all epithets for someone who is not completely covered in "decent," "fly," "fat," "all that," or "safe" clothes ("gear," or "threads") and shoes ("kicks," or "runs").

Sneakers whose soles are beginning to peel back at the toe are said to be "choking for air," "choking," or "talking," because it looks like they have a mouth: Omar once told Andre his "runs got a fat mouth. Listen, you can hear 'em. They saying, 'Can I have a quarter? Can I have a quarter?'" Hand-me-downs are another favorite target: "Hey y'all," Chauntey used to yell when he dribbled up to the basketball hoop, "Georgie got his cousin pants on. His cousin pants and his uncle underwear!" Then he would take a shot while the defending team was incapacitated with laughter and while Georgie sulked off, fuming.

People's houses are also a main target of busses:

> Your house so poor I rung your doorbell, the whole house fell down.

> I went to your house to go to the bathroom, the roaches said, "Hey, wait your turn."

I asked you how to find your house, you said, "Next street on the left, second cardboard box on the right."

At home, if Christmas is generally a disappointing holiday, Easter may be more painful yet. The tradition is to buy new clothes, spend Easter day walking around visiting people, and finish up by going to the movies. Kids who do not have the clothes stay indoors all day, and they usually avoid school for at least a week or so afterward for good measure.

As the story of Fahim and Omar's troubles with school attendance suggests, peer social life in schools is replete with wariness, threat, insult, humiliation, and aggression, based largely on concerns about consumer image. "It's not a school," Fahim likes to say, "it's a big fashion show. That's all people are thinking about is clothes." And, as he made it clear during our early efforts to get him back in school: "I couldn't take it if I knew people was talking about me. . . . I couldn't take that kind of rejection. . . . I'd get into fights."

A prime indicator of the increasing importance of consumer items in inner-city violence is the growing number of assaults between girls, particularly in junior high schools and middle schools in Philadelphia. Most of the slim literature, dating from the 1950s to the early 1980s, on girls fighting in gangs or among themselves has focused on the importance of their relationships with boys and the role of romantic rivalry.[48] While girls I know in Chauntey's neighborhood have reported a number of these kinds of fights, ones over jewelry and other items seem to happen most frequently. For a while when he was in middle school, Omar would come by at the end of nearly each day with new reports of fights between girls "cause they jealous of how they look." He reported, "They be stealing people's earrings, then they get into a fight, and Mr. ——— suspend their ass." He also thinks that girls get into more trouble than boys at school.[49] Theresa tells me that in her junior high, girls get into gangs to protect themselves from other people who are jealous and likely to "snatch your earrings." She has taken a more sensible route and has taken to wearing plastic costume jewelry to school instead of the "formal" gold. In desperate attempts to stop thefts of fur-trimmed "fox coats" in 1987, an inner-city Philadelphia principal outlawed them at school. More recently, eyeglasses with a gold snakeskin motif on the rims became a target of thieves in school.

The eruption of "sneaker murders" in the 1980s, as sportsware companies stepped up their campaign to conquer inner-city feet, is probably the best measure of just how easily the inherent impatience and self-absorption of American consumer ideals can, under the desperate circumstances of the inner city, turn into a passion to kill. To be sure, killings in the search of status symbols have occurred in some Philadelphia inner-city neighborhoods since at least the early 1970s (and probably earlier), when turf-gang members occasionally went to war over incidents involving shoes or clothes. A young relative of one of my neighbors was knifed to death in 1971, partly because of a fight over a pair of pants. But, if police departments' impressions are to be trusted (given a lack of official statistics), the rate of clothing-related armed robberies that turn fatal increased dramatically during the 1980s.[50] Recently the Philadelphia police commissioner issued a warning that "wearing [fashionable gold jewelry] in public places invites attack." His remarks followed the gunning down of a teenage girl for a pair of "jumbo bamboo figure eight" earrings in a subway station.[51]

The single-parent household run by an unmarried woman, also a phenomenon of the late 1960s, 1970s, and 1980s, may itself be an emblem of the same kinds of recent historical changes involved in the rise of sneaker-murders. Indeed the same kinds of feelings and values associated with American consumerism, that have threatened parent-child, peer, neighborhood, and school relationships also dictate much of what happens in adolescent boy–girl relationships where many young inner-city families get their start. I was walking through the neighborhood with Fahim and a couple of his "boys" one spring evening. Fahim had a major crush on a girl, and he could not stop talking about it. "She has such a pretty face," he said, "and she's so nice. I'd like her even if she had bummy clothes on!" "Nah," said one of our companions, "I don't mess with the dirty ones." Fahim had to agree. The rapper L.L. Cool J echoes such thoughts in his ode to the round-the-way girl when he sings that all he needs to put him in a "good mood" is "a girl with extensions in her hair [and] bamboo earrings, at least two pair."[52]

In 1986, Oran "Juice" Jones's rap song "The Rain" hit the top of the *Billboard* charts. It is a song of betrayed love: one rainy day, the protagonist accidentally encounters his lover under another man's umbrella. The jilted man raps that his first instinct was to "do a Rambo," but that he thought twice about getting the mess on his "$3700 lynx coat." The rest of the song is a catalogue of all the expensive things the rapper has bought for the woman ("I gave you silk suits, Gucci handbags, blue diamonds/ I gave you things you couldn't pronounce," etc.) Almost as soon as "The Rain" began to ring out from car stereos and boom boxes everywhere in Chauntey's neighborhood, it faced ridicule from female singers. Fifteen satirical "response songs" came out in the weeks after Jones made the *Billboard* charts, many of which took up his theme of consumption and romantic loyalty. "Thunder and Lightning," sung by Cheryl Sewell, was one of the most biting of these songs:

As for those electro-plated slum-gold chains you gave me last Valentine's Day,
Did they have a sale at Chains R Us?
You walking around like you're so fly in that $37 rabbit coat
Honey, that coat had to be destroyed last week after it bit the neighbor's child
. . .

By the way, my new man got me a gold American Express card
And I never leave home without it.
But as you know, I've been leaving home without you, baby.[53]

The themes of this kind of musical satire echo throughout the romances of young people in Chauntey's neighborhood. In exasperation Omar once told me, "I wish I was white. Them white boys dress up like bums, and they get all those decent girls. Black girls, shoot, they be always talking trash about your shit." For public consumption, boys tap gender stereotypes to rationalize their difficulties in keeping up with girlfriend's demands for commodities: "They just want you for your money," goes the line, "they all golddiggers." "Those girls be bringing the dudes down," Omar told me one day after he left school in exasperation. "That's why all them niggas drop out. They be thinking they bums." "It's the girls' fault?" I exclaimed, incredulously. "Damn straight," he replied. Later he told me: "I don't never trust 'em. They be out to get you, man. The minute you start leakin' [showing up in public without new clothes] . . . , they find another nigga." The deep drive to consume conspicuously and the complex of emotions involved have clearly invaded inner-city teenage dating relationships, giving young kids, especially boys, experiences of humiliation about issues of provision that are much like those that have long been experienced by older people in marriages racked by unemployed men's inability to be breadwinners (see chapter 2). Further study of the impact of American consumerism upon kids' economic identities and romantic relationships may give us more understanding of the increasing numbers of African-American households run by women who cannot depend on the fathers of their children for support.

Probably the most drastic connection between American images of abundance and the growing threat to cooperative community institutions has been inner-city kids' participation in streetcorner drug dealing. The electronic media and rap's outsized fixation on abundance have increased the authority of the streetcorner over-lords of taste. Drug dealers' fast cash, after all, has made it possible for many people to get the items that appear on billboards and TV. Drug dealing is also the only activity boys regularly observe that allows kids to overcome for any satisfying length of time some of the economic and emotional prices of consumer-oriented compensatory identity. Boys like Fahim say they would do anything to dress like a drug dealer (luckily, in Fahim's case that has not yet included selling drugs himself or getting killed), and in the meantime he and his "posse" of friends walk, talk, make "tough" faces, and pretend to drive like a drug dealer. When Omar or someone else gets a twenty-dollar bill, he runs to the bank to change it for twenty ones, which he then stacks and folds into a "fat knot," like drug dealers would have. He can then swagger up and down the street flashing his hard cash. Young boys who dress well are approvingly called "pimps," "bad niggaz," or "drug dealers."

Only the influence of their father and a slightly larger than nor-mal fear of violence have kept Omar and Fahim from responding to the numerous entreaties they face to sell drugs. Chauntey's views on the subject, by contrast, come from vast firsthand experience. In one of his most astonishingly candid moments, he told me, "I just feel so proud. Out on the corner with your nice clothes, a decent rope around your neck. Nobody can't buss on you or nothing no more."

The inherently self-absorbed and competitive nature of American abundance and of the cult of consumption has permeated the emo-tional and cultural life of poor urban African-American kids and the social life of their families and neighborhoods. Commodity worship has been a fundamental part of the compensatory identities that kids have created for themselves, not only to overcome economic and racial humiliation but also to help define their femininity or masculinity. The culture of American affluence helps flesh out other explanations of change in the inner-city social fabric. Material cul-ture, clearly a social force beyond their control, has brought severe emotional and moral pressures upon poor black families—often helping to sustain mainstream philosophies of forceful parenting—thus further belying the theory that families alone have been the source of all inner-city troubles. Furthermore, consumerism and the peer pressure it engenders also help account for the aggressive moral codes and behaviors that have not been accounted for in theories of middle-class black flight to the suburbs. And, inner-city kids' growing embrace of consumer culture is more evidence that today's African-American city life is not an isolated culture deriving solely from either the rural South or the late-nineteenth-century black urban experience. Inner-city kids' enthusiastic adoption of conspicuous consumption is indeed a sign, as the commentator Arthur Kempton recently concluded, that "because the prevailing culture acts upon them most directly, these [inner-city] children are among its purest products." Indeed, in some senses, the kids I know have become "the most American of children."[54] As the upbringing of Darrel the jitterbug, the settlement boys, and Chauntey's friends should remind us, however, compensatory emotional investment in the mainstream too often comes at the stiff price of further alienation for kids who are black and poor. While luring those kids into the wonders of abundance, mainstream America can also expertly castigate the unthrifty and label inner-city folks who like fancy sneakers or who spend their AFDC checks on car payments as "undeserving," "deviant," or criminal. Rap knows this double bind well. In a song about fondness for sneakers, KRS-One warns that such "love's gonna get'cha!" For the most ardent disciples of mainstream consumerism—kids like Chauntey who finally find a sense of pride by dressing fly on the drug corner, then finish their upbringing in prison or by getting killed—the rapper's prophecy is played out only too often.

6

Poor Black Children and American Violence

When the black activist H. Rap Brown made his oft-quoted observation that "violence is as American as cherry pie," he was not only offering an argument for militant action against racial oppression but also pointedly drawing the connections between different kinds of American violence. These connections seemed to many especially plausible in the late 1960s. The inner cities were exploding, many in the civil rights movement were embracing armed struggle, and black hustlers were preying on the streets and forming deadly gangs. Such activity, labeled as subversive or criminal, only imitated or responded to more powerful manifestations of violence in American history that had enjoyed state sanction: the Vietnam War, tanks in Newark and Detroit, Bull Conner's dogs and firehoses in Birmingham, and the John Wayne attitude of southern sheriffs, not to mention the age-old violence of the Klansmen, slaveholders, and slayers of Native Americans.[1]

In chapters 2 and 4 I alluded to the effects of some of these forms of American violence—in particular slavery, racial hatred, and police brutality—on the social life of the late-twentieth-century inner city. A handful of social scientists have attempted to test another piece of Rap Brown's hypothesis as a way of understanding the wide differences in national homicide rates. The criminologists Dane Archer and Rosemary Gartner have noted that national homicide rates in countries at war (whether the country in question won or lost) most often increase in the years during and after the conflict. They argue that war efforts, which glorify violent exploits, also incidently generate broad approval of the kinds of violence on the homefront that gets labeled as criminal. The criminologists Martin Daly and Margo Wilson offered another interpretation of the same statistical evidence: the presence of military veterans may affect murder rates during and after wartime.[2] Indeed, some evidence suggests that American militarism during the post—World War II era may have had consequences for life in places like inner-city Philadelphia. As noted earlier in chapter 1 murder rates in most segments of the black population reached a peak in the five years around 1970, starting when the Vietnam War was at its most ferocious, and increasing when President Richard Nixon began deactivating soldiers (a disproportionate number of whom were black and poor) and sending them home. Many men arrested for violent crimes in the 1970s and 1980s were Vietnam vets. A much more direct result of American militarism and of the international arms race in general was the growing number of assault weapons available to drug lords and their inner-city representatives during the 1970s and 1980s.

In Chauntey's neighborhood, references to various aspects of American militarism appear occasionally in boys' codes of aggressive behavior and in their attempts to construct a compensatory masculine identity. Several of the boys I got to know had older relatives— brothers, fathers, or uncles—who had done stints in the armed forces. When kids mentioned such military experiences, they either did so with a macho pride or told me about the army having driven someone "crazy." The older cousin described in chapter 3 who impressed girls by making Fahim and Omar periodically "hit the deck" and do twenty-five push-ups learned his drill-sergeant routine in the army. On the other hand, Fahim once attributed the gang violence of one of his older relatives and the murder of another to the assailants' Vietnam experiences. In the late 1980s, when I met Chauntey, he could boast about American military strength and disparage the Russians with as much conviction as the crustiest of cold warriors. Other kids followed Operation Desert Storm like they would a video game, periodically asking me, "Did Bush get Saddam Hussein yet?" or boasting that if they were president they would use an atom bomb.

But war is not the principal way that the history of American violence has shaped the emotional, cultural, and social world of inner-city children. Instead, an important segment of corporate America has used television and movies to present and glorify this history in inner-city homes and neighborhoods.

Like messages about conspicuous consumption, messages that

glorify violence have increasingly become a staple of American mass culture. Also, like the merchants of consumer culture, the creators of America's mass culture of violence have increasingly catered to the tastes of poor urban African-American customers. And, like inner-city commodity worship, the American cult of violence has been especially fervid in the inner-city because of young people's need to compensate for their powerful feelings of humiliation and to expressing their nagging frustrations. Whether the amount of violence in films and TV shows has contributed to the recent rise in homicide rates, or for that matter family change, is uncertain, but some of the ethical codes of aggression in Chauntey's neighborhood clearly have depended on the mainstream culture of violence for legitimacy. Also, kids', and especially boys', efforts to compensate for humiliation and frustration owe some of their aggressive qualities to their identification with the heroes and values of the mainstream American culture of violence. Indeed, TV and movie violence has nearly completely replaced the messages and the ways of expressing and concealing pain that had been offered by African-American folklore of the late-nineteenth and early-twentieth centuries. Therefore, American violence must be included alongside racial caricature and mass consumerism in any complete understanding of inner-city residents' unprecedented experience of poverty and racism.

Violence in a variety of forms has always been a staple of American film and television, and many mass media images have been drawn directly from the history of American violence. Westerns have depicted the lawlessness of the frontier and the genocide that "won" the West.[3] D. W. Griffith's ground-breaking movie *The Birth of a Nation* (1915) glorified violent racial oppression. Gangster movies, which came into their own in the 1930s after films acquired sound and directors could create much more realistic gunshots, relied heavily on the perceived chaos of America's ethnically diverse cities. World War II films showcased American military bravura. And, reflecting the other side of the militaristic coin, horror films, film noir, and violent science-fiction thrillers like *Invasion of the Body Snatchers* played on the paranoia, fear of invasion, and panic about uncontrolled technology of the cold war and the atomic age.

Television has been concerned with similar things. The fight against urban crime has dominated the medium's police and detective genres, and the West has been an important source of plots. Television has also thrived on the violence of American sport, especially professional football and boxing, but also hockey, professional wrestling, and (in some of its moments) basketball. In addition, the slapstick humor of American vaudeville pervades much of situation comedy and children's Saturday morning cartoons.

By World War II (the Depression notwithstanding), Hollywood and the film industry had built a gigantic mass audience of about four million viewers a week, thus giving romanticized violence an unprecedented medium and an unprecedented source of legitimacy. But if there was a historical moment when American culture first became saturated with mass-media violence, it was the 1950s, when television became the dominant form of American entertainment. The new medium quickly attracted the same size audience each day that films had claimed each week. It had no box office, it fit conveniently in every living room and then every child's bedroom, and it quickly filled up households' evening hours and kids' weekend morning hours with rituals of viewing. By the late 1960s, researchers had found that most Americans spent between one-fifth and one-sixth of their waking hours in front of the television, mostly during "prime time."[4] The programming they watched was heavily laced with violence: according to "Violence Profiles" compiled by Professor George Gerbner and others at the Annenberg School of Communications from the late 1960s through the 1990s, roughly seven out of ten prime-time programs on average, have contained violence, half of their characters have been involved in acts of violence, and violent acts have occurred at a rate of five or six an hour, two of which typically result in a killing. All of these figures have been consistently much higher for Saturday cartoon programs, almost all of which have included regular portrayals of "comic" violence.[5] Since 1970 by the time an average American child has reached the age of sixteen, he or she has witnessed 33,000 media murders and nearly a quarter-million acts of violence.[6]

The persistence of violence on American TV shows has no doubt reflected some of American consumers' preferences, but such preferences may only contribute marginally to TV producers' decisions. Researchers have found that the promotion of TV shows with appeals containing sex and violence does not affect the shows' ratings, and violent shows do not compete particularly well against less violent ones scheduled on other channels at the same hour. Indeed, violent programming has persisted, despite international condemnations and opposition from parents, educators, and law-enforcement groups, largely because of its inexpensive production costs and perhaps more importantly, the fact that action programs are more easily translated into other languages than other genres like comedy, and therefore are more easily exported abroad, where American television has recouped much of its profit margins.[7]

Television has also managed to help increase the demand for violent shows, especially among the recent generations informed largely by that medium. A second, somewhat less momentous turning point in the saturation of media culture with violence came during the late 1960s and early 1970s in movies. Hollywood had long been searching for attractions that would bring back audiences it had lost to television during the 1940s, and that would restore profits lost since production companies had given up control over local theaters in the wake of antitrust suits.[8] In the late 1960s, movie moguls began to find success in expensive, but widely marketed, action-packed "blockbuster" films. Partly because of these corporate interests, a television-induced taste for violence, and the social upheaval of the era, many of the American movie genres that included the most violence enjoyed substantial comebacks in the form of heavily promoted superproductions starting during the late 1960s. The unexpected success of *Bonnie and Clyde* (1967) and the very profitable *Godfather* (1972) helped bring gangster movies back to the screen after a relative absence that dated from the 1930s. Similar revivals also occurred in horror pictures, science-fiction thrillers, and even film noir. (Westerns, whose decline began during the early 1970s, were the notable exception to the rule, though Clint Eastwood did give celebrity appeal to the few that were produced.) By the 1980s, many films exploring the Vietnam War began to appear, and action-adventure films like *Rambo, Die Hard,* and *Batman* led off annual parades of hugely successful blockbusters that marched across American screens every summer.[9]

The cultivation of violent imagery in the movies that was renewed in the late 1960s can be measured in various ways, not the least of which is the ratings system. Although an "X" (adults-only) rating may be given to movies that include graphic sexual acts, "Parental Guidance" is routinely suggested for extremely violent movies designed for young people. (*Teenage Mutant Ninja Turtles,* in which one researcher documented "133 acts of mayhem *per hour,*" got a PG rating, for example.)[10] The remakes of prewar and 1950s violent genre films have included much more heavy artillery and onscreen carnage than the originals. All eight deaths in the 1930s gangster film *Public Enemy* occurred offscreen, in marked contrast to the showy violence in *Bonnie and Clyde,* for example.[11] (The trend toward showing more weapons and killings may also have affected television police dramas. In the 1950s, in a whole year of "Dragnet," "only 15 bullets were fired, and all of five fights took place"—suggesting a much different kind of show from the 1980s' "A-Team.")[12] Another innovation of the 1980s was movie producers' habit of selling sequels to summer action-adventure blockbusters by increasing the doses of violence. According to the reviewer Vincent Canby's informal survey, the hero of *Robocop* (1987) killed 32 people and returned in *Robocop II* (1990) to massacre 81, Rambo killed nearly twice as many people in *Rambo III* (1989) as in the original (1985), and Bruce Willis's body count in *Die Hard* rose from 18 in the prototype (1988) to 264 in the spin-off (1990).[13]

More important than the growing concentration of violence in American film and TV shows has been the equation of violence with entertainment. Television specializes in sanitizing violence by avoiding portrayals of the psychological and physical consequences to victims and by burying all pain in happy endings. The most violent action-adventure films, which tend also have happy endings, tend to glorify and sanitize violence, making it the vehicle for deliverance of justice and preservation of social order. As the communications expert George Gerbner writes, such "happy endings assure the viewer that although evil and deadly menace lurk around every corner, strong, swift and violent solutions are always available and efficient."[14]

Mass-media violence has also been overwhelmingly masculine: in TV shows, men are much more likely than women to be perpetrators of violence and much less likely to be victims. Most violent genre films focus on a male character—a cowboy, a cop or detective, a soldier, a gangster, or a superhero adventurer—who glorifies violence. Indeed, violent male characters also help uphold a particular image of masculinity: TV and movie superheroes such as Sam Spade, James Bond, Kojak, any one of John Wayne's lone rangers, the Godfather, Rambo, the Terminator, in Batman derive their moral authority from a glorified ability to play it alone and to live outside the realms of humdrum emotional vulnerability, bureaucracy, and other ordinary things that entrap and supposedly undermine less valiant types. In movies and TV shows the main male characters' commitment to the good is often signaled by a celebration of these men's lack of commitment to intimacy, particularly with women, whom they sometimes treat as objects of sexual conquest, and by their willingness to fight for a cause. In turn, their violence often acquires a moral admirability precisely because it is portrayed as the most effective way to cut through red tape and achieve desirable ends. What emerges is a license, derived from gender privilege (if not an obligation derived from gender duty), for men to express pain from encounters with adverse circumstances by withdrawing from intimacy and becoming aggressive. (Also, as media scholar Nancy Signorielli has documented, an overwhelming proportion of male characters in television are unmarried. Although marriage is not a sign of commitment to intimacy per se, this disproportion may signal that TV programmers see a lack of strong day-to-day commitments as important in creating successful male characters).[15]

As well as being a predominantly masculine phenomenon, American mass-media violence has also been largely white. But in the wake of the civil rights movement, both the TV and movie industries began to recruit more racially diverse casts.

In television, these changes affected the content of programming and, hence the portrayal of violence, less than in the movies. In television shows of the 1950s and early 1960s, black characters were relegated to roles either as buffoons modeled after old minstrel-show performers, as in the "Amos 'n' Andy Show," or as characters in sitcoms like "Julia," who represented the realities of whites' communities more than blacks'. The exception that proved the rule was "The Nat King Cole Show," which gave the African-American entertainer considerable authority as host of a talk program, and which attracted widespread black viewership, but was canceled after a single season.[16]

Greater inclusion of black people in TV roles during the late 1960s, however, only changed the content marginally. Some of the most successful shows involving African-American casts—most notably, "The Cosby Show"—have largely followed the pattern set by "Julia" of deracializing the black experience. However, African-Americans on recent TV shows have overwhelmingly appeared in comedic roles, prompting cultural critic J. Fred MacDonald to call the years from the 1970s to the present "the age of the new minstrelsy." No one had more power over the content of shows with predominantly black casts than the production team of Norman Lear and Bud Yorkin, who helped create "Good Times," "Sanford and Son," "Grady," and "The Jeffersons" (in addition to "All in the Family"). Though the black characters in these shows were never quite as clichéd as those on "Amos 'n' Andy," their humor did often derive from racial self-deprecation as well as other ethnic barbs, and from the denigration of welfare and poverty.[17] Indeed, a tradition of racial deprecation in African-American TV comedy dates from this time, with "The Flip Wilson Show," to be imitated in the 1980s by Eddie Murphy on "Saturday Night Live," and in the 1990s by Damon and Keenan Ivory Wayans's "In Living Color."

If television has cultivated a generation of violent black super-heroes, it has been through the growing attention to blacks in pro-fessional sports. Indeed, some of these athletes have gained renown for their especially aggressive style of play, with the football player Jim Brown being the first in the 1960s. Since then such athletes as the football player "Mean" Joe Greene of the Pittsburgh Steelers, the backboard-breaking basketball player Darryl Dawkins of the Philadelphia 76ers, and a pair of later Sixers, Charles Barkley and Rick Mahorn ("Thump and Bump"), have achieved national super-stardom partly through TV coverage of their macho antics and their roughness during games. A host of black boxers like Muhammad Ali, Joe Frazier, George Foreman, Leon Spinks, and Mike Tyson also rose to stardom partly through TV promotions.

In Hollywood, by contrast, increasing participation of black film-makers in the movie industry did result in some more consequential changes in the face of American mass-media violence. As in televi-sion, most black characters in the first sixty-odd years of film history had been modeled after the stereotypes of blacks as childlike, awk-ward, and dependent. Black men tended to be cast as "Uncle Toms," and women overwhelmingly as yes-saying domestics. One important exception was *Birth of a Nation,* which echoed the race-baiting negro-phobia of the early Jim Crow South by portraying blacks during Reconstruction as sexually ravenous and as ruthless when in power. Like TV shows, movies also developed a parallel portrayal of blacks as "dark-skinned whites," notably, in the films of the independent black filmmaker Oscar Micheaux and in many of the roles given to the actor Sidney Poitier.[18]

By the mid-1900s, Hollywood seemed ready for black action-adventure movie stars. Jim Brown was the first to get the nod, and in 1964 when he was still playing as a fullback for the Cleveland Browns, he starred in the "B" movie *Rio Conchos.* His later movie *100 Rifles* (1967) showed that Hollywood was ready to challenge, or play on, racist myths: in the film, Brown has consensual, passionate sex with a character played by Raquel Welch.

A full-fledged black superhero genre was not created until 1971 when the African-American director Melvin Van Peebles, who deeply sympathized with militant black protesters, found financing and distribution for his independent film, *Sweet Sweetback's Baadasss Song*. From the opening credits, Van Peebles let his viewers know that he was offering a film that sprang directly from the black experience, not merely a mainstream imitation: after the cast members' names appear on the screen, a message states that the movie is "a hymn from the mouth of reality." The hero, Sweet Sweetback, played by Van Peebles himself, has many of the masculine attributes of other Hollywood violent heroes: he expresses frustration through violence, then withdrawal (in this case, into the California desert), and his aggression is justified by the desirable ends achieved. The most innovative feature of the movie, however, is the black superhero's reliance on two other traditions of American violence not present in white action-adventures: the armed struggle for racial liberation and the caricature of the aggressive, sexually potent black male. Sweetback's primary opponents are none other than officers of the Los Angeles Police Department, who harass and try to brutalize one of Sweetback's acquaintances but get crushed by the superhero's manacled fists. More importantly, Van Peebles does everything to create his hero in the image of a "Baadasssss Nigger," who, he claims in the final credits, "is Coming Back to Collect Some Dues." In the early scenes, a teenage Sweetback gets his nickname (slang for "penis") from a female lover who is much older than he. Later he achieves superhuman stature and has torrid, forceful, and completely gratuitous sex with several white women. *Sweet Sweetback* thus managed to mix Hollywood's violent superhero with a hatred of white cops and a compensatory inversion of racial stereotype—and to label the whole thing authentically black.[19]

Sweet Sweetback's financial success buoyed the fortunes of several other pictures created by black directors working for Hollywood companies. *Shaft* (1971) and *Superfly* (1972) were the most important of these. In the former, Richard Roundtree plays a sharp-dressing detective who beats up fewer white cops than Sweetback, but has sex with as many white women, and he more clearly imitates the James Bond superhero model. In *Superfly* star Ron O'Neill also relies on cross-racial sex, though little on militancy, as a measure of masculinity, and his superhero image derives more from gangster movies. Whatever the permutations, "blaxploitation" was born. Over two hundred pictures fitting the formula—many written and directed by whites—were released after the early 1970s, including several sequels (and a short-lived TV series) based on *Shaft*.

The blaxploitation film phenomenon petered out quickly, although its legacy would persist in other media. By the end of the 1970s, the first heyday of the black superhero had ended. During the middle and late 1970s inner-city black audiences developed a short-lived interest in martial arts films. By the mid-1980s, in his satire *Hollywood Shuffle*, Robert Townshend could only fantasize—facetiously, to be sure—about the possibility that Hollywood would create a "Rambro." (Later, though, he would persuade a major Hollywood studio to sign him on in the role of "Meteor Man" which appeared in 1993.) If a second age of black superheroes has occurred, it has been in the field of comedy, and it has been dominated by Eddie Murphy's move from television into film. With the tremendous success of *Beverly Hills Cop* (1985), Murphy has given racial humor based on self-deprecation, combined with occasional parodies of the action-adventure genre, a massive audience.

Meanwhile, the search for a more authentic portrayal of the African-American experience in film, begun by Van Peebles in 1971, was revived by Spike Lee in 1986 with his low-budget independent release *She's Gotta Have It*. He and the rising generation of young black filmmakers who benefited from his success have, on the whole, more successfully conveyed the African-American experience than blaxploitation ever did. In their best moments, they have done so by casting out caricature, abandoning the quest for superheroes, and even seeking a potentially more healing representation of inner-city violence.

Though some of the most recent movies, particularly Lee's comedies, have claimed authenticity for certain manifestly buffoon or black-stud stereotypes, the best of these films have tackled topics like inner-city violence by at least beginning to explore the underlying emotional and cultural world. As noted in chapter 3, John Singleton's *Boyz N the Hood* (1991), for example, makes a case for the relation between single-parent families and gang violence, and Ernest Dickerson's *Juice* (1992) explores the ways aggressive behavior enters into boys' search for compensatory respect.

To their credit, neither Singleton nor Dickerson made their protagonists into invulnerable superheroes. The main character of *Boyz* actually breaks down and cries at one point—an inner-city reality that had rarely, if ever, gotten any screen time before. Also, unlike with blaxploitation films, most of the directors of recent movies about inner-city realities have at least attempted to condemn inner-city killing (though in *New Jack City*, Melvin Van Peebles' director-son Mario undermined this message at the end by having a community

activist, frustrated by the leniency of the criminal justice system
shoot down a drug dealer). Some of the films, like Lee's *School Daze,
Do the Right Thing,* and *Malcolm X,* and Singleton's *Boyz N the Hood*
carry an Afrocentric or nationalist message, but one less tied to militant action than in blaxploitation movies.

The recent creation of new genres in African-American film does
offer some hope for representations that convey the complexities of
emotional and cultural life in poor urban black communities. But
the capacity of these new films to spark similar thinking, readjust
identities, and increase self-awareness among inner-city audiences
will depend largely on several factors. First, the films will need to
shed their remaining celebration of caricature and macho (the few
women characters in the films are often dehumanized,[20] and the
films' rap soundtracks often carry contradictory messages). The
filmmakers will also need to explore further the reasons behind
inner-city violence, and they will need to begin actively counteract-
ing the overwhelming effects that the rest of mass imagery has had
on the upbringing of poor inner-city kids.

To get an idea of how complicated and daunting that task may be,
we need to turn to an account of the ways American mass-media violence has helped raise the children of the inner city.

Television and movies have not been passive instruments that have
simply "reflected" real violence already inherent in American society,
nor does the violence portrayed through these media stem solely
from American consumers' insatiable demand for it. After all, television and movies resulted from technological developments, not
from some massive historic upheaval in cultural mores or consumer
demand. Since the advent of these media, directors and programmers have wielded enormous power over the amount and type of
violence portrayed. The power of instant dissemination through
television was historically unprecedented, and those who controlled
it, much more than American consumers, dictated the specific con-
tours of the cultural experience it offered.

Compared to consumers of print media and movies, TV viewers,
and especially the heaviest viewers, have much less control over the
level of violence they encounter. Media analysts have shown that levels of TV viewing tend to be determined by the hour of day much
more than the content of programs, and that switching channels, at
least among the major networks and even most cable stations, does
not appreciably reduce the levels of violence for viewers. The people

who have the least power in determining what they are going to get from television are, of course, children, and many post–World War II youngsters have learned from television much of what they know about the world.[21]

The unprecedented growth in concentrated mass-media violence and the strong influence of television have uniquely shaped the experiences of poor people and black people in post–World War II America. Indeed, poor urban African-American children have grown up more intimately included in the mainstream culture of mass-media violence than any other group in American society. Media expert Paul Carton has noted that television-usage figures for blacks and whites diverged throughout the 1970s and 1980s, and by 1989, African-Americans watched half again as much television as whites. In the average black household in 1990, the television was on for eleven hours a day, and no doubt even longer in poor households (some families I know virtually never turn it off). At these rates, Carton estimates, black children witness a hundred thousand more instances of televised violence, including many more killings, than whites by the time they are sixteen.[22] Marketing analysts have also found that African-Americans, who make up 12 percent of the population, account for a quarter of the movie-going public.[23]

Television shows and movies have affected the upbringing of inner-city children in at least three ways. First, portrayals of violence in these media, according to the nearly unanimous verdict of clinical researchers, help increase aggressiveness in children. Second, the same media have also been shown to "cultivate" memories of fear and promote mistrust. Finally, and for our purposes here, most importantly, American mass-media violence has slowly, subtly, but in crucial ways altered the ways violence has been legitimized in the inner city.

The results from over thirty years of clinical research on children and television have led to an overwhelming scholarly consensus that TV violence does make children more prone to aggression. Some researchers have also reported that poor children are more likely than others to act out aggressively after seeing violent imagery, and that they are more likely to identify with violent characters. The same researchers have nearly universally discredited the theory that television actually minimizes violence by offering viewers an emotional catharsis, or a substitute for actual aggressive behavior.[24]

This research, combined with figures on disproportionate TV usage, allows for only vague speculation that the rise of television might have in some way contributed to disproportionate increases in homicide rates in poor urban African-American neighborhoods. However, it at least bears noting that the generation of young people who brought unprecedented waves of gang violence to Philadelphia and other cities in the late 1960s and early 1970s were part of the first generation of Americans who were raised from birth with television. The increasing frequency of violence at inner-city movie theaters on the opening night for movies like *New Jack City* and *Boyz N the Hood* may reflect similar dynamics.[25]

Mass-media violence does not, however, affect viewers' lives only by increasing their proneness to aggression. Television and other media also help cultivate a compelling emotional and cultural world of their own through controlled dramatic content. In annual surveys taken since 1967, Gerbner, Gross, and Signorielli have documented, for example, that heavy viewers of television are consistently more likely than light viewers to see the world with a sense of fear, foreboding, and alienation. Heavy TV viewers, for instance, show a particular proclivity for guns, locks, and watchdogs, and they are more likely than light viewers of a similar class background, gender, race, and political background to fear crime and subscribe to draconian solutions to social problems.[26] Fear and mistrust are, of course, are big parts of the emotional world in which inner-city kids have grown up, especially since the late 1960s. Though television is not the only reason that kids in Chauntey's neighborhood have acquired those deep, painful memories, media violence may have helped confirm them.[27]

As a historian and ethnographer, I can more easily document the impact of mass-media violence on the inner-city ethical culture. All of the kids in Chauntey's neighborhood passionately enjoy watching violent visual drama. Though their TV-watching habits are relatively nonselective, and the bulk of the TV violence they encounter probably comes from random heavy viewing, the scenes kids remember and talk about with their peers tend to be from shows either with all-black casts or with especially high levels of violence. (A 1976 Arbitron survey on the shows preferred by black audiences found that the top three shows were sitcoms with all-black casts, followed in descending order by "Starsky and Hutch," "The Bionic Man," "Kojak," and "Baretta.")[28]

Similar tastes direct the kids' selection of videocassettes for movie nights at the Kids' Club, although violent adventure films are definitely closer to the top, especially for boys. From very young ages (warnings about "suitability for children" notwithstanding) both girls and boys have gotten to know much of the canon of popular action-adventure flicks from their VCRs. As one young teenage woman, who for a while acted as a role model for some of the more troubled girls at the Kids' Club, once exclaimed to me: "I know y'all don't like violence. But I like my movies violent. Movies that don't got violence is corny to me."

Nothing in my own experience with middle-class fans of slasher flicks and superheroes prepared me for my young inner-city friends' vein-popping conversations about cinematic gore and mayhem, punctuated with fervid reenactments and varied sound effects, which follow their afternoons at the theater or their evenings watching cable. Among the kids I know, moviegoing is a more interactive experience than among white middle-class audiences. Laughter, open encouragement of characters, a running commentary, and shouts of glee are common ways that the kids show their appreciation of the onscreen spectacle. Though excessive demonstrations of enthusiasm are often subject to ridicule, kids reserve some of their least self-conscious expressions of delight for the times they witness people getting beaten up or hacked to pieces on the screen. I once walked into the Kid's Club video room to find Omar Wilkins and a friend playing a scene from the horror picture *Planet of the Dolls* in which one of the alien antagonists furiously grinds some kind of power drill into the human protagonist's skull. Laughing uproariously, the kids paused the movie and replayed the scene over and again, to increasing bursts of mirth.

Kids have seized every bit of control mass media allows them, from movie selection to playing with the replay button, to witness as much screened violence as they can. No doubt their intense interest can be traced to these kids' deeply painful emotions. However, American mass-media violence did not always provide the main behavioral models for inner-city kids' expression of their pain. The Big Brothers Association case reports of the 1950s contain no references to movie or TV stars, let alone to images of mass-media masculine violence. That probably reflects the particular interests of the caseworkers, who were much more concerned about kids' families than about other cultural influences. In the toasts collected by folklorists in the 1950s and early 1960s, male performers did often allude to superhuman male figures as a way of giving violence a heroic cast. Stackolee occasionally made an appearance, suggesting something of a continued connection with the South. More often, however, heroes in the toasts, the Honky-Tonk Buds and Two-Gun Greens, were invented by the performers. The catalogue of toasts collected by the folklorist Dennis Wepman and his colleagues in various men's prisons during the 1950s and 1960s contain only a few references to mass-media characters like Frankenstein and Dracula, and one performer boasts that "I the Hustler can make Astaire dance and Sinatra croon." However none of these references to mass-media figures are particularly flattering, and performers did not actively seek out mass-media heroes to articulate their vision of masculinity or to validate their aggression.[29]

Pinpointing the time when the masculine heroes of American mass-media violence became important spokesmen for aggressive behavior among inner-city teenage boys will require more research. However, by the years of *Sweet Sweetback's* and *Shaft,* and certainly by the 1980s, the available evidence clearly suggests a very different picture from the days of jitterbugs and toasts. Writing about growing up in the age of blaxploitation, the cultural critic Nelson George observed:

> Of course the idea that we highly impressionable ghetto boys would imitate what we saw on the screen was crucial to the controversy these films aroused. And, I must admit, the cultural gatekeepers were right: blaxploitation films did have their lingering effects. Aside from an appreciation for sensual bubble baths, I gained a lingering attachment to turtleneck sweaters, leather pants (only recently overcome) and calling women "baby" or "babe" that now spans decades.[30]

During the late 1970s, when the craze for martial arts movies took over from *Superfly* remakes, I remember my school bus stop being besieged by African-American youngsters brandishing "numchucks," (heavy dowels linked by a chain), and three-inch, handlaunched "death stars" they had made in shop class out of sharp, six-pointed pieces of sheet metal.

For the generation that invented the b-boy in the late 1970s, the cult of violent mass-media heroes has been perhaps even more profound. Indeed, the b-boys' violence has not been modeled only on a compensatory inversion of racial stereotypes and the "nigga" hero, nor has their prestige derived only from conspicuous consumption. Both their codes of behavior and their sense of adequacy are enhanced by the legitimacy they can claim through identification with the heroic, masculine glorification of aggression and withdrawal that pervades the larger American mass-media culture of violence. In Chauntey's neighborhood, children do not know who Stackolee is, and only a few boys I know have any vague memories of the Signifyin' Monkey. Indeed, kids no longer have to invent heroes to glorify sexual conquest and violence or define the realm of the "bad": those heroes have been manufactured on an assembly line for them by the American entertainment industry.

At three and four, kids in my neighborhood tuck sticks into the backs of their T-shirt collars, pretending to have Ninja Turtle shells, and they then pull their weapons and hit each other. They can also draw pictures of their carapaced heroes that are as vicious as those of any of the many preteen contributors to the syndicated "Turtles" comic strip, which appear in the local newspaper. Once when Asmar Greene's mother confronted the seven-year-old for socking one of his peers, Asmar replied that "'a man's gotta do what a man's gotta do.'" His mother then asked, "Where did you get that from?" Asmar said, "From that commercial, you know the one that says 'a man's gotta do what a man's gotta do' and this boy is eating a big bowl of cereal." In their gruesome conversations about Bruce Lee, *Terminator,* or *Die Hard,* boys often compare themselves to their heroes, as they also often do when they threaten to fight someone. When I met Fahim Wilkins, then eleven, he asked me to help him make a six-inch-thick cardboard wrestling belt with the initials of the National Wrestling Association done in tinfoil filigree on the makeshift buckle. Video games are also important references in these kids' conversations and threats: I recently listened slack-jawed to a group of ten- to thirteen-year-olds excitedly boasting about their exploits playing "Streetfighter," with each trying to best the others' prowess by mentioning a greater variety of the games' violent moves. Such comments as "I bit, jabbed, and electrocuted the motherfucker" vied with blood-curdling reports of "slash-kicking," "defensive" and "offensive chokes," the "def-touch," "sucker-punches," and "upside-down helicopter kicks," all terms from the video game.

The evolution of the mass-media ideal of masculine invulnerability and violence into a cult among older adolescents and young men in Chauntey's neighborhood provides the best measure of this ideal's emotional importance in their search for compensatory identities. Indeed, instead of being something kids outgrow, the obligation to keep up with the latest TV shows, films, and heroes has always seemed an even more serious business for older boys than for youngsters in the neighborhood. Moviegoing is especially important to older kids' social lives, and theaters offer an important place for boys to seek recognition from people outside the neighborhood and to take girls and young women they are trying to impress. (This volatile social situation, incidentally, may be more important to understanding movie-theater violence than the actual content of films.)

The earlier one goes to a movie after its release, the more likely one is to be the first on the block to see it, and the easier it is to boast and show an exclusive identification with the protagonists. For those who cannot afford the tickets, bootlegged videotapes, usually shot in the darkness of the theater with a hand-held video camera, are often available from street vendors in shopping districts for less than the admission price (Fahim was able to buy a dim rendition of *New Jack City*, complete with audience noise, several days after the movie came out). Between releases, I have known some of the older brothers of kids in Chauntey's neighborhood to rent out a half dozen videotapes of the previous summers' action-adventures for one evening of entertainment with their girlfriend. As the rapper Big Daddy Kane boasted, "Take her to the crib, turn on the beta / Watch a good flick by Arnold Schwarzenegger, / maybe *Commando* or *The Terminator*."[31] Clothing designed as part of movie or TV promotions—Batman earrings and jeans, Dick Tracy T-shirts, and the jerseys of favorite sports stars, for example—are not relegated to the children's aisles, as is the tradition in middle-class shopping malls; in the inner city, mass-media violence is another sign of the height of fashion. As with younger boys, identification with violent TV, movie, or sports superheroes is a common way for teenage boys to boast about their fighting ability. Chauntey's older brother, who was sixteen at the time, once spent an entire half-hour drive with me by clenching his fists and saying over and over, "I'm like Tyson!"—a line he borrowed from the rapper L.L. Cool J.

Indeed, many of the most popular rap performers have raised to an art form the use of male mass-media superstars' names as references for the legitimacy of inner-city cool and "badness." Unlike the 1950s performers of the toasts, today's performers often introduce themselves by comparing their prowess to that of movie and TV superheroes. Kurtis Blow started the trend in 1979, by comparing his "mucho macho" with the "knack of Kojak, better than Baretta," in a reference to two of the top TV shows on the 1976 Arbitron survey of black viewers. Later, at about the same time that L.L. Cool J claimed the mantle of Mike Tyson, Big Daddy Kane boasted that he was more amusing than "Dynasty" and "Hill Street Blues," and he then compared himself in various songs to Rambo, King Kong, Clint Eastwood, a samurai, Freddy Krueger, and even Tony the Tiger. Rakim, of Eric B. and Rakim, tells his audience in one song that he's "rated R," compares himself in another to "007" (James Bond), and on other occasions warns his audience of his prowess with references to *Apocalypse Now, Death Wish, Friday the Thirteenth,* and *Nightmare on Elm Street.* One of the rap group Black Sheep's favorite affectations is to mutter "Van Damme" (the name of the star of *Kickboxer*) in places that would normally call for a "goddamn," and in the aftermath of the success of the gangster movie *The Untouchables,* Kool G. Rap likened himself to Al Capone; in other songs he identified himself with Freddy Krueger, Rodney Dangerfield, and the Terminator. He warned in yet another song that he'd "get wicked as the Witches of Eastwick," and in a song named after the sick movie *Death Wish,* also said he was like a Ninja.

Rap, of course, even in its most commercialized forms is by no means a mere imitation of Hollywood, and its ethical world is very diverse and complex. Among their many other pursuits, some rappers have endeavored, much like the young African-American directors of movies like *New Jack City, Juice,* and even *Boyz N the Hood,* to transmit a "message" about the futility of inner-city violence. The "Stop the Violence Movement," started by KRS-One in response to the murder of his rap partner, Scott LaRock, has been probably the most celebrated of these efforts, though rappers like Ice Cube, Ice-T, and NWA, who are even more identified with the hardcore "gangsta" style of Los Angeles artists, have offered similar songs. Kids I know often hear these messages, and they respect rappers' and filmmakers' efforts, especially because the advice is offered in a language very familiar to the kids. Also, these messages differ markedly from the didactic points about cooperative behavior and racial unity they hear from parents, old-fashioned members of the community, most educational billboards, and schools. Also, as a practice, streetcorner rapping is a direct descendant of the oral culture of the toasts, which offered what many observers believe to be a nonviolent means to express the agonies of inner-city life.

Ultimately, though, even rap's most outspoken prosocial messages fall short of encouraging the kind of emotional self-awareness necessary for lessons in community to be translated into less violent behavior. In general, rap's message songs have relied upon popularized versions of Afrocentrism or black nationalism, which rightfully preaches about self-esteem and self-reliance, and promotes the search for black heroes, but does not prescribe alternate means of expressing or understanding the painful emotions that kids so regularly experience. Furthermore, rap's nationalism is very often wrapped up in an imagery of armed struggle (like, for example, KRS-One's album cover for *By All Means Necessary*, where he poses with an Uzi in memory of a celebrated photograph of Malcolm X armed with a rifle) and in violent expressions of resentment directed at the police (like NWA's "F*** tha Police" and Ice-T's "Cop-Killer"). Add to that "gangsta" rap's cult of violent mass-media superheroes and its glorified inversion of violent racial stereotypes, and the overall lesson that reaches kids like those growing up in Chauntey's neighborhood more closely resembles that of blaxploitation than of newer black film genres. Indeed, recent black filmmakers' attempts to depart from the genre of *Sweet Sweetback* have often been subverted by their movies' soundtracks, which have been largely the work of hardcore rappers. For example, the subtly conveyed message of director Ernest Dickerson's *Juice*—that violence is no way of seeking power and respect—is accompanied by much less subtle, if not (to use Nelson George's words) "proudly homicidal," raps like M.C. Pooh's "Sex Money & Murder," Too $hort's "So You Want to Be a Gangster," and Rakim's "Juice (Know the Ledge)"—in which he boasts, "I'll chill like Pacino, deal like De Niro, Black Gambino, die like a hero."[32]

American mass-media violence has permeated the social life of post-World War II poor urban African-American neighborhoods. The advent of television in the late 1940s and early 1950s, the rise of the violent blockbuster movie in the late 1960s, and the creation of the blaxploitation genre a few years later may have helped reinforce the fear and mistrust that have pervaded inner-city kids' emotional memories. Though proof will probably have to await the methodological wizardry of social scientists, it seems completely likely that heightened media violence has contributed to the overall rise in inner-city family change and community violence.

What is clearer from the experiences of people who engaged in the toasts during the 1950s, and of rappers and children from Chauntey's neighborhood in the 1980s and 1990s is that American mass-media violence has become the most important source of masculine violent ethical culture in the inner city. The historical persistence of a variety of aggressive values in postwar inner-city life, which

I documented in chapter 1, does indeed mask a transformation in the media that have disseminated them. Inner-city children have abandoned a relatively isolated set of aggressive values, one dependent on African-American folkloric forms like Stackolee legends and oral toasts that were passed down principally in families and on streetcorners, and they have taken on a new culture that much more closely links them with the American mainstream.

This change can only have fortified inner-city children's collective cultural experience with violence. The very mass media themselves, and mainstream America's embrace of them, have given the new culture a sense of legitimacy that could never have been achieved by independent forms and media within the inner-city itself. The new culture is not only more able to concentrate violent images than the old folklore, but it sanitizes them in ways Stackolee stories, with their descriptions of widows' sorrow and murder victims' funerals, never allowed. The new culture also packs much more weaponry into its images than the toasts, where the Colt .45 was the most common instrument of death. Also mass-media images are much more likely to present gratuitous violence, which masters of the toasts tended to avoid (killings in the toasts usually happened at the climax of the story and dictated most of its plotline). All of the new attributes of the Americanized culture of violence have made their way into the ethics of b-boys and drug dealers since the 1980s in ways that contrast with the values of gang members and toast masters of the 1950s. Heavy armament, gratuitous conquest and violence, and sanitization have infiltrated the inverted racial caricature of blaxploitation and rap in ways that were not characteristic of "bad niggers" like Stackolee. The new culture gives kids prefabricated and visual images of violence, not ones that require imagination to construct, as with the old oral folklore. And though rap, like the toasts, continues to offer a form for sublimation of painful feelings in the nonviolent pursuit of creation and performance, creative life in the new culture competes with the anticathartic experience of TV viewing.[33] All of these tendencies have in turn worked against black filmmakers' recent attempts to send a fragile message of healing to the young men and women of poor black urban neighborhoods.

CONCLUSION

Toward the Stemming of a Historical Tide

Long after the disastrous summer of 1988, Chauntey Patterson has continued to pay the price of growing up poor and black in inner-city Philadelphia and, at the same time, of being included in America's traditions of social control and its mainstream of racism, affluence, and violence. Inveigled by the caricatures of American racism, Chauntey had become the ultimate "nigga you love to hate." Enchanted by America's traditions of violence he had added potency to his sense of racial adequacy by dressing up in the trench-coat of a "Black Gambino," and nuzzling an Uzi. Then, in the spring of 1991, seduced by American abundance, he treated himself to a luxurious joyride. Like many similar experiences in his life, this one gave him a fleeting moment of glory before exacting a stiff price. According to Omar Wilkins, who saw the incident from down the street, the cops gave chase to the fancy Oldsmobile Chauntey had cross-wired, then shot at him as he abandoned the car and tried to run down a back alley. At age seventeen, like one-quarter of African-American men, Chauntey Patterson entered the criminal justice system, in his case a prison for youthful offenders, largely because of the grinding memories and the delusions of psychic relief that his American upringing has offered to him and his generation.

* * *

A complex historical tide of tragic proportions has washed over the young lives of today's poor urban African-Americans. For purposes of close analysis, I have examined different eddies of that tide separately. Put back together, its main currents look like this:

To many African-Americans, the years immediately after World War II looked economically and socially promising. The federal government got more serious about ending flagrant racially discriminatory practices in the private sector and black Americans began the second great migration to urban areas. However, the promise soon turned sour, especially for the poor and the unskilled. During the next fifty years the industrial job markets that had long served as fairly effective springboards to economic stability for several generations of white immigrants began to leave American cities. American companies had begun to lose their competitive edge. Corporate preferences drifted to cheaper locations in the suburbs and exurbs, and in some cases, to other countries. Thus, racial inequalities in levels of poverty, welfare dependency, and joblessness that had first been established by cruel, blatant forms of discrimination in the early twentieth century largely persisted and even increased in the years since.

The legal battle against racial discrimination in hiring and firing, meanwhile, has not by any means hindered the historical endurance of other faces of American racism: the language of racial hatred has remained strident in many places, the practices that originally created urban residential and educational segregation still separate the American national community by race, and in recent years hateful and divisive caricatures of black people have once again insinuated themselves into the folklore of white American life and into political rhetoric.

Economically and socially, the post–World War II era has thus been a period of increasing alienation for poor, unskilled, urban African-Americans. As a result, their children have been increasingly likely to experience and remember the physical pain and frustration of material deprivation, the resentment and fear associated with an internalized sense of racial inferiority, and the humiliation stemming from both.

The growing social scope of these emotional experiences, combined with spurts of growth in the youthful population, the growth of drug sales, and the increased availability of guns, would alone have brought about substantial increases in violence and in other behaviors that threaten efforts at community building. But, growing economic and social exclusion has also been accompanied by another transformation, this one in inner-city culture. The direction of this cultural change was the reverse of that of economic and social change: it brought inner-city children closer to the mainstream than they had been before. Greater cultural inclusion has, however, redoubled the tragic effects of economic and social exclusion for poor African American children.

The process of cultural inclusion was directed, like the process of economic and social exclusion, largely by crucial corporate and political leaders who have in turn had far reaching influence over all Americans. While many white political leaders propounded a divisive and demeaning rhetoric of violent black men, corporate America not only played ever more on inner-city kids' desires to consume conspicuously but also organized a massive transfusion of violent imagery into the national culture. All of these quintessentially American habits gained a redoubled corporate or political commitment beginning in the late 1960s.

As a result of growing cultural inclusion in the mainstream, the young people in poor urban African-American communities learned new ways to conceal humiliation, protect themselves from fear, and express frustrations and resentments—with drastic results. During the late 1960s and the 1970s the folklore that young people had relied on, with at least some success, in channeling painful feelings into less aggressive, even communal pursuits began to erode, and many aspects of it disappeared altogether. Self-images of "baaad niggers" based on mainstream caricatures had been part of this older culture, but in their folkloric setting they were largely imagined, and relatively less obsessed with firearms, especially compared to these images that played on movie screens and rap videos of the 1970s, 1980s, and 1990s. The culture of conspicuous consumption had also always played some part in restoring young poor urban African-Americans' otherwise humiliated economic identity, but by the late 1960s that culture too had found a place in TV shows and movies, and advertisers tailored it to fit inner-city kids' specific desires from infancy on. This compensatory identity had always come at the price of long spells of increased humiliation for poor kids, but in recent years its intensified and more deeply internalized emotional contradictions may have invaded social relations in ever more consequential ways. Finally, the inventive, often nonviolently sublimating traditions of dozens and toasts has either disappeared or become, as in the case of hardcore rap, too often a showcase for the devaluation of life, an outlet for the glorification of firearms, and a forum for the victimless violence of the mass media. Although many rap performers have helped perpetuate the expressive and cathartic traditions of earlier folklore, they have had to contend with other media that heighten fear more, and encourage imitation rather than provide healing or models of nonviolent expressions of pain.

Ultimately, the price for this combination of intensified economic and social rejection and cultural delusion has been paid by inner-city children and their communities. Harsh expressions of feelings have invaded family relationships, sustaining mainstream philosophies of forceful parenting in an age when childhood has become all the more vulnerable to the practice of those philosophies. As a result, inner-city homes have become places that are much too rough and hard to help kids understand the other detrimental forces in their lives. At the same time, economic and social alienation, combined with cultural inclusion and fueled by periodic booms in the youthful population of poor African-American urban communities, has made it more likely for inner-city residents to die at the hands of someone else in the community or to suffer sexual conquest and family abandonment.

Such social behavior has not gone unnoticed by America's increasingly overworked and, partly as a result of that, increasingly aggressive enforcers of social order. Their official message to inner-city children conflicts with the other official messages of mainstream culture, and lately it also comes increasingly laden with memories of its forceful transmission as well. Indeed, of late, the mainstream culture of American communities has been most effective only in exacting further psychic and physical costs from inner-city youth. Among the highest of those costs is the profligate waste of human potential brought on by mass incarceration.

My analysis of the causes of the inner city's history of desperation is grim indeed. This book is filled with pessimistic images: vanished opportunities, self-reinforcing racist caricatures, seductive visions of personal adequacy that end up undermining those who put their faith in them, and the social death of imprisonment. Indeed, there has been very little in the history of this country's upbringing of inner-city children that does not seem to put youngsters at high levels of risk. To paraphrase the rapper Grand Master Flash, one must wonder how some poor African-American children today, living much too "close to the edge" do actually "keep from going under."

However, if my explanation of recent inner-city history is filled with a deep sadness and sense of tragedy, I think it also points to at least the outlines of efforts we can take as a nation to reverse the historical tide and rekindle hope.

That task is much more than simply urgent. The recent changes in inner-city social life threaten to take their place among the most devastating of America's extensive collection of social historical calamities. The lives of a number of generations are at stake, especially among the most recent cohorts of poor African-American men. Whole communities may be in danger of foundering, and even when they do find some way of surviving, the life required of survivors is not one we should wish on anyone. Also at stake is America's own sense of national community, which is simply being whittled away by fear, mistrust, and the divisive ways that too many political leaders, scholars, and average citizens have chosen to interpret the fate of late-twentieth-century cities and especially the poor African-Americans who live there.

Renewal and rebirth of the inner-city will depend on two interrelated goals: the creation of employment for poor African-American city-dwellers, and the creation of a national culture of commitment and community that is emotionally expressive, ethnically diverse, and compelling to children and young people.

The availability of employment alone will go a very long way toward reducing some of the most deeply felt kinds of humiliation and frustration kids feel. Higher rates of employment should help lessen some key tensions in many inner-city parent-child relationships and make intimacy more affordable, rendering compensatory identities that rely on inverted racial caricature and intense commodity worship, or that transform men into sexual conquerors, less necessary for individuals' senses of personal adequacy.

In order to bring jobs to the inner city, or give inner-city residents access to jobs elsewhere, America should employ every means available. Business leaders need to be shown how well placed they are for participation in national efforts to reverse the flow of jobs out of American urban areas, and to offer on-the-job training to the unskilled. Extensive federal employment programs and employment education programs, even with the bureaucratic chaos and labor disputes they will inevitably engender, still offer a much better alternative than bloodletting and drug-dealing in city streets. In my years as a volunteer for the Kids' Club, I have been very impressed with the benefits of government-funded summer employment programs for children aged fourteen to eighteen; these should be fully funded. Every teenager with a demonstrable need should be able to get a summer job that at least helps to pay for the things kids need to attend school in comfort.

Employment alone, however, will not reverse all the ill effects of American culture's traditions of forceful parenting, racism, consumption, and violence, not only upon the most recent generations of children in the inner city, but also in the country at large.

There is nothing to gain by calling for the government's wholesale dismantling of American consumer culture, or advertisers' disinvestment from their pioneering efforts to include African-Americans in their advertisements, even if that trend may have sometimes helped to intensify certain emotional conflicts about poverty in the inner-city. There is more wisdom in calling for the self-regulation of Hollywood's production of movie violence, and even more wisdom in calling for television to scale down its oversaturated and oversanitized aggressive imagery.

More important, though, is the process of strengthening and building compelling alternatives to these cultures. My six years in Chauntey's neighborhood have made me an advocate of efforts at national cultural renewal based around a series of core values that can be imparted to kids in the context of a diversity of ethnic and racial traditions. These values include social responsibility to family, community, and the broader society and polity; opposition to violence and the search for alternative forms of expressing pain; and avoidance of the abuse of dominance across lines of gender, race, class, age, sexual preference, or physical and mental ability, and between humans and the environment. Traditions of a variety of cultures can be harnessed to this end. Poor black inner-city children should have ample opportunity to celebrate the ways their own history and culture have helped the nation move closer to those values. The life of Martin Luther King, Jr., Malcolm X, the civil rights movement, and the universal lessons of African-Americans' history of opposition to injustice stand out as only the most obvious kinds of relevant subject matter. Much of the kind of learning suggested by Afrocentric educators may also be helpful here. However, it should be also made clear that all world cultures—whether pan-African, African-American, "Western," Asian, Latino, or Native American—all need to strive harder to preserve the kinds of universal values that alone can make this whole country truly a less violent place.

Indeed, any "values education," no matter what set of historical traditions it is based on, will also need to be supplemented by education in emotional self-awareness. The ability to name painful emotion, locate its origins, and develop nonviolent ways of expressing it should also be part of our educational curricula and an especially important part of the national upbringing of inner-city children.

Afrocentric educators and artists have begun the task of inculcating self-esteem through the rediscovery of accomplished figures from the African and African-American past. In my experience, however, for many inner-city children to experience racial pride or any more general sense of satisfaction with themselves, much more needs to happen for them. They need to learn, as early as they are able, how to identify and understand the pain they experience daily and how to express it nonaggressively. In retrospect, the Kids' Club was most successful when it helped kids learn some of the rudiments of these skills. A deeper reading of the African-American experience than that currently offered by most Afrocentric educators may be also useful for this kind of education. As I and a number of other historians and writers have suggested, many of the African-American folkloric forms that flourished before the mass-media onslaught were devised as a means of identifying hurt and expressing it imaginatively. Black folklore from the rural South has been similarly filled with expressive forms, as have been its even more ancient African roots. The Afrocentric educational movement would do much service to the poorest of African-American children by emphasizing the rediscovery of these forms—from communal ceremonies and drumming, to ring shouts and expressive worship, to the blues and its evocation of vulnerability, to the toasts, and perhaps most importantly, to the performance of rap—and adding to the creative but limited efforts to integrate those traditions into the country's culture of emotional self-awareness.

Ideally, curricula based on values like these would be integrated nationwide into private community efforts and public preschool, primary and secondary education, employment training, and teenage job programs. There may also be wisdom in organizing some form of national service for eighteen-year-olds, as a kind of purposeful rite of initiation into full membership in the polity and community.

Here, the work undertaken by initiates could occur in settings that are integrated by race, class, and educational background, and gender, thus allowing the participants to search for understanding among a diversity of young people and to dispel racial hatred. Ultimately, a year of community service could also be seen as an initiation into national adult job programs for those with relatively few skills who could not otherwise find satisfactory work. In this way, values of community could be linked more closely to those of opportunity, and they might not have to be promoted so often by forceful and ultimately self-defeating means.

These tasks will no doubt put America's democratic capitalist political and economic arrangements to some of their severest tests ever. Indeed, their ultimate viability, and their often-vaunted capacity to deliver equality and liberty, may well rest on their willingness to raise the children of American inner cities in more healthy, more cherishing, more optimistic ways. Both business and political leaders will need to be enlisted on the side of any rebirth of inner-city neighborhoods. They alone currently possess the power essential for that rebirth—not to mention much of the historical responsibility to see it through. Unfortunately, there is ample reason to be skeptical about the desire and the inherent capacity of America's business community to lead the way in search of these goals. The economic incentives that have carried American manufacturing jobs to less expensive job markets in developing nations or to less heavily taxed locations on the suburban rim have on balance outweighed any enterprise-zone incentives, or any other efforts to persuade American business to create jobs in the city and give them to city dwellers who most desperately need them. Similar profit-driven priorities and a similar refusal to visit alternative ethical visions govern the largest private producers of mainstream America's consumer culture and its culture of violence.

Because of American private enterprise's structural commitment to the underemployment of inner-city residents and to poor kids' hypereducation as consumers of status-enhancing goods and violent imagery, we will need to place much of our faith for renewal on another crotchety and unwilling, but structurally more supple, source of power—American democratic government. So far in the late twentieth century, American democracy's record on inner-city rebirth has included half-hearted measures at best, long periods of malign neglect on average, and outright campaigns of hatred at the worst. The federal government has also meanwhile spent itself far into debt by waging the cold war in the most expensive ways imaginable, and it has little extra cash for even the most reasonably priced social programs. Experience has also shown that real movement in political circles may not materialize without considerable popular pressure from poor people themselves, either through increased participation in elections or a renewal of insurgent social movements. However, the American state does have something of a tentative, progressive animus of its own that occasionally inspires a ray of hope. If the American federal government's leaders get enough of an outside push, the whole bulky edifice just might slowly inch its way in directions that will be much more beneficial to poor people in cities. It has a difficult set of tasks ahead of it.

All Americans will have to play a part, though, if dreams of inner-city renewal can ever come true. Changing the political language we use when talking about the inner-city tragedy may be the first step to take. As well as forsaking our habit of making fear of crime turn into racial hatred and dedicating ourselves to greater human understanding we will also have to learn to see signs of hope in inner-city life and learn to cherish them. Here the kids of the inner city can perhaps provide their most important lessons. As the life stories I have recounted from case reports and from Chauntey's neighborhood demonstrate, inner cities like Philadelphia's are filled with youthful dreams, imagination, resourcefulness, friendliness, laughter, and desires for love and life. Ironically, Chauntey Patterson himself may have found some of that hope during his stay in a gang-racked Philadelphia juvenile prison.

The last time I saw Chauntey, he was out again, living in the house of a man who worked as a mentor for the prison. The deal was that Chauntey could hang out for as long as it took to get himself "hooked up" with some work and an apartment of his own. He had meanwhile done a fair amount of inspiring reading: he could quote from the *Autobiography of Malcolm X* and Claude Brown's *Manchild in the Promised Land*. And he could now count on a bear hug from his mentor every time he headed out the door in the morning and every time he returned home at night. Chauntey was full of plans: for himself, his girlfriend, his college, and his ability to "turn away from the crazy stuff on the streets." More importantly, though, his face had regained some of the clarity and some of the eleven-year-old's delight in life that I used to see before the summer of 1988, when he would drop his "tough face" to lick a bowl of frosting, or when, impishly, he would play basketball late on spring nights in only his underpants.

This youthful inner-city hope is a precious commodity often found in places we would least expect. We will need to look carefully to find it, and once we find it we will need to care for it tenderly. But to keep tragic historical tides from washing over the lives of still more generations of poor African-American children, we will need to find a way to remind the rest of the country of the endless possibilities of the fragile hopes that can still be found in the inner city—and dedicate our national energy to their nurture.

APPENDIX A

Statistical Tables

TABLE A.1
Households Run by a Single Woman, by Race, 1930–1983

	Black (%)	White (%)	Bl/Wh Ratio
1930	19.3	12.0	1.6
1940	17.9	10.1	1.8
1950	17.6	8.5	2.1
1960	21.7	8.1	2.7
1970	24.9	9.0	2.8
1975	35.3	10.5	3.4
1980	40.2	11.6	3.5
1983	41.9	12.2	3.4

Sources: Rates for 1930 were calculated from U.S. Bureau of the Census, *Census of the Population: General Characteristics, 1930* (Washington, D.C.: GPO), table 35, p. 27; other rates were compiled from the Census Bureau's *Current Population Reports* by William Julius Wilson in *The Truly Disadvantaged: The Inner City, the Underclass, and Public Policy* (Chicago: University of Chicago Press, 1987), p. 65, table 3.2.

TABLE A.2
Marital Status of All Poor Women Aged 14–44, by Race, 1940–1980

	Married (%)	Never Married (%)	Separated (%)	Divorced (%)	Widowed (%)
1940					
Black	43.5	32.8	21.0	2.6	4.3
White	50.7	41.8	5.9	2.1	12.0
1950					
Black	46.5	25.4	25.0	4.9	7.7
White	54.7	31.9	9.4	5.5	4.8
1960					
Black	35.5	30.6	36.6	6.5	5.8
White	49.9	28.9	14.6	9.0	6.2
1970					
Black	17.4	44.0	49.7	11.6	7.7
White	33.5	37.7	24.2	15.4	6.6
1980					
Black	12.3	60.3	38.5	25.3	5.1
White	30.7	37.3	17.8	30.3	3.0

Source: U.S. Bureau of the Census, "Public-Use Micro-Data Samples" (PUMS). See Appendix B for details on sampling and poverty cutoffs.

TABLE A.3

Marital Status of Poor Women in Northern Cities, Aged 14–44, Heading Households on Their Own, by Race, 1940–1980

	Widowed (%)	Separated (%)	Divorced (%)	Never Married (%)
1940				
Black	38.7	46.7	5.9	8.7
White	40.9	35.3	14.7	9.1
1950				
Black	20.1	54.8	11.5	13.6
White	26.9	38.3	23.1	11.7
1960				
Black	9.1	64.0	11.7	15.2
White	21.2	44.7	28.6	5.5
1970				
Black	8.2	56.1	12.6	23.0
White	11.4	48.1	31.8	8.7
1980				
Black	3.8	28.8	18.6	49.6
White	4.1	24.4	40.9	30.6

Source: U.S. Bureau of the Census, "Public-Use Micro-Data Samples" (PUMS). See Appendix B for details on sampling and poverty cutoffs.

TABLE A.4

Poor Single Mothers Not Receiving Child Support, by Reason, Marital Status, and Race, 1985

	All Reasons[a] (%)	Unable to Locate Father (%)	Unable to Establish Paternity (%)	Did Not Want Support[b] (%)
Never Married	82.1	32.8	4.7	28.3
Separated	65.8	26.0	0.0	12.4
Divorced	28.0	10.7	1.0	8.4
Black	72.9	34.3	3.4	20.3
White	49.8	15.6	1.4	15.6

Source: U.S. Bureau of the Census, "Child Support and Alimony: 1985," *Current Population Reports* (Washington, D.C.: GPO, 1986), ser. P-23, no. 154, table 2, p. 28.

[a]This includes women for whom final agreements are pending, property settlements have been made in lieu of child support, or joint custody has been granted, plus women who did not receive support for other reasons.

[b]Women often elect not to pursue child support because receiving an allotment from the father of their children would diminish their welfare payments, and would thus put them partially at the mercy of a generally less dependable source of income. Many of these women, though, may fall in the category of those who could not locate the father of their children.

TABLE A.5

Marital Status of Poor Black Women Aged 21–30, by Region of Residence, 1940–1980

	Living in Northern Cities		Living in South	
	Born in North (%)	Born in South (%)	Living in Cities (%)	Living in Rural Areas (%)
1940				
Married[a]	39.5	56.0	56.5	64.8
Never Married	41.2	19.5	24.0	21.0
Separated[b]	26.9	22.8	17.2	10.5
1950				
Married	48.5	55.8	56.8	62.8
Never Married	27.6	16.8	16.3	17.9
Separated	26.2	27.4	23.9	16.4
1960				
Married	37.1	47.4	51.6	54.1
Never Married	24.4	16.4	20.8	24.1
Separated	40.6	37.5	27.4	23.6
1970				
Married	21.5	19.0	33.4	40.4
Never Married	30.6	24.1	28.4	29.1
Separated	54.3	58.8	37.8	29.4
1980				
Married	12.9	15.2	21.4	31.2
Never Married	60.2	55.9	49.3	45.3
Separated	40.8	43.8	32.5	25.5

Source: U.S. Bureau of the Census, "Public-Use Micro-Data Samples" (PUMS) for northeastern and midwestern cities, and for southern urban and rural areas. Because the total southern-born black population in the postwar period has, on the whole, been older (hence, more likely to be married and separated) than the northern-born population, I have tried to control for age by focusing on a more restricted age group than in other tables referring to marital status. See Appendix B for notes on sampling and poverty cutoffs.
[a]The married and never-married rates were calculated from the total female or male population. The rates of separation were based on the number of ever-married people.
[b]Separation rates were calculated on the basis of all ever-married women.

TABLE A.6

Rate of Homicide Offenses Committed without Firearms among Total U.S. Population and among 15- to 19-Year-Olds, 1961–1990

	U.S. (per 1 million)	15- to 19-Year-Olds (per 1 million)
1961	15.8[a]	na[b]
1966	17.4	12.1
1968	19.7	15.1
1975	27.3	22.4
1980	30.7	28.1
1990	24.1	21.6

Source: U.S. Department of Justice, Federal Bureau of Investigation, *Uniform Crime Reports,* for relevant years.
[a]These figures are from a group of selected larger municipalities with a total population of 79,711,762.
[b]Data not available.

TABLE A.7

Suicide Rates by Race and Sex for Total Population and for 15- to 19-Year-Olds in Philadelphia, Selected Periods, 1957–1990

	Total Population			
	Men		Women	
	Nonwhite	White	Nonwhite	White
1957–1960	6.7	15.6	2.5	5.8
1961–1965	9.2	22.6	3.3	8.8
1966–1970	14.8	16.7	4.2	9.8
1971–1975	15.5	20.0	4.9	10.6
1976–1980	11.4	22.6	4.3	9.1
1981–1985	14.2	24.0	3.4	8.1
1986–1990	18.3	26.4	3.6	5.1

	15- to 19-Year-Olds			
	Men		Women	
	Nonwhite	White	Nonwhite	White
1957–1960	1.4	1.7	1.4	1.3
1961–1965	6.8	5.8	0.9	0.7
1966–1970	9.0	6.5	2.0	3.3
1971–1975	10.1	10.0	5.2	5.6
1976–1980	8.3	15.0	4.0	5.1
1981–1985	8.0	18.4	3.5	5.2
1986–1990	20.1	16.0	3.4	2.1

Source: Philadelphia Department of Public Health, *Annual Birth and Death Reports for Philadelphia* for relevant years. The rates were calculated by dividing the total number of incidents in each period by the total population of each age/sex/race category during each year of the period (as listed in table 1 of each *Report*), and multiplying the result by 100,000.

TABLE A.8

Homicide Victimization among Children Four and Under, by Race, in Philadelphia, Selected Periods, 1957–1990

	Nonwhite	White
1957–1960	8.7	1.9
1961–1965	11.2	1.5
1966–1970	17.9	1.6
1971–1975	23.4	2.5
1976–1980	15.5	3.7
1981–1985	14.9	5.6
1986–1990	15.9	7.5

Source: Philadelphia Department of Public Health, *Annual Birth and Death Reports for Philadelphia* for relevant years. The rates were calculated by dividing the total number of incidents in each five-year period by the total estimated population of people four years of age and under for each race in each of the same five years (as listed in table 1 of each *Report*), and multiplying the result by 100,000.

TABLE A.9

Homicide Victimization Rates, per 100,000 Women Aged 40–59, by Race, in Philadelphia, Selected Periods, 1957–1990

	Nonwhite	White
1957–1960	8.6	1.5
1961–1965	6.9	1.5
1966–1970	14.1	1.7
1971–1975	17.8	2.2
1976–1980	11.8	2.0
1981–1985	11.6	2.1
1986–1990	10.3	3.3

Source: Philadelphia Department of Public Health, *Annual Birth and Death Reports for Philadelphia* for relevant years. The rates were calculated by dividing the number of reported incidents during each five-year period by the sum of the estimated total number of women aged 40 to 59 of each race for each of the same five years (as listed in table 1 of each *Report*), and multiplying the result by 100,000.

APPENDIX B:

Technical Notes Concerning Public-Use Micro-Data Samples (PUMS)

THE SAMPLE

The Census Bureau's Public-Use Micro-Data Samples were indispensible tools for measuring changes in family structure in the poor urban African-American population. They also provided comparative data for poor black people and poor white people. For every census year since 1940 the bureau has asked especially detailed questions of between 1 percent and 15 percent of the population, and the bureau distributes the resulting data on computer tapes. The samples are thus all large enough that the differences between groups and the changes over time that I observed are statistically very significant. To obtain the data in tables 2, 3, and 5, I used a sample composed of the data from the south-central, southeastern, northeastern, and midwestern states, which includes all of those lying east and including Texas, Arkansas, Missouri, Iowa, and Minnesota. All the states of the former Confederacy (where most of the great migration for African-Americans began) are included, as are all the states with the largest midwestern and northeastern cities. For each census year, I retrieved data for the population living in metropolitan areas.

CALCULATING POVERTY CUTOFFS

The most complicated challenge in using the PUMS data for this project was to measure characteristics of a reasonably consistent sample of poor people in each census year from 1940 to 1980. The problem arises from the fact that government agencies first defined a "poverty line" only in 1959, and the PUMS data do not include poverty as a variable until 1970. In constructing my sample of the population living in poverty, I began with the 1980 poverty cutoffs as defined by the Census Bureau by size of household. I then adjusted each of those levels for changes in the cost-of-living index for each previous census year. The cost-of-living figures I used for 1970, 1960, and 1950 were derived from those listed in Citicorp Database Services' 1990 file tabulation of the consumer price index, as measured by the U.S. Department of Labor's Bureau of Labor Statistics.* The ratios listed are as follows:

1980	1,000.000
1970	485.312
1960	376.756
1950	302.682

To determine the ratio for 1940, I used the figure for "Consumer Prices" listed by Harold Vatter in *The U.S. Economy in World War II* ([New York: Columbia University Press, 1985], p. 91). Based on a 1947–49 average of 100, which I used as a proxy for the 1950 figure, the 1940 rate listed by Vatter was 59.9, which corresponds to a figure of 181.307 in relation to a 1980 average of 1,000. The resulting poverty cutoffs, in dollars, for households of different sizes appear in the following table.

TABLE B.1
Poverty Cutoffs Based on 1980 Figures Adjusted by Consumer Price Index, by Household Size, 1940 – 1980 (In Dollars)

Persons in Household	Census Year				
	1940	1950	1960	1970	1980
1	668	1,113	1,389	1,789	3,686
2	856	1,430	1,779	2,292	4,723
3	1,049	1,752	2,180	2,809	5,787
4	1,344	2,243	2,793	3,597	7,412
5	1,591	2,656	3,306	4,259	8,776
6	1,798	3,001	3,736	4,812	9,915
7	2,037	3,401	4,234	5,453	11,237
8	2,263	3,779	4,703	6,059	12,484
9 +	2,684	4,483	5,581	7,188	14,812

Source: Calculated on basis of 1980 figures, U.S. Bureau of the Census, *1980 Public-Use Micro-Data Samples: Technical Documentation* (Washington, D.C.: GPO), p. K35.

* "Consumer Price Index," *Citibase* (Citicorp Database Services, 1990 file) U.S. Department of Labor, Bureau of Labor Statistics. I owe much to Doug Mills of Princeton University's Computer and Information Technology for helping me locate and retrieve this information.

PUMS family income data are not broken down by unit dollar amounts, except for 1940. The poverty cutoff values I used corresponded to the closest available figures in the census survey, resulting in the following data.

TABLE B.2

Poverty Cutoffs Adjusted to Available Values in Micro-Data Samples (In Dollars)

Persons in Household	Year				
	1940	1950	1960	1970	1980
1	668	1,099	1,399	1,799	3,685
2	856	1,399	1,799	2,299	4,725
3	1,049	1,799	2,199	2,799	5,785
4	1,344	2,199	2,799	3,599	7,415
5	1,591	2,699	3,299	4,299	8,775
6	1,798	2,999	3,699	4,799	9,915
7	2,037	3,399	4,199	5,499	11,235
8	2,263	3,799	4,699	6,099	12,485
9+	2,684	4,499	5,599	7,199	14,815

NOTES

All citations to case reports are in code form, following the agreement I made with all of the agency staff members who gave me permission to use their papers. The following abbreviations apply for coded citations to the case reports:

BB   Papers of the Big Brothers Association of Philadelphia

FS   Papers of the Family Services division of the Protestant Episcopal City Mission

GPFS   Papers of the Greater Philadelphia Federation of Settlements

SA   Papers of the Sheltering Arms program of the Protestant Episcopal City Mission

In the body of the notes I use the following abbreviations, as in the chapters:

BBA   Big Brothers Association

PECM Protestant Episcopal City Mission

INTRODUCTION

1. The term *underclass* was first used by the Swedish social scientist Gunnar Myrdal in the early 1960s. It then fell into disuse, but was resuscitated by popular journalists in 1977. Scholars then latched on to the term with nearly universal enthusiasm in the 1980s. See Gunnar Myrdal, *The Challenge to Affluence* (New York: Pantheon, 1963), pp. 34–49; George Russell, "The American Underclass," *Time*, August 19, 1977, pp. 12–18; and Ken Auletta, *The Underclass* (New York: Vintage, 1982). On current scholars' embrace of the

term, see William Julius Wilson, "Social Theory and Public Agenda Research: The Challenge of Studying Inner-City Social Disloca- tions" in *American Sociological Review* 5 (February 1991), pp. 4–5; Paul Peterson, "The Urban Underclass and the Poverty Paradox," in *The Urban Underclass,* ed. Christopher Jencks and Paul Peterson (Washington, D.C.: Brookings Institution, 1991), pp. 3–4; Christo- pher Jencks, "What Is the Underclass—and Is It Growing?" *Focus* 1 (Spring/Summer 1989): pp. 14–26; and Jencks, *Rethinking Social Policy: Race Poverty, and the Underclass* (Cambridge, Mass: Harvard University Press, 1992). Ken Auletta lauds the word as a conve- nient "abbreviation" in the introduction to his book. At the same time, he said, "I worried about the racial freight the subject car- ried. What was the proper racial etiquette? What were the correct code words? At first I used the word *underclass* gingerly, fearful that it was somehow racist" (p. xii). The social scientist Paul Peterson later wrote in his preface that the term was "powerful" because

> "under" suggests the lowly passive and dismissive, yet at the same time the disreputable, dangerous, disruptive, dark, evil, and even hellish. Apart from these personal attributes, it suggests subjection, subordination, and deprivation. All these meanings are perhaps best brought together in Richard Wagner's *The Ring of the Nibelung.* Wotan goes under the earth to wrest the ring from the malicious Alberich, who has used it to enslave a vile and debased subhuman population. (p. 3)

2. William Julius Wilson, *The Truly Disadvantaged: The Inner City, the Underclass, and Public Policy* (Chicago: University of Chicago Press, 1987), chaps. 2 and 3. Quotation from p. 56. For a fuller discus- sion of these ideas, see chap. 2.
3. See Mike Davis, *City of Quartz: Excavating the Future in Los Angeles* (New York: Vintage, 1990), pp. 221–322.

CHAPTER 1: THE EXPLOSION OF INNER-CITY DESPERATION

1. The story of Johnnie "Bojack" Dungee comes from report BB037.
2. Municipal Court of Philadelphia, Juvenile Division, *Annual Report,* (Philadelphia, 1959), table on "Reasons for Referral to Court, by Race."
3. Philadelphia Department of Public Health, *Annual Birth and Death Report for Philadelphia* (Philadelphia, 1960).
4. The historian Herbert Gutman has demonstrated that among black people, the so-called nuclear family survived the most crushing psy- chological circumstances of the slave plantation and slaveholders'

practice of selling family members to distant locations. After emancipation, those families that had been broken up more often than not reunited, and the two-parent family became the backbone of the sharecropping livelihood in the South. According to Gutman, neither economic peonage under the sharecropping regime nor racial violence and disfranchisement shook the predominance of two-parent families among African-Americans, nor did the supposedly disruptive life as migrant and new settler in northern cities. (*The Black Family in Slavery and Freedom* [New York: Vintage, 1976], chaps. 9–10, and app. A). See also Elizabeth Pleck, *Black Migration and Poverty* (New York: Academic Press, 1979), chap. 6.; and Frank Furstenberg, John Modell, and Theodore Hershberg, "The Origins of the Black Female-Headed Household: The Impact of the Urban Experience," in *Philadelphia: Work, Space, Family, Group Experience in the Nineteenth Century,* ed. Theodore Hershberg (New York: Oxford University Press, 1981), pp. 435–54.

5. In the 1850s and 1880s, Furstenberg and his colleagues found, the overwhelming majority of women who ran households on their own reported themselves to be widows: three-quarters of all black single parents who lived on their own did so after the death of their husband (Furstenberg et al., "Origins of the Black Female-Headed Household," pp. 446–50). The historian Elizabeth Pleck, looking at black families in Boston during the same period, has countered that many of the black women who told census takers that they were widows may have actually been trying to conceal their true status as never-married, separated, or divorced mothers. She, like Furstenberg and his colleagues, tried to match the names of these women with names of men in death records, with contradictory results. Pleck found that rates of widowhood based on death records were much lower than those in the Boston census manuscripts. She dismisses evidence documented by Furstenberg and his colleagues in Philadelphia that suggests the opposite as "less a question of cause and effect than sheer coincidence" (*Black Migration and Poverty,* pp. 17–73). None of these researchers of nineteenth-century black family arrangements checked to see if other racial and ethnic groups had similar tendencies toward dissimulation, so there is no evidence that the immediate circumstances of the formation of single-parent families differed for blacks and whites.

6. On traditions of child fosterage, see Robert Hill, *The Strengths of Black Families* (New York: Emerson Hall, 1971); Carol Stack, *All Our Kin: Strategies for Survival in a Black Community* (New York: Harper, 1972); and Andrew Miller, "Social Science, Social Policy, and the Heritage of African-American Families," in *The "Underclass" Debate: Views from History,* ed. Michael Katz (Princeton N.J.: Princeton University Press, 1993), pp. 254–92.

7. Because much of the detailed published information on poor families of today does not compare racial groups, and because much of the available data on various racial groups is not broken down by economic status, information from long-form questionnaires, and from the "Public-Use Micro-Data Samples" that are based on those questionnaires, has been indispensable for this section. The Census Bureau has distributed this information on computer tape for each census year since 1940.

8. Furstenberg et al., "Origins of the Black Female-Headed Household," pp. 441, 444; Gutman, *The Black Family,* chap. 10 and app. A; Pleck, *Black Migration and Poverty,* pp. 151–97; and Jacqueline Jones, *Labor of Love, Labor of Sorrow* pp. 152–95. Spotty evidence from the early years of the twentieth century suggests that there was little change during the early twentieth century in the circumstances under which families run by single women were formed. Most of the New York City black families that Gutman studied were headed by older women: less than 1 percent of the women running a household on their own were teenagers, and only 18 percent were between ages 20 and 29. Twenty-seven percent were older than 40, despite the fact that only a tenth of the black population was over 45. Most single mothers who ran families on their own, we can infer, did so because their husband had died, or because they were divorced or separated. (Gutman, *The Black Family,* p. 516, table A-45, p. 511, table A-40).

   Information from my 1940 "Micro-Data" sample suggests that, on the eve of the war (as had been true sixty years earlier), most women of both races who headed families on their own were widows:

Marital Status of Urban Female Heads of Household, Philadelphia, 1880, and U.S. Census "Micro-Data Sample," 1940, by Race

	Never Married	Separated	Divorced	Widowed
1880				
Black	5.0	19.1	1.1	74.3
White	2.3	19.8	1.0	77.0
1940				
Black	8.6	25.6	4.2	61.7
White	12.2	14.1	6.8	66.8

9. Stack, *All Our Kin,* pp. 124–25. See also Joyce Ladner, *Tomorrow's Tomorrow: The Black Woman* (Garden City, N.Y.: Anchor, 1971), pp. 60, 70–75; Joyce Aschenbrenner, "Extended Families Among Black Americans," *Journal of Comparative Family Studies,* 4 (1973), 257–68; Harriette Pipes McAdoo, "Black Mothers and the Extended Family Support Network," in *The Black Woman,* LaFrances Rodgers-Rose, ed. (Beverly Hills, Calif.: Sage Publications, 1980), pp. 125–44; Demitri B. Shimkin, Gloria Jean Louie,

and Dennis A. Frate, "The Black Extended Family: A Basic Rural Institution and a Mechanism of Urban Adaptation," in *The Extended Family in Black Societies*, ed. Demitri B. Shimkin, Edith M. Shimkin, and Dennis A. Frate. (Den Haag, Netherlands: Moulton, 1978), pp. 25–149; Joyce Aschenbrenner, "Continuities and Variation in Black Family Structure," ibid., 181–200; Regina E. Holloman and Fannie E. Lewis, "The 'Clan': Case Study of a Black Extended Family in Chicago," ibid., 201–38; Lenus Jack, Jr., "Kinship and Residential Propinquity in Black New Orleans: The Wesleys," ibid., 239–70; and Kiyotaki Aoyagi, "Kinship and Friendship in Black Los Angeles: A Study of Black Migrants from Texas," ibid., 272–354. For a historical discussion, see Gutman, *The Black Family*.

10. See also, Reynolds Farley, *Blacks and Whites: Narrowing the Gap?* (Cambridge, Mass.: Harvard University Press, 1984), pp. 160–63; Mary Jo Bane, "The Politics and Policies of the Feminization of Poverty," in *The Politics of Social Policy in the United States,* ed. Margaret Weir, Ann Shola Orloff, and Theda Skocpol (Princeton, N.J.: Princeton University Press, 1988), pp. 381–96.

11. The rise of African-American single-parent families has often been blamed on high levels of teenage pregnancy among black girls. Actually, though, teenage-pregnancy among young black women has declined rapidly during most of the post–World War II era. The increase in single-parent households reflects the fact that teenage girls who do have a child have been less and less likely to marry after the birth of their child.

12. Mary Jo Bane and David T. Ellwood's "Single Mothers and Their Living Arrangements" (Grant report for U.S. Department of Health and Human Services, grant 92A-82, 1984) contains similar data on women of all economic groups. On the relationship between the increasing rates of marital breakup and the increasing rates of single-parent households, see Phillips Cutright, "Components of Change in the Number of Female Family Heads Aged Fifteen to Forty-four: United States, 1940–1970," *Journal of Marriage and the Family* 36 (November 1974): 714–21, especially tables 2 and 4. During the 1950s, Cutright showed, the likelihood that women who had lived through marital disruption would become heads of households grew dramatically. Cutright found that between 1940 and 1970, and especially in the 1950s and 1960, separated, divorced, and widowed women became increasingly likely to have children and at the same time much more likely to decide to live on their own after their marriage ended. The fertility rate and the "propensity to form separate families" (p. 716) among mothers in disrupted marital statuses increased at about an equal pace for both blacks and whites. In fact, Cutright concluded that

these demographic factors were the most important reasons for the overall growth in the number of families run by single women in the postwar era. However, because blacks were more likely than whites to be separated or divorced, more black women were "at risk" of being single parents. Thus, when the likelihood that divorced and separated women would actually become heads of families increased for both races during the 1950s, the disparity between the proportion of all black and all white women who were family heads grew dramatically.

13. The figures for never-married women who had not been able to find the father of their children might reflect as little as half of the women who had the same problem. A large proportion of poor never-married women with children who took part in the Census Bureau survey claimed they did not want support. This may reflect their anxiety about reductions in welfare checks, as well as their desire to avoid less reliable sources of income like child support, or the fact that they made some kind of informal arrangement for paternal support. However, many, or even most, of these women may also have had trouble locating the father of their children.

14. There has been much controversy surrounding measurements of violence in black communities. I have relied exclusively on homicide rates, for several reasons. Because murder is overwhelmingly committed by perpetrators who are the same race as their victims, these statistics clearly focus on life within African-American communities. Also, unlike rates of black arrests for burglary, robbery, sexual assault, and other crimes, which have also been on the increase in cities, the rate of death by homicide has not been subject to inflation due to the racial biases of police officers or the courts. (This is less true in the South, where black-on-black murder was, for much of this century, generally ignored by authorities who also often covered up white-on-black homicide, such as lynchings.) See Roger Lane, *The Roots of Violence in Black Philadelphia, 1860–1900* (Cambridge, Mass.: Harvard University Press, 1986), pp. 134–35; and Lane, *Violent Death in the City: Suicide, Accident and Murder in Nineteenth Century Philadelphia* (Cambridge, Mass.: Harvard University Press, 1979), pp. 113–14.

15. See Ted Robert Gurr, "Historical Trends in Violent Crime," in *Violence in America*, vol. 1, *The History of Crime*, ed. Ted Robert Gurr (Newbury Park, Calif.: Sage, 1989), pp. 22, 36.

16. See Lane, *Roots of Violence*, pp. 2–3; and Gurr, "Historical Trends," pp. 38–40. In the immediate aftermath of World War II, African-Americans were about twelve times as likely as whites to be victims of homicide in Philadelphia. However, the rate of 26.4 per 100,000 tabulated by the Philadelphia Department of Public Health for death by homicide among nonwhite residents was probably some-

what off the peak of the 1920s and 1930s, when bootlegging and other organized criminal activities had brought a wave of violent death to the streets and other public spaces of the city. Most of the wide gap between black and white murder rates probably reflected restrictions on immigration, which had helped bring the white murder rate down dramatically during the 1930s nationwide. Actual rates of murder *victimization* have not been tabulated for the 1920s. However, if the historian Eric Monkonnen's data for New York are any indication, the level for blacks was about 30 per 100,000 in the early thirties (see Gurr's calculations, in "Historical Trends," p. 39). The historian Gloria Count-van Manen gives a homicide arrest rate in 1930 among blacks in Washington, D.C., of forty in her study *Crime and Suicide in the Nation's Capital: Toward-Macro-Historical Perspectives* ([New York: Praeger, 1977], pp. 200–201). Lane lists a black homicide conviction rate of 13.3 for 1921 through 1928 (*Roots of Violence*, p. 166). Rates of convictions are usually at least half as high as victimization rates. See Margaret Zahn's tabulation of national murder rates from *Vital Statistics* and *Uniform Crime Reports* figures, ("Homicide in the Twentieth Century," in *Violence in America*, ed. Gurr, p. 219).

17. See the following *Philadelphia Inquirer* articles: "Philadelphia Gangs: Slow Death on the Killing Ground," February 16, 1975; "Battle in the Streets," March 18, 1973; "Handful of Gang Members Affects Lives of All," July 19, 1971; "'Nothing Better to Do So We Get Together and Rumble,'" July 20, 1971; and "Other Cities Curb Gang Violence; 'Band-Aid' Approach Fails Here," July 18, 1971. For a comparison between Philadelphia and New York gangs, see "The Street Fighters," *Philadelphia Inquirer Magazine*, October 14, 1973, pp. 23–29. All of these articles are filed at Temple University's Urban Archives, clippings files for *Philadelphia Evening Bulletin* and *Inquirer* box on "gangs."

18. See "One Family Conquers Gang War," *Parade*, May 4, 1980, pp. 8–9; and "New Direction Helps Curb Turf 'Wars,'" *Philadelphia Evening Bulletin*, June 24, 1980, pp. 1, 5.

19. See Daniel Lazare, "How the Drug War Created Crack," *Village Voice* (January 23, 1990, pp. 22–29; and Bruce D. Johnson and Ali Manwar, "Towards a Paradigm of Drug Eras: Previous Drug Eras Help to Model the Crack Epidemic in New York City during the 1980s" (Paper presented at the Forty-seventh Annual Meeting of the American Society of Criminology, San Francisco, November 1991). See also Terry Williams, *The Cocaine Kids: The Inside Story of a Teenage Drug Ring* (Reading, Mass.: Addison-Wesley, 1989); Arthur Kempton, "Native Sons," *New York Review of Books*, April 11, 1991, pp. 55–57; Tom Mieczkowski, "Understanding Life in the Crack Culture," *National Institute of Justice Reports*, no. 212

(November–December 1989): 7–9; and Leon Bing, *Do or Die* (New York: Harper Perennial, 1991).

20. See David Zucchino, "Agents Go after the Zulu Nation, a Drug Gang Known for Its Terrorism," *Philadelphia Inquirer,* December 3, 1992, p. A-1.

21. See Lazare, "Drug War Created Crack"; Mike Davis, *City of Quartz* (New York: Vintage, 1990), pp. 267–322; and Williams, *Cocaine Kids*. On the relationship between drugs and violence, see Paul J. Goldstein, "Drugs and Violent Crime," in *Pathways to Criminal Violence*, ed. Neil A. Weiner and Marvin E. Wolfgang (Beverly Hills, Calif.: Sage Publications, 1989), pp. 16–48; Paul J. Goldstein, Henry Brownstein, Patrick J. Ryan, and Patricia A. Belucci "Crack and Homicide in New York City, 1988: A Conceptually Based Event Analysis," *Contemporary Drug Problems* 16 (Winter 1989): 651–87; Mario De La Rosa, Elizabeth Y. Lambert, Bernhard Gropper, "Drugs and Violence: Causes, Correlates, and Consequences" (Washington National Institution on Drug Abuse Research, Washington, D.C., 1990, Monograph 103), 177–207.

22. The criminologist Marvin E. Wolfgang, in his seminal study, "Criminal Homicide with Special Reference to Philadelphia, 1948–1952" (Ph. D. diss., University of Pennsylvania, 1955), found that killings between black husbands and wives occurred at seventeen times the rate of whites—at a time when the overall black murder rate was less than twelve times as high, according to my calculations of average annual rates using figures in Wolfgang's table 25 (p. 218) and U.S. Census figures of total population. Tracing changes in homicide rates between people in marriages and other intimate relationships is particularly difficult, given the lack of information and variations in measurement. Comparing Wolfgang's detailed Philadelphia figures with national rates compiled for 1976 to 1985 by the policy analysts James A. Mercy and Linda Saltzman at the Centers for Disease Control ("Fatal Violence among Spouses in the U.S., 1976–85," *American Journal of Public Health* 79 [May 1989]: 595–600), it appears that there may have been at least a gradual increase in domestic murder rates during the postwar period. In Wolfgang's study, the marital murder rate was 11.2 per 100,000 married black Philadelphians; and by 1976, a year of declining violence in the streets, the normally much lower national rate was about at 1950 levels. (My calculations for 1948 to 1952 are based on Wolfgang's figures and the total married black population listed in the 1950 census. National rates are from Mercy and Saltzman, "Fatal Violence," p. 597. fig. 3.) Because these rates are based on the married population, they have become less significant indicators of domestic homicide as marriage has become rarer. The psychologist Angela Browne and the

criminologist Kirk R. Williams have charted increases in national murder rates for unmarried partners in their "Trends in Partner Homicide by Relationship Type and Gender: 1976–87" (Paper presented at the annual meeting of the American Society of Criminology, Baltimore, November 1990). However, the criminologist Carolyn Block found that "spousal/intimate homicide" in Chicago decreased steadily from a peak in 1967 throughout the 1980s. ("Trends in Homicide Syndromes and Economic Cycles in Chicago over Twenty-five Years: Maps and Charts to Accompany a Presentation to the American Society of Criminology, Session on Disaggregating Homicide" [Paper presented to the annual meeting of the American Society of Criminology, San Francisco, November, 1991]). See also Margaret Zahn, "Homicide in the Twentieth Century," *Violence in America*, ed. Gurr, p. 229.

23. See app. A, tables 6–9. For similar trends in various kinds of homicide in another city, see Richard Block and Carolyn Block, "Homicide Syndromes and Vulnerability: Violence in Chicago Community Areas over Twenty-five Years" (Paper presented at the Forty-seventh Annual Meeting of the American Society of Criminology, San Francisco, November 1991) and Block, "Trends in Homicide Syndromes."

24. Charles Silberman, *Criminal Violence, Criminal Justice* (New York: Random House, 1978), pp. 119–23. Researchers who have conducted more systematic statistical studies to determine whether the high rates of violence among African Americans are due solely to disproportionate poverty have found contradictory results. However, in a review of the abundant social-scientific literature on this subject, the sociologist Augustine Kposawa has suggested that the studies showing a high proportion of blacks in a population to be a better predictor of high murder rates than economic variables tend to be studies that focus on cities. These contrast with studies that include rural jurisdictions, where poverty is often a better predictor of homicide. In his own study of homicide rates on the county level, Kposawa found that the proportion of blacks in any urban or rural county was by far the best predictor of high rates of violence, and that the percentage of people in poverty was a strong predictor of homicide only in rural areas. He also noted, however, that counties with high Hispanic and Native American populations also tended to have relatively high homicide rates, though never as high as those among African-Americans. Part of the reason for high rates of violence in urban America evidently is the way the country has excluded various racial or ethnic groups ("A Comparative Analysis of U.S. Homicide Rates: Subculture of Violence and Poverty" [Description of data set presented at Haverford College, January 1990]). See also Gary LaFree, Kriss A. Drass,

and Patrick O'Day, "Race and Crime in Postwar America: Determinants of African-American and White Rates, 1958–1988" (Paper presented at the annual meeting of the American Society of Criminology, Baltimore, November 1990), pp. 5–6.

25. Characters like Brer Rabbit and the Signifyin' Monkey, who may have even more ancient roots in West Africa, were virtuosos of ruse and indirection, and they apparently served as role models for slaves and then freedmen in artful and devious relations with white people. See Lawrence Levine, *Black Culture and Black Consciousness* (Oxford: University of Oxford Press, 1977), pp. 300–366; and John W. Roberts, *From Trickster to Badman: The Black Folk Hero in Slavery and Freedom* (Philadelphia: University of Pennsylvania Press, 1989), pp. 17–64.

26. From "The Fall," a toast recorded in Attica prison by Dennis Wepman, Ronald B. Newman, and Murray B. Binderman (*The Life: The Lore and Folk Poetry of the Black Hustler* [Philadelphia: University of Pennsylvania Press, 1976], p. 80). See also Roger Abrahams, *Deep Down in the Jungle . . . : Negro Narrative Folklore from the Streets of Philadelphia* (Chicago: Aldine, 1963), pp. 61–87.

27. See Thomas Kochman, "Rapping in the Ghetto," in *The Black Experience: Soul* ed. Lee Rainwater (New Brunswick, N.J.: Transaction Books, 1973), p. 66. In his autobiography, Piri Thomas used "to cop" as a synonym for the more familiar "hustle": "What have you got now? Nothing. / What will you ever have? Nothing. . . . / Unless you cop for yourself" (*Down These Mean Streets* [New York: Signet, 1967], p. 10).

28. Quotation from Edith Folb, *Runnin' Down Some Lines: The Language and Culture of Black Teenagers* (Cambridge, Mass.: Harvard University Press, 1980), p. 71.

29. See also Folb, *Runnin' Down Some Lines,* chap. 4.

30. Levine, *Black Culture,* pp. 214–15, 240–53, 267, 344–50.

31. Abrahams, *Deep Down in the Jungle,* p. 47; Ulf Hannerz, *Soulside: Inquiries into Ghetto Culture and Community* (New York: Columbia University Press, 1969), pp. 129, 218; Folb, *Runnin' Down Some Lines,* pp. 92–95. See also Herbert Foster, *Ribin', Jivin', and Playin' the Dozens* (Cambridge, Mass.: Ballinger, 1986).

32. On the cathartic function of earlier toasts, see John Dollard, "The Dozens: The Dialect of Insult," *American Imago* 1 (1939): 3–24; Samuel Sperling, "On the Psychodynamics of Teasing," *Journal of the American Psychoanalytic Association* 1 (1953): 470; and Abrahams, *Deep Down in the Jungle,* pp. 52–56.

33. SA338, 10.

34. BB042, 14–14A. Elsewhere in the case reports, the imperative of a response to victimization also frequently galvanized gang loyalties. "Malcolm explained that some time ago he and a friend were walk-

ing passed [*sic*] a street corner and were verbally abused by a small group of boys. He said he became angry but could do nothing about it because there were too many boys in the group. Several days later Malcolm stated that he and five of his friends saw two of these boys on a corner and began fighting them. The parents of the boys had them arrested" (BB031, 12). See also BB001, 21; BB023, 16; BB048, 14; BB094, 3 among other examples.

35. BB042, 9A.

36. See SA999, 8, about mail-order guns.

37. See SA048, 5, 27; SA478; SA009, 12; SA609, 4; SA629, 4; and SA999, 8. See also Ann Campbell, *The Girls in the Gang: A Report from New York* (Oxford: Oxford University Press, 1984), chap. 1; and Welm Brown, "Black Female Gang Members in Philadelphia," *International Journal of Offender Therapy and Comparative Criminology* 21 (1977): 221–28.

38. FS070. For other territorial references, see BB010, 3A; BB021, 5; BB025, 2A; BB081, 15.

39. BB024, 1. See also BB023, 19, among many other similar examples.

40. BB023, 6. See also 16.

41. SA048, 27.

42. Quoted in Lewis Yablonski, *The Violent Gang* (New York: Macmillan, 1962), pp. 8, 22–23.

43. "Badman Dan and Two-Gun Green" quoted from Binderman et al., *The Life*, pp. 130–31. On the Signifyin' Monkey, Stackolee, and Shine, see Roger Abrahams, *Deep Down in the Jungle*, pp. 97–172; on the Signifyin' Monkey, Duriella du Fontaine, Honky-Tonk Bud, and Stagger Lee (another name for Stackolee), see Binderman et al., *The Life*, pp. 21–29, 44–50, 54–71, and 135–38.

44. See FS069, 8.6, 26.8.

45. SA048, 4.

46. FS069, 8.6, 26.8.

47. Quoted portions from BB001, 19, 31, 33, 34, 35, 38. See also BB028, 9; BB031, 3; BB020, 10; BB095, 13.

48. After Marty was chased by police for stealing money from parking meters with his buddies, he explained to his social worker that "'we believe when you are caught by police you are chicken.' I [The caseworker] said to Marty the fact that you run away from the policeman shows that you are a worse chicken' [*sic*]. He looked and smiled and said, 'Oh, that's not the way we believe. Our leader said if we are caught we are chicken'" (FS069, p. 8.5). Another fellow, aged fifteen, who "tends to dress as a jitterbug and emulates them in words and deeds," had his career as a client of BBA interrupted by five months in a local institution on an armed robbery charge. Upon his return into the neighborhood, he

"seemed quite boastful of the fact that he had been in a reform school and has been making it sound attractive for the rest of the youngsters" (BB038, pp. 9–10).

49. Lew Yablonski, in his career as a gang worker with the New York City Youth Board, found that, much to his frustration, the gang he was assigned to welcomed his arrival as a sign of increasing legitimacy in the street. At the same time, it was also clear that the nature of his mission was no mystery to the gang members. "Having a worker makes you a real 'down' club. All 'bad' clubs have a 'man' trying to change them." The gang leader Yablonski got to know played along with a slate of "positive activities" like baseball games and dances, and even accepted the title of "social club" for his gang because he expected to get Yablonski's help in getting parole for several incarcerated members of the group. Though this did not happen, Duke, the gang leader, did manage to parlay his group's legitimacy, achieved by being associated with the Youth Board, into increased membership and increased potential for violent activity. See Yablonski, *Violent Gang*, pp. 44, 51–69.

50. BB037, 16; 7–8. See also BB042, 14; BB085, 10; and BB090, 13.

51. For more on the link between "badness" and racial identity, see chap. 4.

52. Explorations of the role of emotional factors in inner-city social life are not new. African-American essayists and novelists like W. E. B. Du Bois, James Baldwin, Ralph Ellison, and Toni Morrison have long sought to uncover the roots of desperation among poor black people in the cities. Their lead was also followed by a few academic anthropologists. For the ethnographer Elliot Liebow, a sense of "failure" and "humiliation" undergirded all of the "shadow values" he saw expressed on a Washington, D.C., streetcorner:

> Sometimes [the streetcorner man] sits down and cries at the humiliation of it all. Sometimes he strikes out at [his wife], or the children. . . . Increasingly he turns to the street corner where a shadow system of values constructed out of public fictions serves to accommodate just such men as he, permitting them to be men once again provided they do not look too closely at one another's credentials (*Tally's Corner*, pp. 212–13).

The sociologist and ethnographer Lee Rainwater also wrote eloquently of inner-city residents' obligation to "find ways of living with the knowledge that they are embarrassments in their own world" and Rainwater even declared that their "identity problems . . . make the soul-searching of middle-class adolescents and adults seem like a conspicuous consumption of psychic riches" (*Behind Ghetto Walls*, p. 373). People who work in education and social services in Philadelphia and elsewhere have also pointed the way toward this kind of analysis. The caseworkers who wrote the reports I read were keenly interested in the emotional life of the children they encountered, and many of the more forward-looking school administrators, health workers, and social workers I have met in connection with the kids in my neighborhood also have developed a keen awareness for evidence of self-esteem and caring in children's lives. More recently, the psychologists Richard Majors and Janet Mancini Billson have offered a complex picture, based on interviews, of black men's coping styles in living with pain; these men's experiences closely resemble those of many boys I have met in Chauntey's neighborhood. (See Majors and Bilson, *Cool Pose: The Dilemmas of Black Manhood in America* [New York: Lexington, 1992].)

Following the lead of all of these researchers, I have based my own conclusions in this chapter overwhelmingly on long personal contact and friendship with a group of children, namely, Chauntey Patterson and his peers. In fact, it was only after spending a lot of time with kids in my neighborhood that I could even begin to grasp that the emotions they felt were enormously important to understanding the history of inner-city community life. When I describe kids' feelings in this and future chapters, I try not only to tell their stories but also to present my observations in the context of my own intervention into kids' lives.

53. The quoted phrases are from Charles A. Valentine, *Culture and Poverty: Critique and Counter-Proposals* (Chicago: University of Chicago Press, 1968), p. 143. One even more optimistic observer of the ethics of black hustlers wrote that "in effect the hustler's society represents the lower-class black's original and indigenous means of waging a 'war on poverty.' Members of this subculture, and numerous ghetto residents, feel that the hustler's anti-poverty program is considerably more successful than the government's" (Julius Hudson, "The Hustling Ethic," in *Rappin' and Stylin' Out: Communication in Urban Black America*, ed. Thomas Kochman et al. (Urbana: University of Illinois Press, 1972), p. 121.

On resistance in general see James C. Scott, *Domination and the Arts of Resistance: Hidden Transcripts* (New Haven, Conn.: Yale University Press, 1990). The historian Robin D. G. Kelley has answered Scott's call to study the "infrapolitics" of the poor (though he disagrees with Scott that the concept of hegemony ought to be discarded) by uncovering the ways that black people in twentieth-century urban settings have created a variety of ordinary strategies of resistance to social inequity. Indeed, these strategies often take the form of noncooperative or aggressive acts. See Kelley's review of Scott, "An Archaeology of Resistance," *American Quarterly* 44 (June 1992): 292–97.

Throughout the early twentieth century, Kelley tells us, domestic and factory workers in southern cities silently protested low wages by pilfering from their employers' coal stocks or larders. Urban commuters during World War II resisted the exploitative treatment of Jim Crow bus drivers by demanding to pay lower bus rates for inferior service, or by changing the position of the "color boards" that separated the races in the bus, or simply by insulting white passengers ("The Black Poor and the Politics of Opposition in a New South City, 1929–1970," in *The "Underclass" Debate: Views from History,* ed. Michael B. Katz [Princeton, N.J.: Princeton University Press 1993], pp. 293–333). Zoot-suiters in the 1940s reacted to the demeaning racial epithet "boy" by calling each other "man," and like many other black workers, they saw dressing up as a way of "collapsing status distinctions between them and their oppressors." Also see Stuart Cosgrove, "The Zoot-Suit and Style Warfare," *History Workshop Journal* 18 (Autumn 1984): 77–91. And in the 1980s hard-core rappers have decried police brutality and racism by calling for armed retaliation (Kelley, "Straight from the Underground," *Nation,* June 8, 1992, 793–96).

54. Here my assessment more closely resembles that of Richard Majors and Janet Mancini Bilson in *Cool Pose.* As explained in chapters 4–6, when I discuss compensatory strategies that involve the pursuit of mainstream values and images to counteract the pain from poverty and racism, much of the psychic relief that kids gain comes at the high price of relegitimating the very forces that created their hurtful memories.

CHAPTER 2: THE LIMITS OF ALIENATION

1. For liberal and social-democratic analyses of economic and social alienation, see William Julius Wilson, *The Truly Disadvantaged: The Inner City, the Underclass, and Public Policy* (Chicago: University of Chicago Press, 1987); Christopher Jencks, *Rethinking Public Policy: Race, Poverty, and the Underclass* (Cambridge. Mass.: Harvard University Press, 1992). Charles Murray's analysis of the effects of welfare and other "liberal social programs" is contained in his *Losing Ground: American Social Policy 1950–1980* (New York: Basic Books, 1984). "Cultural" analyses can be found in Thomas Sowell, *Race and Economics* (New York: McKay, 1975); Glen Loury, "Crisis in Black America," *American Family* 9 (May 1986); Nicholas Lémann, "The Origins of the Underclass" *The Atlantic,* June and July 1986 (see esp. the June installment, p. 35); and Roger Lane, *The Roots of*

Violence in Black Philadelphia, 1860–1900 (Cambridge, Mass: Harvard University Press, 1986), esp. pp. 144–74.

2. The overall decline in national and African-American poverty rates between 1960 and 1990 has barely affected the lives of people living in single-parent households. While the poverty rate among members of black two-parent households decreased overall from 52 percent to 14 percent in the thirty years after the poverty line was invented, it remained virtually steady, between 60 percent and 70 percent among members of single-parent households. Largely because black people are more likely to live in one-parent homes, the poverty rates of black women and children have been much higher than those of whites. About 44 percent of all African-American children were poor in 1989, compared to about 16 percent of all white children.

3. As yet, we do not know how much the exceptionality of poor urban African-American's social experience reflects the exceptionality of their experience of poverty. According to Mary Jo Bane and David Ellwood, black children have tended to live in poverty for much longer periods of time than white children. Using data collected over fifteen years at the University of Michigan, they found that, at any point in time, the average poor black child "appears to be in the midst of a poverty spell which will last for almost two decades" ("Slipping in and out of Poverty: The Dynamics of Spells," *Journal of Human Resources* 21 [Winter 1986]: 21). The authors caution that poverty rates in the supposedly representative Michigan sample were somewhat lower than rates derived by the U.S. Census. Thus, what they discovered in their work must be interpreted as a slightly optimistic portrait of long-term poverty. Two main questions suggest themselves: Does longer-term poverty cause higher rates of family troubles? Does it make kids more likely to act out violently as they grow up?

4. The historical argument the social scientist Charles Murray posits in *Losing Ground* (New York: Basic Books, 1984) is based on evidence that rates of female-headed households grew among the poor from the late 1960s onward, beginning at the same time that liberal welfare reform efforts took effect (pp. 124–34). Though Murray makes no mention of the slower growth in the number of poor female-headed households starting in the 1950s, his argument may account for the more dramatic changes that began a decade or so later. However, for Murray's theory to hold true, the number of families on AFDC should have continued to rise into the 1980s at the same rate as the rise in the number of families run by single mothers. As a number of observers have pointed out, this simply never occurred. (See, for example, Robert Greenstein, "Losing Faith in 'Losing Ground,'" *New Republic*, March 25, 1985,

12–17.) The sociologists David Ellwood and Lawrence Summers have found that the number of children living on AFDC stabilized in about 1973, and actually peaked and then declined somewhat among blacks, but the number of kids living with a single mother continued to surge well into the 1980s. See Ellwood and Summers, "Poverty in America: Is Welfare the Answer or the Problem?" in *Fighting Poverty: What Works and What Doesn't* (Cambridge, Mass.: Harvard University Press, 1986), Sheldon H. Danziger and Daniel H. Weinberg pp. 78–105, esp. pp. 92–98. See also Kathryn Neckerman, Robert Aponte, and William J. Wilson, "Families, Unemployment, and American Social Policy," in *The Politics of Social Policy in the United States,* ed. Margaret Weir, Ann Shola Orloff, and Theda Skocpol (Princeton, N.J.: Princeton University Press, 1988), pp. 397–419; and Wilson, *Truly Disadvantaged* pp. 77–81. The rise in female-headed families also occurred against the backdrop of declining monetary value of welfare benefits, suggesting that AFDC incentives could not possibly be the only reason for family change. See Neckerman, Aponte, and Williams, "Families, Unemployment," pp. 402–3; and William A. Darity, Jr., and Samuel L. Myers, "Does Welfare Dependency Cause Female Headship? The Case of the Black Family," *Journal of Marriage and the Family* 46 (November 1984): 765–779.

These critiques are upheld in a much more detailed study of the statistical correlation between welfare and family structure (conducted simultaneously with Murray's research) by Elwood and Bane. They found that welfare had no effect on trends in childbearing among single mothers, a small effect on patterns of marital life that might give rise to single-parent families, and a somewhat stronger effect on the decision of single mothers to live on their own and not with relatives. Thus, "the more significant the family structure or living arrangement change, the less influence AFDC seems to have" (The Impact of AFDC on Family Structure and Living Arrangements" [Grant report prepared for the U.S. Department of Health and Human Services, grant 92A-82, March 1984], p. 6).

If Murray's theory about the influence of social programs does not provide a sufficient explanation for the chronology of family change, neither does it help us understand the exceptionality of the poor black social experience. In fact, *Losing Ground* presents no information comparing the experiences of poor blacks and poor whites. The main reason Murray shies away from this kind of analysis is his insistence on the notion that families are structured according to rational, economic choices made by parents. Family arrangements "may be seen . . . simply, . . . naturally, as the behavior of people responding to the reality of the world around them and making the decisions—the legal, approved, and even encouraged decisions—that maximize their quality of life" (p. 162). Intuition alone suggests problems with this idea: having children and getting married are not only very complex processes, involving emotional, cultural, and personal political considerations, they often are not the result of "decisions" at all, let alone "rational choices." (I am thinking here of unplanned or forced pregnancies, single mothers who remain unmarried because the father of their child deserted, and marriages that end in the same way.) While Murray grudgingly acknowledges that "when economic incentives are buttressed by social norms, the effects on behavior are multiplied" (p. 162), implying that family difference between the races may have to be explained by factors other than welfare or other economic incentives, he then quickly retreats: "the main point is that the social factors are not necessary to explain behavior" (p. 162). This line of thinking leaves us begging for answers as to why poor blacks are more likely to live in single-parent homes than poor whites; or, to ask the same question more precisely, why black single mothers' rates of childbirth have decreased while whites' rates have increased, and why racial differences have persisted in marital life among the poor. Nor can we explain evidence analyzed by Bane that black women tend to be poor before they become a single mothers, whereas white women are more likely to become poor as a result of becoming single parents. ("The Feminization of Poverty," in Weir, Orloff, and Skocpol, *Politics of Social Policy*, p. 384–85.) To all these questions Murray's breezy answer is that "in this account of rational choices among alternatives, . . . it makes no difference whether Harold is white or black" (*Losing Ground*, p. 162).

5. See Stanley Lieberson, *A Piece of the Pie: Black and White Immigrants since 1880* (Berkeley: University of California Press, 1980), pp. 299–319; Edwin Harwood and Clair Hodge, "Jobs and the Negro Family: A Reappraisal," *Public Interest* 23 (Spring 1971): 126, Edward Greer, *Big Steel: Black Politics and Corporate Power in Gary, Indiana* (New York: Monthly Review Press, 1979), pp. 85–87; Kenneth Kusmer, *A Ghetto Takes Shape: Black Cleveland 1870–1930* (Urbana: University of Illinois Press, 1976), pp. 66–90, 190–205; and August Meier and Elliot Rudwick, *Black Detroit and the Rise of the UAW* (New York: Oxford University Press, 1979), pp. 3–33. On race riots, see Rudwick, *Race Riot in East St. Louis, July 2, 1917* (Urbana: University of Illinois Press, 1982); and Allan M. Spear, *Black Chicago: The Making of a Negro Ghetto* (Chicago: University of Chicago Press, 1967), pp. 214–22.

6. Stanley Lieberson, in *A Piece of the Pie*, p. 243. Also, see Alexander Keyssar, *Out of Work: The First Century of Unemployment in Massachu-*

setts (Cambridge: Cambridge University Press, 1986), pp. 88–89, for data about unemployment rates before the depression.

7. These figures are from John Kasarda, "Urban Change and Minority Opportunity," in *The New Urban Reality*, ed. Paul E. Peterson (Washington, D.C.: Brookings Institution, 1985), tables 1, 3, 4 on pp. 44, 48, 50; and, for 1977–1987 (figures for the whole Philadelphia metropolitan area) from Carolyn Adams, David Bartelt, David Elesh, Ira Goldstein, Nancy Kleniewski, and William Yancey, *Philadelphia: Neighborhoods, Division, and Conflict in a Postindustrial City* (Philadelphia: Temple University Press, 1991), p. 21. See also Charles Killingsworth, "The Continuing Labor Market Twist," *Monthly Labor Review* 91 (September, 1968): 12–17; Killingsworth, "Negroes in a Changing Labor Market," in *Employment, Race and Poverty*, ed. Arthur Ross and Herbert Hill (New York: Harcourt, Brace, and World, 1967), pp. 49–70; and William Julius Wilson, *The Declining Significance of Race* (Chicago: University of Chicago Press, 1978), pp. 104–9.

8. David Bartelt, "Housing the 'Underclass'," in *The "Underclass" Debate: Views from History*, ed. Michael Katz (Princeton, N.J.: Princeton University Press, 1993), pp. 118–160; Tom Sugrue, "The Structures of Urban Poverty: The Reorganization of Space and Work in Three Periods of American History," in *The "Underclass" Debate* ed. Katz, pp. 85–117, and Arnold Hirsch, *Making the Second Ghetto: Race and Housing in Chicago, 1940–1960* (Cambridge: Cambridge University Press, 1985). On indices of segregation, see Lieberson, *A Piece of the Pie*, pp. 253–93; and Reynolds Farley, "Residential Segregation of Social and Economic Groups among Blacks," in *The Urban Underclass* ed. Christopher Jencks and Paul E. Peterson (Washington, D.C.: Brookings Institution, 1991), pp. 274–98.

9. See David T. Ellwood, "The Spatial Mismatch Hypothesis," in *The Black Youth Unemployment Crisis*, ed. Richard B. Freeman and Harry J. Holzer (Chicago: University of Chicago Press, 1986), p. 155; John Kasarda, "Urban Change and Minority Opportunities," in *The New Urban Reality*, ed. Paul E. Peterson (Washington, D.C.: Brookings Institution, 1985), pp. 33–67; and Wilson, *Declining Significance of Race*, pp. 92–99. Kasarda writes that

> as industries providing [blue-collar and entry-level] jobs have dispersed to the suburbs, exurbs, and non-metropolitan peripheries, racial discrimination and inadequate incomes of inner-city minorities have prevented many from moving with their traditional sources of employment. Moreover, the dispersed nature of job growth sites makes public transportation from inner-city neighborhoods impractical, requiring virtually all city

residents who work in peripheral areas to commute by
personally owned automobiles.

As late as 1980, less than half of all Philadelphia black households
owned a car ("Urban Change," pp. 55–56, and table 1.3).

10. See Herman Schwartz, "Affirmative Action," in *Minority Report*, ed.
Leslie Dunbar (New York: Pantheon, 1984), pp. 58–74; and Wilson, *Declining Significance of Race*, pp. 99–104.

11. Joleen Kirschenman and Kathryn M. Neckerman, "'We'd Love to
Hire Them, But...,': The Meaning of Race for Employers," in
Jencks and Peterson, *Urban Underclass*, pp. 203–34.

12. See Wilson, *Truly Disadvantaged*, esp. tables 2.7 and 2.8, on pp.
42–43.

13. Freeman and Holzer, *Black Youth Employment Crisis*, p. 7.

14. Wilson, *Truly Disadvantaged*, pp. 82–83.

15. Ibid., p. 83.

16. The language of failure and blame dominates marital disputes in
the FS cases. Sixty-seven of the reports I read concerned young
married couples (under thirty years old) who had sought help for
marital troubles. In those sixty-seven reports, the issue of inadequate provision by the male partner was a principal source of dis-
agreement in forty-eight. Of the remaining nineteen, only a handful contained a clear indication that the ways either partner carried
out his or her role as provider for the family did not enter into the
conflict in some way. In the SA case reports, little information was
typically given about the economic status of teenage fathers. Similar questions of family provision do occasionally come up in discus-
sions of marriage. For examples, see SA378; SA878; SA298; SA798;
SA109; SA739.

17. Women's complaints about men's role as providers pervade the FS
case reports, and they appear often in those SA reports that provide information about teen fathers. In the sixty-seven FS reports I
reviewed, I catalogued 119 separate citations of such complaints.
Several case reports stand out as good examples: FS008, FS022,
FS026, FS030, FS034, FS035, FS044, FS050, FS060, and FS064. See
also FS039, 3.4; FS045, 8.4; FS051, 2.1; FS063, 3; and FS064, 3.7.
Among SA reports, see especially 3A878, and 3A298. The BBA case
reports also contain dozens of similar expressions of disgust. For
examples, see BB071, 2; BB085, 2, 5; BB091, 2.

18. On the issues of nagging and insults about welfare, see FS010, 1, 4;
FS018, 5.3; FS022, 20.8; FS023, 8.2; FS031, 12.2; FS032, 4.9; FS039,
3.4; FS043, 3.9; FS046, 2.7; and BB089, 11A. On issues of women
and work, see FS001, 20; FS002, 3, 15, 18; FS005, 17; FS008, 10;
FS011, 5.2; FS015, 8.0; FS018, 5.5; FS035, 17.0; and FS062, 6.6.

19. BB001, 39.

20. In thirty-nine of the sixty-seven case reports, the man in the house
    reacted to marital trouble resulting from disputes over provision
    by leaving the household, and in some cases women who did not
    work outside the home endured abandonment by several different
    men. Battering occurred very often, probably more often than the
    twenty-seven citations recounted by women in the FS reports. In
    FS013, 1.3, a man whose wife had turned him in for child support
    nearly shot her. See also FS0001, 2, 4, 7, 23; FS002, 8; FS005, 14,
    17, 18; FS008, 4, 7; FS013, 1.2, 2.6; FS015, 22.7; FS017, 3.5; FS018,
    7.4; FS020, 3.5; FS026, 2.1, 2.5, 3.5, 4.7; FS033, 2.1, 3.5; FS034, 4.9;
    FS037, 1.3; FS039, 3.4; FS045, 8.4; FS050, 1.9; FS056, 14.4, 16.2;
    FS059, 2.7; FS065, 2.2; and FS067, 2.8, 6.9, 8.3.

21. Elliot Liebow, *Tally's Corner: A Study of Negro Streetcorner Men*
    (Boston: Little and Brown, 1967), pp. 72–160, 208–31; and Elijah
    Anderson, *Streetwise: Race, Class, and Change in an Urban Community*
    (Chicago: University of Chicago Press, 1990), pp. 112–37; also Lee
    Rainwater, *Behind Ghetto Walls: Black Family Life in a Federal Slum*
    (Chicago: Aldine, 1970), pp. 155–87, 316–97.

22. My samples from the U.S. Census long-form questionnaires consis-
    tently show that unemployed or jobless men have higher separa-
    tion and divorce rates, and lower marriage rates, than employed
    men. See also Wilson, *Truly Disadvantaged*, chap. 3; Neckerman,
    Aponte, and Wilson, "Families, Unemployment," in Weir, Orloff,
    and Skopcol, *Politics of Social Policy*, pp. 397–420; W. E. B. Du Bois,
    The Philadelphia Negro: A Social Study (1899) (Millwood, N.Y.: Kraus-
    Thompson, 1973), pp. 66–72; Heather L. Ross and Isabel Sawhill,
    Time of Transition: The Growth of Families Headed by Women (Wash-
    ington, D.C.: Urban Institute, 1975), pp. 74–75.

23. The calculation of Wilson and Neckerman's "Male Marriageable
    Pool Index" (MMPI) depends not only on relatively clear econo-
    mic measures of joblessness, like rates of unemployment, and
    less clear gauges, like absence from the workforce, but it also
    reflects the greater numbers of men, relative to women, who are
    incarcerated, who have died prematurely, or who have been
    missed altogether by census enumerators. Indeed, other explana-
    tions may be needed to understand the predicament of all of these
    supposedly "unmarriageable" men. These include the variety of
    reasons men leave the workforce, including college attendance,
    injury or illness, and abandonment of a search for jobs. Since
    crime and homicide account for much of the high incarceration
    rates and early death among men, particularly poor black men,
    the rate of "joblessness," in the MMPI calculation, in part reflects
    the high levels of violence in inner-city communities. And family
    outcasts, the homeless, drug addicts, and criminals all swell the
    numbers of men whom the census never even counts. The close

correlation Wilson and Neckerman measure between black joblessness and single-parent families does suggest that inner-city men are not getting married, or are dissolving their marriages, even as they experience a variety of difficulties, the most important of which is probably joblessness. The index also suggests that other factors may be involved in the historical increase of family change.

24. In a study that concurs with my findings, Heather Ross and Isabel Sawhill, writing on families run by single women across the country, documented that only a third of the racial difference in rates of marital separation in 1970 was due to racial differences in "earnings, education and occupation" (*Time of Transition,* pp. 74–77).

25. Neckerman, Aponte, and Wilson, "Families, Employment," p. 416.

26. Unlike marriage rates and measures of family structure, indices of murder or other violent acts are not collected along with information about the economic status of individuals involved, so statistical connections between joblessness and individuals' likelihood to commit murder, or become a murder victim, are difficult to make. Criminologists have therefore relied on correlations between murder rates and the economic health of communities, and analyses that chart connections between changes in murder rates and unemployment rates over time. See John Hagan, "The Poverty of a Classless Criminology: Presidential Address to the American Society of Criminology," *Criminology* 30 (February 1992): 1–19.

27. Robert Sampson, "Urban Black Violence: The Effect of Male Joblessness and Family Disruption," *American Journal of Sociology* 93 (September 1987): 348–82.

28. On differences in measurements and statistical techniques, see M. Dwayne Smith, "Variations in Correlates of Race-Specific Urban Homicide Rates" (Revised version of a paper presented at the Forty-third Annual Meeting of the American Society of Criminology, San Francisco, November 1991). For several different interpretations, see Smith; Gary LaFree, Kriss A. Drass, and Patrick O'Day, "Race and Crime in Postwar America: Determinants of African-American and White Rates, 1957 1988," *Criminology* 30 (1992): 157–87; Colin Loftin, David McDowall, and James Boudouris, "Economic Change and Homicide in Detroit, 1926–1979," in ed. Gurr, *Violence in America, Volume 1: The History of Crime,* pp. 163–77; and Kenneth C. Land, David Cantor, and Stephen T. Russell, "Unemployment and Crime Rate Fluctuations in the Post-World War II United States: Statistical Time-Series Properties and Alternative Models" (Paper presented at the Forty-third Annual Meeting of the American Society of Criminology, San Francisco, November 1991).

29. Quotations from Jay Corzine and Lin Huff-Corzine, "Racial Inequality and Black Homicide: An Analysis of Felony, Nonfelony and Total Rates" (Revised version of a paper presented at the Forty-third Annual Meeting of the American Society of Criminology, San Francisco, November 1991). For the debate on economic inequality, see Judith R. Blau and Peter M. Blau, "The Cost of Inequality: Metropolitan Structure and Violent Crime," *American Sociological Review* 47 (February 1982): 114–29; Kirk R. Williams, "Economic Sources of Homicide: Reestimating the Effects of Poverty and Inequality," *American Sociological Review* 49 (1984): 283–89; James W. Balkwell, "Ethnic Inequality and the Rate of Homicide," *Social Forces* 69 (1990): 53–70. On the frustration-aggression hypothesis, see John Dollard, Leonard R. Doob, Neal E. Miller, O. H. Mowrer, and Robert R. Sears, *Frustration and Aggression* (New Haven: Yale University Press, 1939); and Leonard Berkowitz, "Frustration-Aggression Hypothesis: Examination and Reinterpretation," *Psychological Bulletin* 106 (1989): 59–73.

30. Wilson, *Truly Disadvantaged*, pp. 46–62. The seventy-six "community areas" Wilson analyzed are those delineated by the authors of the *Local Community Fact Book: Chicago Metropolitan Area, 1970 and 1980* (Chicago: Chicago Review Press, 1984). For maps, see Wilson, pp. 51–54.

31. Wilson, *Truly Disadvantaged*, pp. 56, 58–59.

32. William Julius Wilson, "Social Theory and Public Agenda Research: The Challenge of Studying Inner-City Social Dislocations," *American Sociological Review* 5 (February 1991): 6–12. See also Martha Van Haitsma, "A Contextual Definition of the Underclass," *Focus* 12 (Spring/Summer 1989): 27–31.

33. Paul Jargowski and Mary Jo Bane, "Ghetto Poverty: Basic Questions," in *Inner-City Poverty in America*, ed. Lawrence E. Lynn and Michael G. H. McGeary (Washington, D.C.: National Academy Press, 1990), pp. 16–67.

34. In Detroit the increase was from 11.5 percent to 20.6 percent; in Cleveland, from 32.8 percent to 36.6 percent; in Saint Louis, from 32.3 percent to 32.9 percent; in Milwaukee, from 15.5 percent to 24.0 percent; and in Buffalo, from 3.4 percent to 30.6 percent; in Miami, from 28.1 percent to 29.5 percent; and in Atlanta, from 31.3 percent to 32.3 percent (Jargowski and Bane, "Ghetto Poverty," pp. 59–67).

35. The figures are from Jargowski and Bane, pp. 59–67. The only exception on the West Coast was Portland, Oregon, which had a rate of 11 percent in 1980. San Francisco's rate stayed the same, at 9 percent. In the South, the proportion of poor blacks living in high-poverty tracts declined during the 1970s in Dallas, Houston, San Antonio, Jacksonville, Memphis, and Tampa, and remained

stable at 8.6 percent in Washington, D.C. The same rate declined
from 19.6 percent to 9.8 percent in Boston during the 1970s.

36. Karl E. and Alma F. Taeuber, *Negroes in Cities: Residential Segregation
    and Neighborhood Change* (Chicago: Aldine, 1965), p. 164; see tables
    with information on Philadelphia on pp. 156–63; Farley, "Trends,"
    p. 14.

37. See Jargowski and Bane, "Ghetto Poverty," pp. 59–67.

38. Though "concentration effects" do not appear to provide a suffi-
    cient explanation for racial differences, we cannot rule out the
    possibility that, in some cities, and in certain periods, the flight of
    nonpoor people may have contributed somehow to the increases
    that all American urban poor people—regardless of race—have
    experienced in levels of noncooperation and aggression. More
    research is needed to determine exactly how much of a role class
    segregation has played in changes in the community life of the
    poor, and my doubts do not by any means close the question. Life
    in high-rise public housing projects, which have much higher
    poverty rates than most high-poverty census tracts, may be missed
    in analyses of neighborhoods. Recency of migration may also help
    determine the ways people interact in poor communities. Finally,
    as we shall see in connection with the efforts of kids in my neigh-
    borhood to define their racial identities, the physical deterioration
    of neighborhoods (which, of course, depends not so much on the
    disappearance of middle-class morals as on the disappearance of
    middle-class money) may also have played an important historical
    role in the experience of inner-city poverty.

39. For earlier formulations of the idea, see Allison Davis, *Social Class
    Influences upon Learning* (Cambridge, Mass.: Harvard University
    Press, 1948), pp. 10–11; Walter Miller, "Lower-Class Culture as a
    Generating Milieu of Gang Delinquency," *Journal of Social Issues* 14,
    (1958): 5–6. Oscar Lewis's most concise elaboration of the con-
    cept of the culture of poverty is in "The Culture of Poverty," in *On
    Understanding Poverty: Perspectives from the Social Sciences,* ed. Daniel
    Patrick Moynihan (New York: Basic Books,1969) p. 188. See also
    Daniel Patrick Moynihan, *The Negro Family: The Case for National
    Action* (Washington, D.C.: Government Printing Office, 1965), esp.
    pp. 5, 30, 47. For Marvin Wolfgang and Franco Ferracuti's some-
    what different notion of the "subculture of violence," which has
    received enduring discussion in the field of criminology, see *The
    Subculture of Violence: Toward a Unified Theory in Criminology* (Lon-
    don: Tavistock, 1967).

40. Glen Loury, "Crisis in Black America," *American Family* 9 (May
    1986): 3. Pundits in the popular press have taken up these argu-
    ments most strongly. See CBS Reports, "The Vanishing Family:
    Crisis in Black America," with correspondent Bill Moyers (New

York: CBS Transcripts, January 25, 1986); Charles Krauthammer, "Crime and Responsibility," *Time*, May 8, 1989, 104; and George Will, "Wilding: Evil in the Park," in his *Suddenly: The American Idea Abroad and at Home, 1986–1990*, ed. (New York: Free Press, 1990).

41. Stanley Lieberson has criticized cultural analyses for this same reason in *A Piece of the Pie*, pp. 8–9. The same criticism is made by Wolfgang and Ferracuti in *The Subculture of Violence*, pp. 157–58. For an exception, see Linda Datcher-Loury and Glenn Loury, "The Effects of Attitudes and Aspirations on the Labor Supply of Young Men," in Freeman and Holzer, *Black Youth Employment Crisis*, pp. 377–401.

42. Daniel Patrick Moynihan, *The Negro Family: The Case for National Action*, reprinted in Lee Rainwater and William L. Yancey, *The Moynihan Report and the Politics of Controversy* (Cambridge, Mass.: M.I.T. Press, 1967), pp. 5, 30, 47.

43. Charles S. Johnson, *Shadow of the Plantation* (Chicago: University of Chicago Press, 1934), pp. 31, 188; Hortense Powdermaker, *After Freedom: A Cultural Study of the Deep South* (New York: Viking, 1939), pp. 143–46; John Dollard, *Caste and Class in a Southern Town*, 3rd ed. (Garden City, N.Y.: Doubleday/Anchor, 1957), pp. 274–79; E. Franklin Frazier, *The Negro Family in the United States* rev. ed. (Chicago: University of Chicago Press, 1966). See also W. E. B. Du Bois, *Philadelphia Negro*, pp. 72, 192, 196.

44. Nicholas Lemann, *The Promised Land: The Great Black Migration and How It Changed America* (New York: Knopf, 1991), p. 29. Lemann previously argued a case for the determinative importance of southern sharecropping "culture" on the North in "The Origins of the Underclass" (*Atlantic*, June 1986, esp. p. 35).

45. Herbert Gutman, *The Black Family in Slavery and Freedom* (New York: Vintage, 1976), pp. 495–96, tables A-21 and A-19. Although these data were derived from a very small sample, they also fit with the observations of Frank Furstenberg and his colleagues on Philadelphia. See "The Origins of the Female-Headed Black Family," in *Philadelphia: Work, Space, Family, and Group Experience in the 19th Century* ed. Theodore Hershberg (New York: Oxford University Press, 1981), pp. 438–44, tables 4, 6, 7.

46. The only years in which marriage statistics from the rural South approach those among northern-born city dwellers are the never-married rates in 1960 and 1970, when the collapse of sharecropping had become virtually complete, and when still extremely low welfare expenditures in southern states left the poor black rural South in a particularly acute state of economic crisis.

47. These statistical patterns were also noted for nineteenth-century Boston by Elizabeth Pleck (*Black Migration and Poverty: Boston 1865–1900* [New York: Academic Press, 1979], pp. 166, 168, tables

6-1 and 6-2); and by Ross and Sawhill in the twentieth century (*Time of Transition,* pp. 77, 86–87).

48. Lemann, *Promised Land,* p. 48.

49. James Comer, "Black Violence and Public Policy," in *American Violence and Public Policy: An Update on the National Commission on the Causes and Prevention of Violence,* ed. Lynn A. Curtis (New Haven, Conn.: Yale University Press, 1985), p. 76. See Charles Silberman, *Criminal Violence, Criminal Justice* (New York: Random House, 1978), pp. 155–60; and Alvin Poussaint, *Why Blacks Kill Blacks* (New York: Emerson-Hall, 1972), p. 72.

50. Frazier, *Negro Family,* p. 363.

51. Lemann, "The Origins" (June installment), p. 48.

52. See Pleck, *Black Migration and Poverty,* pp. 174–76; Ross and Sawhill, *Time of Transition,* pp. 77–78; and Roger Lane, *Roots of Violence in Black Philadelphia, 1860–1900* (Cambridge, Mass.: Harvard University Press, 1986), pp. 144–61.

53. Lane, *Roots of Violence,* pp. 157–58, 146. Others dispute the northern origins of Stackolee stories, which, according to some reports, were originally modeled on the exploits of a Memphis dockworker. John Robertson thinks badmen stories resulted from the change from slavery to sharecropping, but Lawrence Levine gives that change a later date, toward the turn of the century, which may link them more to the rise of rampant "negrophobia," lynching, and disfranchisement in the South. On the origins of Stackolee, see John A. Lomax and Alan Lomax, *American Ballads and Folk Songs* (New York: Macmillian, 1934), pp. 93–94; Roberts, *From Trickster to Badman: The Black Folk Hero in Slavery and Freedom* (Philadelphia: University of Pennsylvania Press, 1989), pp. 171– 219; and Levine, *Black Culture, Black Consciousness* (Oxford: Oxford University Press, 1977), pp. 407–20.

54. Quotations from Lane, *Roots of Violence,* pp. 157–8, 173.

55. Lane, *Roots of Violence,* p. 169. Here, he is restating the hypothesis suggested by Ted Robert Gurr in "On the History of Violent Crime in Europe in America," in *Violence in America: Historical and Comparative Perspectives,* rev. ed., ed. Hugh Davis and Ted Robert Gurr (Beverly Hills, Calif.: Sage Publications, 1979), pp. 353–74.

CHAPTER 3: THE AMERICAN TRADITIONS OF POOR BLACK FAMILIES

1. For the history of biblical philosophies of child rearing and their influence on the American mainstream, see Philip Greven, *Spare the Child: The Religious Roots of Punishment and the Psychological Impact of Physical Abuse* (New York: Knopf, 1991); John Demos, *A Little Commonwealth: Family Life in Plymouth Colony* (New York: Oxford University Press, 1970): 100–106; and Harold G. Grasmick,

Elizabeth Davenport, Mitchell B. Chamlin, and Robert J. Borsik, Jr., "Protestant Fundamentalism and the Retribute Doctrine of Punishment," *Criminology* 30 (February 1992): 21–45. For the history of "progressive" or "sacralized" childhood in the United States, see Mary Ryan, *Cradle of the Middle Class: the Family in Oneida County, New York, 1790–1865* (Cambridge: Cambridge University Press, 1981), pp. 70–75, 91–92, 98–102; and Viviana Zelizer, *Pricing the Priceless Child: The Changing Social Value of Children* (New York: Basic Books, 1985), pp. 3–21.

For analyses of physical punishment in African-American families, see Barry Silverstein and Ronald Krate, *Children of the Dark Ghetto: A Developmental Psychology* (New York: Praeger, 1975), pp. 21, 24–25, 30–31, 41–51; Marie Peters, "Parenting in Black Families with Young Children: A Historical Perspective," *Black Families,* ed. Harriett Pipes McAdoo (Beverly Hills, Calif.: Sage, 1981), pp. 211–24; and Virginia Meyer Young, "Family and Childhood in a Southern Negro Community," *American Anthropologist,* 72 (April 1970): 269–88.

2. See Ryan, *Cradle of the Middle Class,* pp. 70–75, 91–92, 98–102; and Zelizer, *Priceless Child,* pp. 3–21.

3. See, for example, Janice Hale, "The Black Woman and Child Rearing," in *The Black Woman,* ed. La Frances Rodgers-Rose, (Beverly Hills, Calif.: Sage, 1980), pp. 79–87; and Gloria Wade-Gayles, "She Who Is Black and Mother: In Sociology and Fiction, 1940–1970," in Rodgers-Rose, *Black Woman,* pp. 89–106. Virginia Heyer Young, in her article "Family and Childhood in a Southern Negro Community" writes all too vaguely that in the rural community she studied, parents employed techniques of discipline in which "love and aggression and control of aggression are linked in an unusual way," but concluded, without giving any evidence, that "childhood experience ... does not show the origins of the aggressiveness found in much adult Negro behavior" (p. 285).

For a more direct view, see Barry Silverstein and Ronald Krate, *Children of the Dark Ghetto: A Developmental Psychology* (New York: Praeger, 1975), pp. 21, 24–25, 30–31, 41–51; and Marie Peters, "Parenting in Black Families," in McAdoo, *Black Families,* pp. 211–24.

4. E. Franklin Frazier, "Problems and Needs of Negro Children and Youth Resulting from Family Disorganization," *Journal of Negro Education* (Summer 1950): 276–77; Kenneth Clark, *Dark Ghetto: The Dilemmas of Social Power* (New York: Harper, 1965), pp. 47–50; Daniel Patrick Moynihan, *The Negro Family: The Case for National Action,* reprinted in Rainwater and Yancey *The Moynihan Report and the Politics of Controversy* (Cambridge, Mass.: M.I.T. Press, 1967), pp. 36–40, and Moynihan, *Family and Nation: The Godkin Lectures at*

Harvard University (San Diego: Harcourt, Brace Jovanovich, 1986), pp. 92–93; Thomas P. Monahan, "Family Status and the Delinquent Child," *Social Forces* (March 1957): 254; Frank J. Sciara and Richard K. Jantz, "Father Absence and Its Apparent Effect on the Achievement of Black Children from Low Income Families," *Journal of Negro Education* 43 (Spring 1974): 221–27; Urie Bronfenbrenner, "The Origins of Alienation," *Scientific American,* August 1974, p. 53; Timothy F. Hartnagel, "Father Absence and Self-Conception among Lower-Class White and Negro Boys," *Social Problems* 18 (Fall 1970): 152–63; W. Mischel, "Father Absence and the Delay of Gratification: Cross-Cultural Comparisons," *Journal of Abnormal and Social Psychology* 63 (July 1961): 116–24; and Frank F. Furstenberg, Jr., J. Brooks-Gunn, and S. Philip Morgan, *Adolescent Mothers in Later Life* (Cambridge: Cambridge University Press, 1987), pp. 115–19.

On family structure and its relationship to murder rates, see James Q. Wilson, *Thinking about Crime* (New York: Basic Books, 1975), pp. 206–7; William B. Harvey, "Homicide among Black Adults: Life in the Subculture of Exasperation," in *Homicide among Black Americans,* ed. Darnell Hawkins, (Lanham, Md.: University Press of America, 1986), pp. 164–65; and Robert J. Sampson, "Urban Black Violence: The Effect of Male Joblessness and Family Disruption," *American Journal of Sociology* 93 (September 1987): 348–82.

5. Robert E. Anderson, "Where's Dad? Paternal Deprivation and Delinquency," *Archives of General Psychiatry* 18 (June 1968): 641; Henry B. Biller, "A Note on Father Absence and Masculine Development in Lower-Class Negro and White Boys," *Child Development* 39 (September 1968): 1003–6; and "The Effects of Father-Absence on Norwegian Boys and Girls," *Journal of Abnormal and Social Psychology* 59 (1959): 258–62. For a useful list of further citations, see Timothy Hartnagel, "Father Absence and Self Conception among Lower Class White and Negro Boys," *Social Problems* 18 (1970): 152–63.

6. Roger Abrahams, *Deep Down in the Jungle . . . : Negro Narrative Folklore from the Streets of Philadelphia* (Chicago: Aldine, 1963), pp. 30–31.

7. See Moynihan, *Negro Family,* pp. 29–48.

8. Hartnagel, "Father Absence," p. 162. For a detailed empirical study of these factors, see Furstenberg, Brooks-Gunn, and Morgan, *Adolescent Mothers,* pp. 77–129.

9. See Furstenberg, Brooks-Gunn, and Morgan, *Adolescent Mothers,* pp. 102–3.

10. Moynihan, *Family and Nation,* p. 98.

11. Quotation from Christopher Jencks and Paul Peterson, *The Urban*

Underclass (Washington, D.C.: Brookings Institution, 1991), p. 19; Sanford M. Dornbusch, J. Merrill Carlsmith, Stephen J. Bushwall, Philip L. Ritter, Herbert Leiderman, Albert H. Hastorf, and Ruth T. Gross, "Single Parents, Extended Households, and the Control of Adolescents," *Child Development* 56 (April 1985): 326–41. See also Paul Jargowski and Mary Jo Bane, "Ghetto Poverty in the United States," in Jencks and Peterson, *Urban Underclass,* p. 247.

12. Chester Finn, *Ten Tentative Truths* (Minneapolis: Center of the American Experiment, 1990), quoted in William Raspberry, "A Stiff Dose of Truth-Speaking Is Needed to Save the Children of the Underclass," *Philadelphia Inquirer,* August 13, 1990, p. A12; George Will, "Bayonets Won't Help the Cities," *Washington Post,* April 9, 1989, p. B7.

13. BB042, 1.

14. BB002, 32, 19.

15. BB003, 13.

16. See, for example, BB091, 5A; BB093, 1; BB039, 3.

17. BB091, 5A. See also BB083, 6.

18. BB064, 10. There are many other instances in the case reports where boys express resentment over maternal control. In most of these cases, however, it is hard to tell whether this has to do with their mothers taking on a traditionally male role, as disciplinarians, or whether the resentment stems from the severity of discipline or some other fault kids perceive in their mothers' parenting—resentment that could be directed at fathers just as easily as at mothers.

19. BB063, attached letter. See BB029, 2; BB071, 3.

20. The data are from my counts of 110 families in BBA case reports where the father did not live in the same home as the client. Twenty-five of the reports made no mention of relatives or friends helping the single mother in question, and a few other clients seemed to be living with another single female relative. Another twenty-one clients had frequent contact, or lived off and on with their father, or lived with an uncle, their mother's "paramour" or a stepfather; another eleven moved back with their father to stay after their case was opened; and twenty-seven kids lived with multiple extended relatives, including grandmothers, grandfathers, older male and female cousins, brothers-in-law, or aunts and uncles.

21. Furstenberg et al., *Adolescent Mothers,* pp. 106–8, 126.

22. See Vance Packard, *Our Endangered Children: Growing Up in a Changing World* (Boston: Little, Brown, 1983), pp. 185–201; and William J. Goode, *After Divorce* (Glencoe, Il.: Free Press, 1956), pp. 307–30.

23. See BB002, 19; BB003, 32; BB031, 1; BB042, 2, 4; BB060, 1–2; BB067, 1–2; BB075, 1; and BB098, 2.

24. Quotations from BB090, 2, 7A, 10. See also BB032, 1; BB036, 2; BB038, 1; BB039, 1; BB043, 10; BB059, 1; BB081, 13; BB089, 2; BB097, 12; BB100, 2; BB104, 5; and FS001, 2. On batterers and their childhood experiences, and on the effects of domestic violence on children, see Richard M. Tolman and Larry W. Bennett, "A Review of Quantitative Evidence on Men Who Batter," *Journal of Interpersonal Violence* 5 (March 1990): 87–118; Marsha Kleinman, "Children—Witnesses to, and Victims of, Domestic Violence," *New Jersey Psychologist* (Fall 1987): 13–16; and David A. Wolfe, Peter Jaffe, Susan Kaye Wilson, and Lydia Zak, "A Multivariate Investigation of Children's Adjustment to Family Violence," in *Family Abuse and Its Consequences,* ed. Gerald Hotaling and D. B. Sugarman (Newbury Park, Calif.: Sage, 1988), pp. 228–39.

25. BB071, 2, 4, 8. See also BB016, 1; BB062, 20; BB091, 2–3; BB095, 9; and BB097, esp. 2.

26. BB004, 11. See also BB070, 12; BB083, 3, 4.

27. BB027, 25. See BB009, 11; and BB003, 26. See also BB009, 11; BB014, 1; BB018, 5; BB083, 3; BB084, 3; BB098, 5; BB100, 2; BB104, 2, 5.

28. BB089, 3, 6, 8, 9A, 13A. For similar situations see BB019, 6; and BB023, 12.

29. BB011, 2; and BB010, 4. See also BB003, 10; BB004, 5; BB005, 8; BB017, 1, 2; BB023, 1, 9, 10; BB026, 1; BB027, 1; BB028, 1; BB031, 3; BB033, 10; BB037, 3; BB058, 4, 7; BB094, 2; BB095, 3, 4; BB098, 3; BB104, 7; BB105, 9.

30. See BB039, 13; BB023, 2; BB015, 10; BB010, 9; and BB073, 16.

31. See for example, BB009, 1A, 2.

32. BB018, 3. See also BB004, 6; BB006, 1, 4; BB063, 15; BB085, 2, 4, 5, 8.

33. BB048, 2.

34. FS070, 37.9–38.2, 16.1.

35. BB073, 10, 10A, 14, 43.

36. BB073, 9, 14, 16, 17A, 18, 29. For some less dramatic expressions of resentment, see BB002, 21, 23; BB026, 5; BB042, 12A; BB043, 5; BB046, 2; BB093, 1; BB095, 5; BB103, 4.

For runaways who left out of fear of parents, see BB001, 16; BB006, 1; BB009; BB010, 2; BB018, 6; BB023, 7, 18; BB027, 7; BB031, 3; BB034, 15; BB044, 9; BB048, 7; BB062, 4, 22; BB066, 2, 12; BB070, 14; BB080, 5; BB081, 2, 4, 9, 10, 14, 19, 20; BB089, 1; BB091, 2; BB092, 2; BB100, 2A; BB103, 1.

For more on kids' violence against abusive parents, see BB003, 13; BB004, 14, 23, 24; BB012, 12; BB023, 7, 19; BB027, 22, 26; BB048, 14; BB053, 1; BB070, 18; BB073, 17, 29; and BB090, 10, 13.

37. BB073, 29, 36, 44.
38. A similar progression of events happened in one case where a boy's mother reported that his stepfather "is trying very hard to be a father to Michael. . . . However, her husband is becoming very discouraged because Donald does not respond to their talks. On several occasions both she and her husband have spanked Michael but this does no good either. . . . Mrs. G. said she is at her wits [sic] end and does not know what she will do with this youngster. She said she may ask the court to place him in an institution for his own good" (BB070, 12). For other instances when police or court authorities were called into a family situation by parents, see BB001, 8; BB003, 13, 18; BB006, 10; BB012; BB73, 11, 35; BB075, 15; BB081, 16, 17; BB089, 3, 17, 24; BB083, 13; BB089, 7; FS70, 37.9–38.2.
39. BB089, 3.
40. BB090, 13; BB089, 3; BB006, 5.
41. BB075, 2, 5.
42. BB039, 1.
43. BB023.
44. See Elijah Anderson, *Streetwise: Race, Class, and Change in an Urban Community* (Chicago: University of Chicago Press, 1990), pp. 123–28.
45. Janice Hale-Benson, "The Black Woman and Childrearing," in Rodgers-Rose, *Black Woman*, p. 87.
46. An early study of parental behavior and court-referred children, which suggests some of the problems of using single-parent family structure as a predictor of behavior, is that of Sheldon and Eleanor T. Glueck. Using their "social prediction table," they claimed to be able to spot future delinquents on the basis of factors like "discipline of boy by father [or mother]" and "affection of mother [or father] for boy" (*Unraveling Juvenile Delinquency* [Cambridge, Mass.: Harvard University Press, 1950], pp. 125–27). In a special attempt to apply the Gluecks' table to single-parent homes run by mothers, Maude M. Craig and Selma J. Glick found that boys who experienced "firm but kindly" discipline from their mothers were one-tenth as likely to be "delinquent" as boys from similar families who experienced "erratic" discipline, one-twelfth as likely as sons of "overstrict" mothers, and one-thirteenth as likely as boys from "lax" single-parent households. These figures very closely paralleled their findings among boys in two-parent households who had similarly characterized relationships with their fathers and mothers. ("Ten Years' Experience with the Glueck Social Prediction Table," *Crime and Delinquency* [July 1963]: 249–61).

On batterers, see G. T. Hotaling and D. B. Sugarman, "An

Analysis of Risk Markers in Husband to Wife Violence: The Current State of Knowledge," *Violence and Victims* 1 (2): 101–24; and Richard M. Tolman and Larry W. Bennett, "A Review of Quantitative Research on Men Who Batter," *Journal of Interpersonal Violence,* 5 (March 1990): 97–98.

On sex offenders, see A. Nicholas Groth, "Sexual Trauma in the Life Histories of Rapists and Child Molesters," *Victimology* 4 (1979): 10–16.

On homicidal youth, see Charles Patrick Ewing, *When Children Kill: The Dynamics of Juvenile Homicide* (Lexington, Mass.: Lexington Books, 1990), pp. 22–23, 32–35, 38–42, 129–31; Kathleen M. Heide and Eldra Solomon, "Responses to Severe Childhood Maltreatment: Homicidal Fantasies and Other Coping Strategies"; and Heide, "Child Maltreatment and Adolescent Parricide: Intervention and Prevention Strategies" (Both papers presented to the Forty-third Annual Meeting of American Society of Criminology, San Francisco, November 1991).

CHAPTER 4: POOR BLACK CHILDREN AND AMERICAN RACISM

1. Kenneth B. Clark and Mamie P. Clark, "Racial Identification and Preference in Negro Children," in *Readings in Social Psychology,* ed. Theodore M. Newcomb and Eugene L. Hartley (New York: Holt, 1947), pp. 169–78.
2. Quote from Kenneth B. Clark, "The Social Scientists and the Brown Decision, and Contemporary Confusion," in *Argument: The Oral Argument before the Supreme Court in* Brown v. Board of Education of Topeka, *1952–55,* ed. Leon Friedman (New York: Chelsea House, 1969), p. xxxvi. See also Esther Milner, "Some Hypotheses concerning the Influence of Segregation on Negro Personality Development," *Psychiatry* 16 (1953): 291–97; and David P. Ausubel, "Ego Development among Segregated Negro Children," *Mental Hygiene* 42 (1958): 362–69.
3. Kenneth B. Clark, "Color, Class, Personality and Juvenile Delinquency," *Journal of Negro Education* 28 (1959): 247.
4. Kenneth B. Clark, *Dark Ghetto: Dilemmas of Social Power* (New York: Harper Press, 1965), p. 27.
5. For example, see Robert Staples, *Black Masculinity: The Black Male's Role in American Society* (San Francisco: Black Scholar Press, 1982), pp. 43–49, 53.
6. See Staples, *Black Masculinity,* chaps. 4, 5; and Michelle Wallace, *Black Macho and the Myth of the Superwoman* (New York: Warner, 1978).
7. Alvin Poussaint, *Why Blacks Kill Blacks* (New York: Emerson Hall, 1972), p. 77.

8. Quotation from Robert Coles, *Children of Crisis: A Study of Courage and Fear* (Boston: Little, Brown, 1964), vol. 1, p. 63. See ibid., pp. 37–71, esp. figs. 12 and 15 and pp. 63–65 for the story of "a mother of five in Jackson, Mississippi." See also *Children of Crisis Volume 3: The South Goes North* (Boston: Little, Brown, 1964), p. 495, esp. figs. 3 and 14.

9. Joyce Ladner, *Tomorrow's Tomorrow* (Garden City, N.Y.: Doubleday, 1971) pp. 77–108. See Poussaint, *Why Blacks Kill Blacks*, pp. 25–34.

10. William Julius Wilson, *The Truly Disadvantaged: the Inner City, the Underclass, and Public Policy* (Chicago: University of Chicago Press, 1987), p. 11.

11. Jonathan Rieder, *Canarsie: The Jews and Italians of Brooklyn against Liberalism* (Cambridge, Mass.: Harvard University Press, 1985); J. Anthony Lukas, *Common Ground: A Turbulent Decade in the Lives of Three American Families* (New York: Vintage, 1985); Ronald P. Formisano, *Boston against Busing: Race, Class and Ethnicity in the 1960s and 1970s* (Chapel Hill, N.C.: University of North Carolina Press, 1991). See also Peter Binzen, *Whitetown, USA: A First-Hand Study of How the "Silent Majority" Lives, Learns, Works and Thinks* (New York: Vintage, 1970).

12. Joleen Kirschenman and Kathryn M. Neckerman, "'We'd Love to Hire Them, But . . . ': The Meaning of Race for Employers," in *The Urban Underclass,* ed. Jencks and Peterson (Washington, D.C.: Brookings Institution, 1991), pp. 203–32.

13. Elijah Anderson, *Streetwise: Race, Class, and Change in an Urban Community* (Chicago: University of Chicago Press, 1990); Studs Terkel, *Race: How Blacks and Whites Think and Feel about the American Obsession* (New York: New Press, 1992). See also Rieder, *Canarsie,* pp. 13–26, 37–95; Formisano, *Boston against Busing,* pp. 184–87; Andrew Hacker, *Two Nations: Black and White, Separate, Hostile, Unequal* (New York: Scribner's, 1992), pp. 179–98; Bill Bradley, "Race Crime and the Future of Cities," *Philadelphia Inquirer,* April 5, 1992, p. C7.

14. William E. Cross, Jr., *Shades of Black: Diversity in African-American Identity* (Philadelphia: Temple University Press, 1991).

15. E. Franklin Frazier, *Negro Youth at the Crossways: Their Personality Development in the Middle States* (1940; reprint, New York: Schocken, 1967), pp. 70–90.

16. Arnold Hirsch, *Making the Second Ghetto: Race and Housing in Chicago, 1940–1960* (Cambridge: Cambridge University Press, 1983), pp. 1–100. See also Domenic Capeci, *Race Relations in Wartime Detroit* (Philadelphia: Temple University Press, 1984) for an account of the 1943 race riot in Detroit.

17. Frazier, *Negro Youth at the Crossways,* pp. 41, 51–61, 79–80. See also St. Clair Drake's introduction to this edition, pp. xvii–xviii.

18. BB042, camp record, entries on August 12, 16, and 24.

19. BB001, p. 12.

20. E. Franklin Frazier, *Black Bourgeoisie: The Rise of a New Class in the United States* (1957; reprint, New York: Collier, 1962), pp. 28, 176–91.

21. BB073, pp. 33, 34; BB104, p. 4. See also BB009, p. 8.

22. Ladner, *Tomorrow's Tomorrow,* pp. 86, 88.

23. See, for example, the *Gallup Poll Monthly,* June 1990, p. 27. In 1990, only 8 percent of nonblacks who were asked "if colored people/black people came to live in great numbers in your neighborhood would you move?" answered "yes, definitely"; in 1963 nearly 50 percent had given this response. See also Gerald David Jaynes and Robin M. Williams, eds., *A Common Destiny: Blacks and American Society* (Washington, D.C.: National Academy Press, 1989), pp. 113–60.

24. *Philadelphia Inquirer,* November 21, 1985, pp. 1–A, 23A. On racial hatred, see also Michael Riley, "White and Wrong: New Klan, Old Hatred," *Time,* July 6, 1992, pp. 24–27.

25. Nancy Boyd-Franklin writes about the deeply personal nature of concerns about women's racial appearance in "Recurrent Themes in the Treatment of African-American Women in Group Psychotherapy," *Women and Therapy* 11 (1991): 25–40. See also Calvin Hernton, *Sex and Racism in America* (New York: Grove, 1965), pp. 130–35; William H. Grier and Price M. Cobbs, *Black Rage* (New York: Basic Books, 1968), pp. 32–46.

26. See also Reynolds Farley and Walter Allen, *The Color Line and the Quality of Life in America* (New York: Russell Sage Foundation, 1987); Farley, "Residential Segregation of Social and Economic Groups Among Blacks: 1970 to 1980," in *The Urban Underclass,* ed. Jencks and Peterson, pp. 274–98; and David Theo Goldberg, "The World Is a Ghetto: Racial Marginality and Urban Location" (Paper delivered at the Forty-third Annual Meeting of the American Criminology Society, San Francisco, November, 1992). On Philadelphia, see "Black Segregation up in Philadelphia, Census Shows," *Philadelphia Inquirer,* April 11, 1991, pp. B1–B2.

27. See Clark, "The Social Scientists" p. xxxvi.

28. *New York Times,* April 1, 1987, quoted in Andrew Hacker, "American Apartheid," *New York Review of Books,* December 3, 1987, p. 31.

29. *Chicago Sun-Times* survey, October 16, 1983, quoted in Gary Orfield, "Ghettoization and Its Alternatives," in *The New Urban Reality,* ed. Paul E. Peterson (Washington: Brookings Institution: 1985), pp. 169–70.

30. George Frederickson, *The Black Image in the White Mind* (New York: Harper and Row, 1971), pp. 51–58.

31. See Eric Foner, *Free Soil, Free Labor, Free Men: The Ideology of the Republican Party before the Civil War* (London: Oxford, 1970), pp. 263–66, 284–88. Quote on p. 263.

32. Quotations from Dr. William Lee Howard and "Pitchfork" Ben Tillman in Frederickson, *The Black Image,* pp. 276, 279; Joel Williamson, *The Crucible of Race: Black–White Relations in the American South since Emancipation* (New York: Oxford University Press: 1984), pp. 111–258, 285–326; Lillian Smith *Killers of the Dream* (New York: Norton, 1949), pp. 77–154; Thomas F. Gossett, *Race: The History of an Idea in America* (New York: Schocken, 1965), pp. 253–86; I. A. Newby, *Jim Crow's Defense: Anti-Negro Thought in America, 1900–1930* (Baton Rouge: Louisiana State University Press, 1963), pp. 42–44, 122–25.

On Reconstruction, see Leon Litwack, *Been in the Storm So Long: The Aftermath of Slavery* (New York: Knopf, 1979), pp. 291–307. On the rising negrophobia in the 1890s, see Frederickson, *The Black Image,* pp. 256–282.

33. Elliott Rudwick, *Race Riot at East St. Louis, July 2, 1917* (1964; reprint, Urbana, Ill.: University of Illinos Press, 1982), pp. 25–26; Capeci, *Race Relations in Wartime Detroit,* p. 88; Bruce M. Tyler, "Black Jive and White Repression," *Journal of Ethnic Studies,* 16 (1988): 31–66; and Hirsch, *Making the Second Ghetto,* p. 144.

34. Figures from Andrew Hacker, *Two Nations,* p. 183.

35. See Ralph Wiley, "Robert, Willie, David, Marion and Charles," in *Why Black People Tend to Shout: Cold Facts and Wry Views from a Black Man's World* ed. Ralph Wiley (New York: Penguin, 1991), pp. 79–91.

36. Rieder, *Canarsie,* pp. 57–94. See also Peter Binzen, *Whitetown, USA.*

37. Terkel, *Race,* p. 3.

38. See Ralph Wiley's wry commentary on the incident in *Why Black People Tend to Shout,* pp. 88–91.

39. Tom W. Smith, "Ethnic Images," *GSS Topical Report,* No. 19 (Chicago: National Opinion Research Center, December 1990).

40. See Robert B. Fogelson, *Big City Police* (Cambridge, Mass.: Harvard University Press, 1977), pp. 34, 240, 256–74; Eric Monkkonen, *Police in Urban America, 1860–1920* (Cambridge: Cambridge University Press, 1981), p. 158; Roger Lane, *The Roots of Violence in Black Philadelphia* (Cambridge, Mass.: Harvard University, Press, 1986), p. 87; Elliott Rudwick, *Race Riot in East St. Louis,* pp. 12, 24–25, 37–40.

41. On contemporary attitudes, see Donald J. Black, *Manners and Customs of the Police* (New York Acadamic Press, 1980), pp. 10–17, 118–19, 137; and Elijah Anderson, *Streetwise,* pp. 193–98, 203–5. On fatal violence, see Ralph Knoohuizen, Richard P. Fahey, and Deborah J. Palmer, "The Police and Their Use of Fatal Force in Chicago: A Report" (Chicago: Chicago Law Enforcement Study Group, 1972).

42. Andrew Hacker, *Two Nations,* p. 189.

43. Pamela Irving Jackson, *Minority Group Threat, Crime, and Policing* (New York: Praeger, 1989), p. xii.

44. See Joseph Daughen and Peter Binzen, *The Cop Who Would Be King: Mayor Frank Rizzo* (Boston: Little, Brown, 1977), pp. 94–95, 99–100; Jackson, *Minority Group Threat,* pp. 33–35, 75–79.

45. Eli Anderson treats this subject in great detail. He concludes that the police only helped to "increase rather than diminish" "tensions between the lower-class black ghetto and the upper-class white community" of Eastern City. See chapter 7 of *Streetwise.*

46. Quotations from Anderson, *Streetwise,* pp. 206, 210, 217, 220.

47. Patricia Williams, *The Alchemy of Race and Rights: Diary of a Law Professor* (Cambridge, Mass.: Harvard University Press, 1991).

48. Anderson, *Streetwise,* pp. 159–61.

49. See Jackson, *Minority Group Threat,* p. 78.

50. On Stackolee, see John and Alan Lomax, *American Ballads and Folk Songs* (New York: Macmillan, 1934), pp. 93–99; and John Roberts, *From Trickster to Badman: The Black Folk Hero in Slavery and Freedom* (Philadelphia: University of Pennsylvania Press, 1989), pp. 171– 219. On Pruitt-Igoe, see Lee Rainwater, *Behind Ghetto Walls: Black Family Life in a Federal Slum* (Chicago: Aldine, 1970), pp. 384–89. Joyce Ladner, *Tomorrow's Tomorrow,* pp. 85–95; on Erik Erikson's conclusions, see "A Memorandum on Identity and Negro Youth," *Social Issues* 20 (October 1964): 34–36; and *Identity: Youth and Crisis* (New York: Norton, 1968), pp. 295–325. On "blaxploitation" movies, see James P. Murray, *To Find an Image: Black Films from Uncle Tom to Superfly* (Indianapolis, Ind.: Bobbs-Merrill, 1973), pp. 61–82, 150–66; Daniel J. Leab, *From Sambo to Superspade: The Black Experience in Motion Pictures;* Claude Brown, "The Language of Soul," in *Rappin and Stylin' Out: Communication in Urban Black America,* ed. Thomas Kochman (Urbana, Ill.: University of Illinois Press, 1972), pp. 134–39.

51. Signithia Fordham, "Racelessness as a Factor in Black Students' School Success: Pragmatic Strategy or Pyrrhic Victory?" *Harvard Educational Review* 58 (February 1988): 54–84; Fordham and John U. Ogbu, "Black Students' School Success: Coping with the Burden of 'Acting White,'" *Urban Review* 18 (1986): 176–206; Sophronia Scott Gregory, "The Hidden Hurdle," *Time,* March 16, 1992, pp. 44–45. On this tendency in Philadelphia schools, see "Fear of 'Acting White' Blocks Some Black Students' Success," *Philadelphia Inquirer,* July 22, 1992, pp. A1, A13.

52. The title of the movie *White Men Can't Jump* (1992) refers to a white basketball player and conman who cannot dunk the ball through the net.

53. Robin D. G. Kelly emphasizes this aspect in his much more optimistic portrayal of Los Angeles rappers entitled "Straight from the Underground," *Nation,* June 8, 1992, pp. 793–96.

54. See John Leland, "Rap and Race," *Newsweek,* June 29, 1992, pp. 47–52. On critics of Public Enemy, see David Solomon, "The Real

Face of Rap," *New Republic,* November 11, 1991, pp. 24–29; and
Brad Lips, "Who Stole the Soul?" (Senior thesis, Princeton University, 1992).

CHAPTER 5: POOR BLACK CHILDREN
AND AMERICAN ABUNDANCE

1. On children's wages and family income, see Claudia Goldin, "Fam-
    ily Strategies and the Family Economy in the Late Nineteenth Cen-
    tury: The Role of Secondary Workers," in *Philadelphia: Work, Space,
    Family, and Group Experience,* ed. Theodore Hershberg (New York:
    Oxford University Press, 1981), p. 284; Viviana Zelizer, *Pricing the
    Priceless Child* (New York: Basic Books, 1985), pp. 57–58. See also
    Michael R. Haines, "Poverty, Economic Stress, and the Family in a
    Late-Nineteenth-Century City: Whites in Philadelphia, 1880," in
    Hershberg, *Philadelphia,* p. 261. On African-American children, see
    John Bodnar, Roger Simon, and Michael P. Weber, *Lives of Their
    Own: Blacks, Italians, and Poles in Pittsburgh, 1900–1960* (Urbana, Ill.:
    University of Illinois Press, 1982), pp. 91–95; Jacqueline Jones, *Labor
    of Love, Labor of Sorrow: Black Women, Work, and the Family from Slavery
    to the Present* (New York: Vintage, 1985), pp. 160–64.
2. See Roy Rosenzweig, *Eight Hours for What We Will: Workers and
    Leisure in an Industrial City, 1870–1920* (Cambridge: Cambridge
    University Press, 1983), pp. 46–47, 179–81.
3. On the 1920s, see Robert S. and Helen Merrell Lynd, *Middletown:
    A Study in Modern American Culture* (1929; reprint, New York: Vin-
    tage, 1956), pp. 153–80, 225–314. For a historical portrait of the
    origins of installment plans and financial corporations, see Edwin
    R. A. Seligman, *The Economics of Installment Selling: A Study in Con-
    sumer's Credit, with Special Reference to the Automobile,* vol. 1 (New
    York: Harper, 1927), pp. 14–54.
4. Stewart and Elizabeth Ewen, *Channels of Desire: Mass Images and the
    Shaping of the American Consciousness* (New York: McGraw Hill,
    1982), pp. 72–77, 96–105, 228–32; and Paula Fass, *The Damned and
    the Beautiful: American Youth in the 1920's* (Oxford: Oxford Univer-
    sity Press: 1977), pp. 228–34.
5. Lizabeth Cohen, "Encountering Mass Culture at the Grassroots:
    The Experience of Chicago Workers in the 1920's," *American Quar-
    terly* (March 1987): 6–33.
6. See Robert T. Bower, *Television and the Public* (New York: Holt, Rine-
    hart, and Winston, 1973), p. 3; and Bradley S. Greenberg and
    Joseph R. Dominick, "Racial and Social Class Differences in Teen-
    Agers' Use of Television," *Journal of Broadcasting* 13 (1968/1969):
    331–44; and Paul Carlton, "Mass Media and the Breakdown of Val-
    ues among Inner-City Youth," *Future Choices* 2 (Winter 1991): 11–22.

7. For some especially infamous examples, see Guy B. Johnson, "Newspaper Advertisements and Negro Culture," *Social Forces* 3 (1924/1925): 706–9.

8. See Raymond A. Bauer and Scott M. Cunningham, "The Negro Market," in *Perspectives in Consumer Behavior* ed. Waltraud M. Kassarjian and Thomas S. Robertson (Glenview, Ill.: Scott Foresman, 1973), p. 494.

9. See "Business and Government Leaders to Aid Study of Negro Market," *Sales Management* 28, (January 28, 1931); and the famous study by Paul K. Edwards, *The Southern Negro as a Consumer* (New York: Negro Universities Press, 1932).

10. On saving, see Marcus Alexis, "Some Negro-White Differences in Consumption," *American Journal of Economics and Sociology* 21 (January 1962): 11–28. A dissenting view is expressed by Alan R. Andreasen in *The Disadvantaged Consumer* (New York: Free Press, 1975), pp. 32–42.

    Quotation on racial stereotypes is from David Sullivan, "Don't Do This If You Want to Sell Your Product to Negroes," *Sales Management* 52 (March 1, 1943), p. 46. A listing of other marketing reports from the 1920s through 1970 is given in Kassarjian and Robertson, *Perspectives in Consumer Behavior,* pp. 503–4. A more complex, integrationist approach to advertising for blacks was articulated by Alan Bullock, "Consumer Motivations in Black and White—Part 1," *Harvard Business Review* 39 (May–June 1961): 89–104.

11. See Waltraud Kassarjian, "The Role of Blacks in the Mass Media," in Kassarjian and Robertson, *Perspectives in Consumer Behavior,* pp. 504–14; George Comstock and Robbin E. Cobbey, "Television and the Children of Ethnic Minorities," *Journal of Communication* 29 (Winter 1979): 104–15; Arnold M. Barban, "The Dilemma of 'Integrated' Advertising," *Journal of Business* 42 (October 1969), 496.

12. On radio, see Raymond A. Bauer and Scott M. Cunningham, *Studies in the Negro Market* (Cambridge, Mass.: Marketing Studies Institute, 1970), pp. 121–23.

13. See Nelson George, *Where Did Our Love Go?: The Rise and Fall of the Motown Sound* (New York: St. Martin's, 1985); David Moran, *Motown and the Arrival of Black Music* (New York: Collier, 1972); and Gerri Hershey, *Nowhere to Run: The Story of Soul Music* (New York: New York Times Books, 1984).

14. See Charles H. Brown, "Self Portrait: The Teen-Type Magazine," *Annals of the American Academy of Political and Social Science* 338 (November 1961): 13–21; and James L. C. Ford, *Magazines for the Millions: The Story of Specialized Publications* (Carbondale, Ill.: Southern Illinois University Press, 1969), pp. 35–39.

15. Alexander Wolff and Armen Keteyan, *Raw Recruits: The High Stakes Game Colleges Play to Get Their Basketball Stars and What It Costs to Win* (New York: Pocket Books, 1991), esp. pp. 73–96.

16. Arthur Kempton, "Native Sons," *New York Review of Books,* April 11, 1991, p. 59.

17. See Leon Litwack, *Been in the Storm So Long* (New York: Knopf, 1979) p. 343; Robin D. G. Kelly, "The Black Poor and the Politics of Opposition in a New South City," in *The Underclass Debate: View from History,* ed. Michael B. Katz (Princeton N.J.: Princeton University Press, 1993), pp. 293–333.

18. Bruce M. Tyler, "Black Jive and White Repression," *Journal of Ethnic Studies* 16 (1988): 31–39. On the zoot-suit riots, see Mauricio Mazon, *The Zoot-Suit Riots: The Psychology of Symbolic Annihilation* (Austin, Tex.: University of Texas Press, 1984); and Stuart Cosgrove, "The Zoot-Suit and Style Warfare," *History Workshop Journal* 18 (Autumn 1984), pp. 77–91.

19. "Why Negroes Buy Cadillacs," *Ebony,* September 1945, p. 34; Bauer and Cunningham, *Studies in the Negro Market,* pp. 156–78.

20. Cited in Bernard Portis, "Negroes and Fashion Interest," in *The Negro Consumer: Dimensions of Behavior and Strategy,* ed. George Joyce and Norman P. Govoni (New York: Random House, 1971), p. 298. Characteristics of "high fashion interest" included "reading the fashion magazines, such as *Vogue* and *Harper's Bazaar,*" "discussing fashions with other women," "observing what other women wear," and "going to fashion shows." See p. 294 for a complete list of characteristics.

21. Raymond A. Bauer, Scott M. Cunningham, and Lawrence Wortzel, "The Marketing Dilemma of Negroes," in Joyce and Govoni, *The Negro Consumer,* pp. 245–46.

22. James E. Stafford, Keith K. Cox, and James B. Higginbotham, "Some Consumption Pattern Differences between Urban Whites and Negroes," in Joyce and Govoni, *The Negro Consumer,* p. 281.

23. See Cohen, "Encountering Mass Culture," pp. 30–33.

24. Malcolm X, with Alex Haley, *The Autobiography of Malcolm X* (1964; reprint, New York: Ballantine, 1990), p. 46.

25. *Ebony,* September 1949, p. 34. See also C. Eric Lincoln, "The Negro's Middle-Class Dream," in Joyce and Govoni, *The Negro Consumer,* pp. 100–108; and the section on "need to belong" in Bullock, "Consumer Motivations," pp. 163–68.

26. Roger Abrahams, *Deep Down in the Jungle,* pp. 37–38. Quotation from "The Pool-Shootin' Monkey" from Wepman, Newman, and Binderman, *The Life: The Lore and Folk Poetry of the Black Hustler* (Philadelphia: University of Pennsylvania Press, 1976), p. 31. Their collection of toasts contains numerous extravagant examples of boasting about clothes. See especially "Good-Doing Wheeler," on pp. 73–74.

27. See Tyler, "Black Jive and White Repression," pp. 32–37; and Joseph S. Himes, "Negro Teen-Age Culture," *Annals of the American*

Academy of Political and Social Sciences 338 (November 1961): 89–101.

28. Malcolm X, *Autobiography,* pp. 52–55.

29. See Malcolm X, *Autobiography,* for his discussion of the "conk," a similar marcelling process, and its relation to a desire to imitate Caucasian hair. Roger Abrahams noted a possible connection between the popularity of straightened hair among men and the influence of boxer Sugar Ray Robinson (*Down in the Jungle. . . ,* p. 37).

30. GPFS006, 1.

31. Malcolm X, *Autobiography,* p. 55.

32. BB004, 5, 7; BB058, 4; BB034, 6; BB097, 2; BB001, 27; BB092, 4. See also BB012, 18.

33. BB104, 6.

34. BB042, 1.

35. BB003, 14, 22, 23, 29. See also BB089, 5.

36. See, for example, BB004, p. 16.

37. See Zelizer, *Pricing the Priceless Child,* pp. 22–55, 208–28. "Sacralization" refers to the adoption of parenting practices that were based on emotional, not just moral, explanations of children's behavior, which saw children as emotionally fragile and not morally pernicious, and which tended to discourage forceful control of kids' behavior.

38. BB019, 13; BB069, 1, 3, 5B (see also p. 9); BB001, 35 (see also p. 37). Compare BB012, 13; BB020, 1; BB043, 5; BB091, 4A.

39. BB028, register, 6, 9, 10, 11, 12, 13, 16, 17. See also BB001, 35, 37; BB091, 6, 7, among others.

40. See the picture of Slick Rick in Janette Beckman and B. Adler, *Rap: Portraits and Lyrics of a Generation of Black Rockers* (New York: St. Martin's, 1991), p. 38.

41. "Gettin' Money," by Dr. Jeckyll and Mr. Hyde. Copyright by Protoons Inc./ASCAP.

42. On the sneaker cult, see Bobbito, "Confessions of a Sneaker Addict," *Source* 20 (May 1991): 21–22.

43. See Amy S. Rosenberg, "City Students Get Off the Gold Standard," *Philadelphia Inquirer,* January 11, 1992, p. B1.

44. The short-lived interest in male "jeri-curls" is something of an exception. See the filmmaker Robert Townsend's spoof on the style in the film *Hollywood Shuffle* (1987).

45. See Richelle Turner-Collins, "Low-Cost Hair-Care Can Ultimately Cost More," *Philadelphia Tribune,* February 20, 1992, p. 44A.

46. Ibid.

47. On the "baby clubs" of Eastern City, see Elijah Anderson *Streetwise,* pp. 123–26.

48. See Anne Campbell's summary of this literature in *Girls in the Gang: A Report from New York City* (New York: Blackwell, 1984), pp. 4–32.

49. This perception is shared by some observers recently interviewed by Felicia Lee; see "For Gold Earrings and Protection, More Girls Take Road to Violence," *New York Times* November 25, 1991, pp. A1, B7. Lee cites a huge rise in arrests of girls for assault in New York.

50. Rick Telander quotes Atlanta police reports of fifty apparel-related robberies in four months, and similar reports of fifty thefts of sports jackets and a dozen of gym shoes every month from one police district in Chicago in his exposé entitled "Senseless"; see *Sports Illustrated,* May 14, 1990, pp. 36–46.

51. See "Promising Teenager Slain for Pair of Gold Earrings," *Philadelphia Inquirer,* October 23, 1991, p. A1; "Warning: Don't Flaunt It," in *Philadelphia Inquirer,* October 24, 1991, p. 1-B; Amy S. Rosenberg, "City Students Get Off the Gold Standard," *Philadelphia Inquirer,* January 11, 1992, pp. 1–2B; and "Fashion to Die For?" *Philadelphia Daily News,* October 24, 1991, pp. 1, 3.

52. L.L. Cool J, "Around the Way Girl," *Mama Said Knock You Out,* 1990, sound cassette.

53. Oran "Juice" Jones, "The Rain"; and Robin Halpin, Doug Wimbish, Monica Lynch, "Thunder and Lightning." See Joe Logan, "A Song Aimed at Men Gets a Rapid Reply from Women," *Philadelphia Inquirer,* September 30, 1986, pp. 1C–3C.

54. Kempton, "Native Sons," p. 61.

CHAPTER 6: POOR BLACK CHILDREN AND AMERICAN VIOLENCE

1. On a connection made between H. Rap Brown's statement and Vietnam, see Clayborne Carson, *In Struggle: SNCC and the Black Awakening of the 1960's* (Cambridge: Harvard University Press, 1981), pp. 259–60. See also Dick Gregory's account of his days in Mississippi during the voter registration drives in Howell Raines, *My Soul Is Rested* (New York: Putnam, 1977), pp. 291–96.

2. Dane Archer and Rosemary Gartner, *Violence and Crime in Cross-National Perspective* (New Haven: Yale University Press, 1984), pp. 63–97; Martin Daly and Margo Wilson, *Homicide* (New York: Aldine de Gruyter, 1988), pp. 277–78.

3. See Ralph E. Friar and Natasha A. Friar, *The Only Good Indian . . . : The Hollywood Gospel* (New York: Drama Specialists, 1972).

4. See George Gerbner and Nancy Signorielli, "Violence Profile, 1967 through 1988–89: Enduring Patterns" (Unpublished report, Annenberg School of Communications, Philadelphia, January 1990), figs. from p. 6. See also Gerbner, assisted by Michael Eleey and Nancy Tedesco, *Violence in Television Drama: A Study of Trends and Symbolic Functions* (Philadelphia: Annenberg School of Communications, 1970).

5. Gerbner and Signorielli, "Violence Profile," pp. 7–9.
6. See Paul Carton, "Mass Media Culture and the Breakdown of Values among Inner-City Youth," *Future Choices,* 2 (Winter 1991), p. 11.
7. As Bruce Gordon, the president of Paramount International TV, recently told *Broadcasting Magazine* (June 15, 1992, p. 19): "The International demand never changes. It's usually action series and films. Comedy series are never easy because in most of the world most of the comedies have to be dubbed and wind up losing their humor in the dubbing." I am indebted to George Gerbner for pointing out in personal conversations much of the information in this paragraph. See also George Gerbner, "Violence and Terror in and by the Media," in *Media Crisis and Democracy: Mass Communication and the Disruption of the Social Order,* ed. Marc Raboy and Bernard Dagenais (London: Sage Publications, 1992), pp. 94–107.
8. Robert Sklar's, *Movie-Made America: A Cultural History of American Movies* (New York: Vintage, 1975) contains a discussion of the *Paramount* case and the impact of television (pp. 269–85) and of the rise of the blockbuster (pp. 286–89).
9. For thumbnail histories of each of these genres, see Wes D. Gehring, ed., *Handbook of American Film Genres* (New York: Greenwood Press, 1988), which also includes much more detailed bibliographical notes. The revival of each of the genres and the eclipse of Westerns in the late 1960s and early 1970s are detailed on pp. 11 (action-adventure), 35–36 (Westerns), 47–57 (gangster), 73–74 (film noir), 217–19 (horror), and 236–38 (science fiction).
10. Gerbner, "Violence and Terror," p. 105.
11. See Vincent Canby, "Now at a Theater Near You: A Skyrocketing Body Count," *New York Times,* July 16, 1990, pp. C11, C13.
12. Brooks Robards, "The Police Show," in *TV Genres: A Handbook and Reference Guide,* ed. Brian Rose (Westport, Conn: Greenwood Press, 1985).
13. Counts by Canby, "Now at a Theater," p. C11.
14. Gerbner, "Violence and Terror," p. 102; see also pp. 98–99.
15. Signorielli, "Television and Conceptions," pp. 348–51.
16. See Bart Andrews and Ahrgus Juilliard, *Holy Mackerel! The "Amos 'n' Andy" Story* (New York: Dutton, 1986). On "The Nat King Cole Show," see J. Fred MacDonald, *Blacks and White TV: Afro-Americans in Television since 1948* (Chicago: Nelson-Hall, 1983), pp. 57–64.
17. MacDonald, *Blacks and White TV,* pp. 172–91.
18. See James P. Murray, *To Find an Image: Black Films from* Uncle Tom *to* Super Fly (Indianapolis: Bobbs-Merrill, 1973); Dan Leab, *From Sambo to Superspade: The Black Experience in Motion Pictures* (Boston: Houghton Mifflin, 1975), pp. 59–82; Thomas Cripps, *Black Film as Genre* (Bloomington, Ind.: Indiana University Press, 1978), pp. 3–61; Cripps, *Slow Fade to Black: The Negro in American Film, 1900–42*

(New York: Oxford University Press, 1977), pp. 70–89, 170–202; James R. Nesteby, *Black Images in American Films, 1896–1954: The Interplay between Civil Rights and Film Culture* (Washington, D.C.: University Press of America, 1982), pp. 65–96, 157–70; Melvin Burke Donalson, "The Representation of AfroAmerican Women in the Hollywood Feature Film, 1915–1949" (Ph.D. dissertation, Brown University, 1981).

19. Similar, if more detailed, readings of *Sweetback* can be found in Murray, *To Find an Image,* pp. 72–82; Leab, *From Sambo to Superspade,* pp. 247–49; Cripps, *Black Film as Genre,* pp. 128–140; and Lerone Bennett, "The Emancipation Orgasm: Sweetback in Wonderland," *Ebony,* September 1971, pp. 106–18. Nelson George is more favorable toward the film; see "The Complete History of Post-Soul Culture," *Village Voice,* March 17, 1992, p. 26.

20. See, for example, Bell Hooks's critique of *She's Gotta Have It,* entitled "Whose Pussy Is This: A Feminist Comment," in *Talking Back: Thinking Feminist, Thinking Black* (Boston: South End Press, 1989), pp. 134–41.

21. See Gerbner, "Violence and Terror," p. 101.

22. Carton, "Mass Media Culture," pp. 6–7, and by personal communication. See also Bradley S. Greenburg and Joseph R. Dominick, "Racial and Social Class Differences in Teen-Agers' Use of Television," *Journal of Broadcasting* 13 (1968/1969): 331–44; Carolyn A. Stroman, "The Socialization Influence of Television on Black Children," *Journal of Black Studies* 15 (September, 1984): 79–100.

23. Figures quoted from Ken Smikle, of *Target Market News,* in Karen Grigsby Bates, "'They've Gotta Have Us: Hollywood's Black Directors," *New York Times Magazine,* July 14, 1991, p. 18.

24. The literature on this subject is much too vast to be catalogued here. Researchers' consensus about TV violence's effects on aggression, as well as the failure of other alternative theories, is described in Eli A. Rubenstein, "Television Violence: A Historical Perspective," in *Children and the Faces of Television: Teaching, Violence, Selling,* ed. Edward L. Palmer and Aimee Dorr (New York: Academic Press, 1980), pp. 113–37; Carmen Luke, *Constructing the Child Viewer: A History of the American Discourse on Television and Children, 1950–1980* (New York: Praeger, 1990). The findings of the 1969 Task Force on Mass Media and Violence to the National Commission on the Causes and Prevention of Violence, edited by R. K. Baker and S. J. Ball, and released as *Violence and the Media* (Washington: D.C.: Government Printing Office, 1969), reflects this consensus, as does the so-called Surgeon General's Report, *Television and Growing Up: The Impact of Television Violence* (Washington, D.C.: Government Printing Office, 1972). On the catharsis hypothesis, see S. Feshbach, "The Catharsis Effect: Research and

Another View," in Baker and Ball, *Violence and the Media,* pp. 461–72.

25. See Carton, "Mass Media Culture," p. 6.
26. Gerbner, "Violence and Terror," pp. 102–3; Gerbner and Signorielli, "Violence Profile," pp. 11–16, tables 12–14. The authors also document that among heavy viewers there is less diversity of opinions across class, gender, race, and political groups than among similar groups of light viewers, suggesting that telvision also contributes to a homogenizing of opinion.
27. Gerbner and Signorielli found that "non-whites are so likely to express interpersonal mistrust that [heavy] television viewing adds little or nothing to that perception" ("Violence Profiles," p. 13).
28. Cited in MacDonald, *Blacks and White TV,* p. 184.
29. Quotation from p. 157. See Abrahams, *Down in the Jungle . . . : Negro Narrative Folklore from the Streets of Philadelphia* (Chicago: Aldine, 1963), and Wepman, Newman, and Binderman, *The Life: The Lore and Folk Poetry of the Black Hustler* (Philadelphia: University of Pennsylvania Press, 1976), pp. 134–37 ("Staggerlee"), p. 103 (Lone Ranger), pp. 111–12 (Frankenstein and Dracula).
30. Nelson George, "Cool vs. Chilly," *Village Voice,* March 24, 1992, p. 75.
31. Quoted from "Just Rhymin' with Biz," *Long Live the Kane* (Copyright 1988 by Cold Chillin' Records, Inc.).
32. "Power" and "respect" are quoted from the promotional billboards for the movie ("Power. Respect. JUICE. How Far Will You Go to Get It?"), which were plastered all over Philadelphia when the movie came out. The quotation from Nelson George comes from his review of the soundtrack for *Juice;* see "Cool vs. Chilly," p. 76. Quotation from Rakim is from "Juice (Know the Ledge)," a song featured in the movie.
33. In this paragraph I am responding to Charles Silberman's hypothesis that the rage of the inner city outgrew the "sublimating" capacities of southern folklore, with its violent fantasies and its dozens playing. See Silberman, *Criminal Violence, Criminal Justice* (New York: Random House, 1978), pp. 152–65.

INDEX